The Hero
in French Decadent Literature

by
George Ross Ridge

University of Georgia Press

To

My wife DAVY

and

My friend JULES C. ALCIATORE

Copyright © 1961 by University of Georgia Press
Library of Congress Catalog Card Number: 61-17538
Publication of this book was aided by a grant from the Ford Foundation
Printed in the United States of America
by Foote & Davies, Inc., Atlanta

The Hero
in French Decadent Literature

CONTENTS

PREFACE

WHAT IS the French decadence? It is a term bandied about, a glib characterization of a gilded epoch, the Second Empire of Napoleon III. The word "decadence" is at once a sobriquet for the historian, a reproach for the moralist, a condemnation for the literary purist. There immediately emerges the cliché of the superannuated aesthete, the dandy twirling his gold-headed cane, as he leers over his absinthe at a voluptuous woman strolling down the boulevard. Hence in the popular mind the literature of the decadence, exuding decay, is superficially preoccupied with the exotic and the erotic. The decadent hero is a kind of pervert, and the decadent writer, by consensus, is obsessed with the strange and the inconsequential.

Such a picture is almost totally false. The decadent writer is most often a Péladan who, wretched novelist though he is, piously laments the collapse of French morality; or a Huysmans, who yearns for and, in his labyrinthine ways, returns to his natal Catholicism; or a Verlaine, who, torn between flesh and the spirit, etherealizes the most carnal pleasure and ever remains at heart a religious poet. So it is that, paradoxically, the decadence is fundamentally a literature of deep religious concern. Its protagonist, or hero, incarnates the problem.

The decadent is a type of the last man, the supremely sophisticated man, who self-consciously dallies with the frills of life while nature prepares its retribution—death at the hands of the barbarians who wait outside the gates. The decadent is a somber man. He does not enjoy his obsessive pursuit of pleasure. He detests the great city, his megalopolis, which holds him captive through the fatal appeal of its artificiality. His perversion is not merely a clinical aberration; it cannot be understood solely in psychological terms. It rather reflects a metaphysical sterility. It signifies that the decadent (who confesses as much) has reached the limits of his possibilities. A deathwish seizes him and impels him on an active quest of damnation, destruction, annihilation. Love becomes impossible for him. The woman of the French decadence is no longer a wife to man or a mother to children. She incarnates activity, he passivity, in an extraordinary reversal of roles. Their attraction for each other is destructive and sado-masochistic. Love leads to death, not life; it ceases to fructify, to yield possibility. It, too, is an aspect of the deathwish and of the total collapse of hearth and home, of religion and society, during the cataclysmic last days, *the decadence,* of Western civilization.

Such is the fatalistic message of the French decadence. And fundamentally it is a religious message.

Over the years several men have been invaluable to me as catalysts. I am especially grateful to Dr. James M. Smith (Emory University), mentor and friend, who first interested me in the subject of French decadence and let me profit from his vast erudition. I am indebted to Dr. A. E. Carter (University of South Carolina) with whom I threshed out many a problem. His criticism was always incisive. To Dr. Jules C. Alciatore (University of Georgia), who generously gave of his time and knowledge, in the midst of his own work on Stendhal, I am deeply grateful. Two faithful catalysts have been Dr. Maxwell A. Smith (University of Chattanooga) and Dr. Howard Sutton (Vanderbilt University). Their cogent comments and their encouraging influence have been deeply appreciated through the years. To Dr. Renato Poggioli

PREFACE

(Harvard University) and to Dr. R. H. Anacker (University of Chattanooga) goes my gratitude for reading parts of the manuscript and for making valuable notations. Dr. Julian Harris (University of Wisconsin) has graciously given permission to draw upon material published in an article, *"The Femme Fatale* in French Decadence," in *The French Review,* February, 1961.

Four agencies have been instrumental by subsidizing time for me to write this book. The Society for French-American Cultural Services and Educational Aid awarded me a grant to spend a summer at the Bibliothèque Nationale; the Southern Fellowships Fund gave me another summer grant; and the Georgia State College Research Committee gave me a free quarter to work on the manuscript. But most of all I am indebted to the American Council of Learned Societies for a most helpful and generous grant-in-aid. To these worthy societies, as to my catalysts, my deepest thanks.

GEORGE ROSS RIDGE

Georgia State College
Atlanta, Georgia

ONE

WHAT IS FRENCH DECADENCE?

BY THE 1850s the French literary scene was stirring uneasily. Romanticism as a movement had been dead for more than a decade, but French writers were not as yet moving in a clearly defined direction. There were only isolated men and splinter groups with no unifying principle. This brief post-romantic calm was to prove the eye of a hurricane. Parnassianism and symbolism, realism and naturalism, *l'école romane* and innumerable côteries were soon to sweep the scene.

Perhaps all these movements can be best understood under the concept of decadence. This thesis may at first seem strange, for the decadents were largely dismissed by their critics as dope-addicts, drunkards, perverts, or minor figures outside the mainstream of literary development. They were considered the beatniks of their time—surely a ludicrous judgment when applied to great poets like Baudelaire, Rimbaud, Verlaine. Yet the idea of decadence is cardinal while not exclusive, and it preoccupies, even obsesses, most writers during the second half of the century. For naturalist and parnassian, for symbolist and realist, decadence is common ground, however differently it may be perceived. It therefore assumes a new importance. A synthesis of the various move-

1

ments becomes possible. Decadence is their common metaphysical concern, with deep roots that have been obscured, for the most part, right up to the present day.

These "decadent" writers—symbolist, realist, parnassian, for all are concerned with decadence—were in fact haunted by the fear that Western civilization was fast drawing to an end because of man's moral, social, political, and religious decay. In different ways they elaborated upon this idea in their fiction, but it remained a catholic concern. However, their depictions of decadent men and women, i.e., their literary heroes and heroines, have prompted many critics to assume, erroneously, that the writers were in fact what many of them were actually protesting against. Although few decadent authors possessed Goethean tranquillity—how many writers ever have?—it is certainly a mistake to equate them, as many observers have done, with their decadent heroes. The truth of the matter is quite complex.

A Problem in Semantics

Its complexity can be seen even in attempting to define the elusive word "decadence." For most readers it has a connotative, pejorative meaning, not a denotative meaning designating certain men, particular movements, peculiar ideas. This confusion endures. Arthur Symons, for one, drew attention to the essential problem from the actual scene:[1]

The latest movement in European literature has been called by many names, none of them quite exact or comprehensive—Decadence, Symbolism, Impressionism, for instance. It is easy to dispute over words, and we shall find that Verlaine objects to being called a Decadent, Maeterlinck to being called a Symbolist, Huysmans to being called an Impressionist. These terms, as it happens, have been adopted as the badge of little separate cliques, noisy, brainsick young people who haunt the brasseries of the Boulevard Saint-Michel, and exhaust their ingenuities in theorizing over the works they can not write. But, taken frankly as epithets which express their own meaning, both Impressionism and Symbolism convey some notion of that new kind of literature which is perhaps more broadly characterized by the word Decadence.

By distinguishing between the essential and the unessential, the permanent and the transient, Symons, who has been in disrepute of late, points to the problem which many others have ignored: The connotative meanings are numerous, certainly, but they must be dismissed, for the moment, if the idea of decadence is to be probed with understanding. With this in mind Symons formulates his own concept along denotative lines:[2]

The most representative literature of the day—the writing which appeals to, which has done so much to form, the younger generation—is certainly not classic, nor has it any relation with that old antithesis of the Classic, the Romantic. After a fashion it is of no doubt a decadence; it has all the qualities that mark the end of great periods, the qualities that we find in the Greek, the Latin, decadence: an intense self-consciousness, a restless curiosity in research, an over-subtilizing refinement upon refinement, a spiritual and moral perversity.

In retrospect Symons' definition rests upon superficial qualities. But it is at least denotative. He has definite attributes in mind when he writes about decadence, and significantly he does not use the term in opprobrium.

Decadence is, denotatively, much broader than the minor school which briefly carried its flaming banner. Its ramifications extend throughout the entire literature of the period. The idea of decadence subsumes the pessimism and fatalism of Flaubert and Taine; it includes the psychological degeneracy of Zola and the Goncourts. Decadence is common ground for all writers concerned with deterioration in any form.

Concern with decadence was, of course, not new in French literature. Rousseau devoted his entire life to expounding the enigma that modern civilization, for all its progress, was truly decadent. Montesquieu drew obvious parallels with Europe in his *Considérations sur les causes de la grandeur des Romains et de leur décadence*. The infamous Marquis de Sade was preoccupied with the problem of progress and decadence. And so were many others in the eighteenth century. There are deep roots of concern.

But decadence as the guiding spirit of a literary epoch appears only in the nineteenth century—and for reasons, possibly, that will be examined in the conclusion. Its precise point of impetus, when the thrust of a genius brings the dormant subject to full bloom, is difficult to say. But the honor seems to belong to the gigantic figure of Baudelaire. Critics have sensed this instinctively when they make him the terminus of romanticism and the beginning of the new, yet undefined movement. Madeleine Rudler, for instance, observes of Baudelaire that "ce précurseur mort en 1867 représente bien, comme l'a vu M. John Charpentier, le point où le *Romantisme* a bifurqué pour aboutir, d'une part au *Parnasse*, d'autre part au *Décadisme* et au *Symbolisme*."[3] The judgment is obvious in retrospect and it can stand. After making her generic point Mrs. Rudler then touches upon decadence proper:[4]

La critique et la presse eurent beau jeu pour se railler de ces innovations, sans comprendre tout ce que cette fermentation préparait pour l'avenir de l'art. Félicien Champsaur, dans un article qui eut du retentissement, traita tous ces esthètes de *Dé-cadents*; le mot fit fortune. Par bravade, ils adoptèrent ce titre et devinrent le point de mire de tous les persifleurs.

Here connotation merges with denotation, and the basic problem of definition must be resolved.

In one sense the decadents are simply those who are so named. This is an attractive solution, just as one is tempted to call a "Christian" anyone who thinks of himself as one despite the obvious differences in belief and practice. But in both instances, with Christian and decadent, history must clarify the definitions.

The word "decadence" had been current since 1880, and it was implicit long before that. Still, "decadence" and the so-called decadent schools, in the narrowest sense, have a technical slot to fill in literary history. Roosbroeck, for instance, discusses it with precision. He notes that[5]

A group of young artists decided about that date, after a few bottles of wine and innumerable cigarettes, that the existing circle, *Les Hydropathes,* was dominated by a number of old tyrannical whigs, like Guy de Maupassant and François Coppée, and that there was a real need for periodical gatherings of really congenial spirits. These "congenial spirits" were mostly the future symbolists. There was among them, as usual, considerable disagreement, and they found that the shortest way out of it was to found three artistic circles: *Les Hirsutes* (the hairy ones); *Le Chat noir* (of Cabaret fame); and, finally, *Le Décadent.* The same year *Les Hirsutes* died; and *Le Décadent* split up into several other ephemeral associations as *Les Jeunes* (1883) and *Les Zutistes,* who aimed openly and avowedly at eccentricity and, in 1884, transformed their name into the significant one of *Les Jemenfoutistes.*

The description is concise, colorful, and accurate. In time the breakdown in decadent schools becomes ludicrous; the patient reader may follow its winding trail in Kenneth Cornell's *The Symbolist Movement.* But Roosbroeck's note is essentially correct: it points out the specific meaning that the term "decadent" had for one brief moment. Matters were never again to be so simple. The initial confusion voiced by Symons would again cloud the issues.

As an example of the devious paths of decadence, Leconte de Lisle was "le maître incontesté" of both the decadent and symbolist youth, and parnassian influence was astonishingly strong:[6]

Pendant dix ans, l'influence des Parnassiens fut prépondérante en poésie et leur éditeur Lemerre publia d'eux une belle série d'oeuvres qui les mirent au premier plan. Quelques-uns comme Banville, Coppée, Mendès, se firent une célébrité au théâtre; d'autres comme A. France furent des maîtres du roman ou des critiques influents dans la presse. Enfin pendant plus de dix ans, on ne connut pas d'autres écoles poétiques que la leur.

To what extent, then, was parnassianism "decadent"? To assess the influence and to pigeonhole each of the multitudinous schools is like cutting the Gordian knot. Just who is the decadent? The incredible Cénacle of Xavier de Ricard included such an unlikely group as Edmond Lepelletier, Catulle Mendès, François Coppée, José-Maria de Heredia,

Léon Valade, Albert Mérat, Léon Dierx, Armand Silvestre, Villiers de l'Isle-Adam, Anatole France, Paul Verlaine, Sully-Prudhomme, and Stéphane Mallarmé. There is a fantastic juxtaposition of men, movements, and ideas—all to some extent "decadent." Manifestoes and counter-manifestoes, sudden conversion and frequent heresies come with bewildering rapidity. The credos, moreover, convey little besides polemics, and even that much with sublime confusion.

The history of the decadents, in the broad view, is the history of the epoch, made confusing because of the often contradictory chronicles of the men who lived through it. These writers were not impartial historians. Gustave Le Rouge, for instance, records the official party line, names bistro chieftains as great thinkers, and castigates the heretics in *Verlainiens et décadents.* Gustave Kahn records his own prejudices as truth in *Symbolistes et décadents,* as when he reminisces over the verbal confusion surrounding the word "decadent":[7]

En 1885, il y avait des décadents et des symbolistes, beaucoup de décadents et peu de symbolistes. Le mot de décadent avait été prononcé, celui de symboliste pas encore: nous parlions de symbole, nous n'avions pas créé le mot générique de symbolisme, et les décadents et les symbolistes c'était autre chose, alors. Le mot de décadent avait été créé par des journalistes, quelques-uns l'avaient, disaient-ils, ramassé comme les gueux de Hollande avaient arboré l'épithète injurieuse; pas si injurieuse et si inexacte.

The note overplays the number of "décadents" and under-emphasizes the importance of "les symbolistes"; it shows, in short, a familiar partisanship.

Although the journalists had in fact described all these writers pejoratively as "décadents," many of them relished the sobriquet while others vehemently rejected it for various reasons. The confusion is on. It becomes increasingly difficult to ascertain what is pose and what fact, what is connotation and what denotation. In this grand mêlée, moreover, the decadents themselves change their own tenets with lightning rapidity, like Jean Moréas:[8]

Quelques mois plus tard, Moréas brûlait ses vaisseaux; reniant le *Symbolisme* qui l'avait porté aux nues, il fondait l'Ecole romane et publiait dans *Le Figaro* du 14 septembre 1891, un manifeste qui définissait ses nouvelles théories.

The critic is tempted to exclaim that it is all sound and fury, signifying nothing. Most critics did so. But they had lost sight of the central idea of the decadent writers.

Their common philosophical concern, under many names, was much more important than the one small movement which briefly and technically bore the misunderstood name "decadent." These writers were no less "decadent" for their various names. Decadence included in historical fact both parnassianism and symbolism as well as the many smaller movements, and to a large extent it shared a common ideology with naturalism. Zola's interest in *la tare* and pathological degeneration is certainly not coincidental with the spirit of the times. And the Goncourt brothers, among other realists, echo their own psychologically oriented concern.

Thus decadence is the preoccupation in some degree of nearly all French writers in the last half of the nineteenth century. Just why this is so and how it is so is the point in question. But first the concept of decadence must be defined, by sifting critical opinion on the facts we have acquired, and by examining the phenomenon of decadence itself. Ultimately we must know the decadent worldview in order to formulate an accurate notion of decadence.

DECADENCE AND STYLE

Style is one of the most salient characteristics of the French decadence. Hence many commentators have tended to interpret this period wholly in terms of style. By this they refer to "decadent" innovations in prose rhythm and vocabulary, which are involuted and dazzlingly rich. The decadent style is *faisandé*—gamy, even suppurating. It exerts the morbid fascination of being overly ripe, unhealthy, tainted. The rich decadent style glows like a diseased person flushing beautifully with fever. Indeed, the disease accounts for the beauty.

To be decadent, a style must therefore have deteriorated from a previous state of excellence. This is a verity which all commentators have accepted. James M. Smith speaks for them by succinctly discussing the evolutional development of style:[9]

In the development of the fine arts, including literature, one can distinguish three fairly distinct phases in the growth of a particular movement or form of expression. The first of these phases may be called the *formative* period, in which there are generally found various forms of expression competing for dominance, during which time artistic procedures are elaborated,—and attacked and defended. One of these will eventually triumph, and there follows a phase of comparative artistic stability—a *formal* period, when the majority of the artists are in general agreement concerning the aims and purposes of art and on the means for achieving them. This formal period is followed by a period of *decadence,* when the conventional, established forms seem to be exhausted, and the artists, in an effort to avoid servile imitation of their immediate predecessors, break down these established forms, exaggerate and embroider upon them, sacrificing the unity of the whole to an emphasis on the part.

A decadent style, then, is an expression of "breakdown" in technique as opposed to subject matter. It emphasizes the etymological meaning of the word "decadence." It elaborates upon and distorts the preceding healthy elements of a culture's classical period. Bourget observes epigrammatically:[10]

Un style de décadence est celui où l'unité du livre se décompose pour laisser la place à l'indépendance de la page, où la page se décompose pour laisser la place à l'indépendance de la phrase, et la phrase pour laisser la place à l'indépendance du mot.

This pointed definition of the decadent style is to some extent accurate. It describes much writing of the French decadence.

Nisard believes a decadent age may be diagnosed, like a disease, through the symptoms of its style. In a long study entitled *Etudes sur les Poëtes latins de la décadence* he compares the Late Roman Age with the contemporary scene in nineteenth century France. The same malignant forces are at work, he finds, and are marked by a strikingly similar style

—one which he terms decadent: "J'y remarque le même goût pour l'érudition, et presque la même espèce d'érudition."[11] He further elaborates: "Autre ressemblance, profusion des descriptions. Après l'érudition, la description est la marque la plus certaine de décadence."[12] He draws up an entire list of parallels between the two periods, then concludes somberly: "Mais c'est surtout par les procédés du style que les deux époques se ressemblent."[13] France lies mortally ill with a disease, he concludes, whose corruption is reflected by its literature and whose decadent style is its glaring symptom. The criticism is of course arrant nonsense, especially for a good Latinist like Nisard: if erudition and description are the certain marks of decadence, then he should have chosen Horace and Virgil as his chief decadents. But Nisard had a point to make, mistaken as it is, and his opinion has been influential.

Gautier describes the new style from an opposite point of view. In the most important single document, stylistically, of the French decadence, his preface to Baudelaire's *Les Fleurs du mal,* Gautier writes in 1868:[14]

Le poète des *Fleurs du mal* aimait ce qu'on appelle improprement le style de décadence, et qui n'est autre chose que l'art arrivé à ce point de maturité extrême que déterminent à leurs soleils obliques les civilisations qui vieillissent: style ingénieux, compliqué, savant, plein de nuances et de recherches, reculant toujours les bornes de la langue, empruntant à tous les vocabulaires techniques, prenant des couleurs à toutes les palettes, des notes à tous les claviers, s'efforçant à rendre la pensée dans ce qu'elle a de plus ineffable, et la forme en ses contours les plus vagues et les plus fuyants, écoutant pour les traduire les confidences subtiles de la névrose, les aveux de la passion vieillissante qui se déprave et les hallucinations bizarres de l'idée fixe tournant à la folie. Ce style de décadence est le dernier mot du Verbe sommé de tout exprimer et poussé à l'extrême outrance. On peut rappeler à propos de lui, la langue marbrée déjà des verdeurs de la décomposition et comme faisandée du bas-empire romain et les raffinements compliqués de l'école byzantine, dernière forme de l'art grec tombé en déliquescence; mais tel est bien l'idiome nécessaire et fatal des peuples et des civilisations où la vie factice a remplacé la vie naturelle et développé chez l'homme des besoins inconnus.

In this vivid passage Gautier seizes the essence of the decadent style more firmly than any commentator before or since. Kahn adds an historical note by connecting it with the Latin decadence:[15]

Cette idée de décadence, elle tenait encore à de vieux errements. Baudelaire avait longuement parlé d'une traduction de Pétrone qu'il n'écrivit pas, ce qui serait la perte irréparable d'un grand et raffiné plaisir d'art si mon cher ami, Laurent Tailhade, ne terminait pas une traduction de Pétrone. . . . On parlait assez couramment, entre autres Paul Adam qui réalisa son désir, de romancer sur Byzance.

Kahn even brings the recurrent comparison up to date by explicitly concluding:[16]

Il y avait aussi l'idée que les Prussiens de 70 avaient été les barbares, que Paris c'était Rome ou Byzance; les romans de Zola, *Nana,* avaient souligné la métaphore, et il y avait donc des décadents; on parlait du roman de la pourriture, du roman médical; sous cette influence de Verlaine, de Huysmans, de Zola surtout, et beaucoup aussi de Mendès conteur, dont les tableautins étaient alors fort goûtés, marchait un groupe d'écrivains plus prosateurs que poètes.

The decadent style begins to merge with decadent subject matter. Through a striking parallel of Rome and Paris, Kahn enunciates a kind of doctrine of the eternal recurrence which Nisard perceives and discusses stylistically. Certain malignant states in a cultural ethos repeat themselves, evoking the decadent style as the natural expression of the inevitable end of a civilization. Decadence is the *Götterdämmerung,* and the decadent style its hymn, with the image of a mad Nero fiddling away while a smoking Rome lies at his feet. The idea of decadence, even stylistically, is closely tied to that of destruction and death, as Gourmont hastens to point out: "L'idée de décadence n'est donc que l'idée de mort naturelle."[17]

The decadent style, then, is the agonizingly beautiful lament of the dying civilization. It portrays the civilized man, with exquisite though involuted taste, expiring like a perfect gentleman—the archetypal Petronius banqueting with choice friends before slowly opening his veins, a deliberate smile playing upon his lips, while he utters a final epigram. Such is the spirit of decadence.

The decadent style is fascinatingly perverse. Indeed this is why A. E. Carter discusses it as the "glamour of syntax."[18] Its luxurious sophistication appeals to the over-civilized man, whose jaded taste is whetted only by the rare, the exotic, the perverse. The decadent style becomes an elaborate device to capture and maintain the weary reader's interest. He is bored by the usual and the normal. His senses have been dulled by continuous excitement, and only the strongest stimulations affect him. Consequently the decadent style becomes ever more strained and twisted, with uniqueness in diction its primary aim. An image, once used, must never be repeated, for through usage it becomes banal and loses its power to evoke sensation. The decadent reader demands headier and headier stimuli.

The decadent style twists like a vine through jungles of strange imagery. Synaesthesia and the transposition of art forms become a familiar decadent product, neatly packaged in a gilded vocabulary.[19] Carter details such stylistic *tours de force* in the decadent and symbolist writers. But parnassians and realists, too, use the same devices. Heredia and Zola are, in their ways, no less decadent stylists than Huysmans and Louys. Style, finally, becomes a way in which the decadent hero, like Des Esseintes of Huysmans' *A Rebours,* not only vents his world-weariness but also titillates his tired and super-refined sensibility. Style becomes a perversion.[20]

The decadent style is clearly a form of art for art's sake. The decadent aesthete is interested exclusively in style, not in didactic themes or moral values, at least in theory. The decadent style even ceases, ultimately, to have a subject content, and the decadent writer can have, by definition, no explicit vision of the world. He is not concerned with it except as an object of sense sensation recorded in style. The decadent style, delicately honed to elicit sensation, is his sole interest. Hence Des Esseintes plays with his perfume atomizer, contemplates abstract patterns, and lingers over lovely words which have lost all relationship with things. This state is the final breakdown. One can go no further, as Huysmans admits in his note to *A Rebours* written twenty years after publication. But many decadents go to this extreme limit of neurosis and hypersensibility. In this connection Smith reflects the critical consensus by observing:[21]

The Classical concept, then, of the fundamental ethical value of art is rejected by the Decadents. In some there is a complete inversion of this ideal in that art is made to serve fundamental immorality. In discarding the ethical side of art many of these writers cultivate the purely aesthetic or formal values. The Classical ideal of a limited, abstract, highly select vocabulary gives way to an extensive literary language into which thousands of new words are introduced, while the regularity of Classical syntax is deliberately distorted, the better to purvey exquisite nuances of sensation. In this pursuit of the sensuously beautiful there is an attempt to rival other art forms, to produce through literature sensations generally associated with other graphic arts, the plastic arts or music. Literary form itself becomes the intimate expression of the author's personality, with little reference to the firm outlines of the Classical genres. The precision and clarity of the Classicists are often deliberately abandoned in favor of subtle ambiguity and wilful obscurity. There is as well an inversion of the Classical doctrine of absolute beauty, reflected in criticism as well as in creative writing, which leads to complete individualism in aesthetic perception and critical interpretation.

Thus the decadent style, in short, represents a clear reversal of classical values. This is only to say that the decadent values are antipodal. It is uncertain, ultimately, how deliberate this inversion is, or whether it is deliberate at all, for the reader can never really know any author's intention. But there is no doubt that, in form alone, content and intention disregarded, the decadent style is antithetical to the classical. It is also true that decadent literature has been most often so called because of its style, since that is its most recognizable characteristic. Indeed, most commentators have tended to have style in mind when writing about the French decadence.

But are they justified in identifying style with decadence?

DECADENCE AND SOCIETY

Decadence may also refer to social deterioration. The diverse views derived from this social, political, and religious "falling away" are manifold, and the whole philosophy of decadence is nebulous. Various writers obviously have different states of being in mind when they write about decadence.[22] For Nietzsche, decadence is Judaeo-Christianity; for Gobineau, the ascent of inferior races; for Montesquieu, a decline in political and commercial power; for Rousseau, civilization with its artifices; for Gautier, super-refined art and fine sensibility; for Bourget, unadaptable individuals in an unhealthy society; for Max Nordau and Edmond Seillière, mental disease; for Anatole Baju, himself a decadent, a quest for new artistic strength. Furthermore, each writer's position must be fully schematized before his actual meaning becomes clear. Gobineau, for instance, does not really have a man's color in mind, primarily, when he writes about race. All the semantic pitfalls of definition are glaringly obvious.

Yet no less obvious is the fact that words symbolize reality: in their language the French decadents are expressing definite ideas about real or supposed social decay. The scene in the last half of the nineteenth century, for all the glitter of the Second Empire, is not propitious for France.[23] The Revolutionary and Napoleonic Wars have exhausted the nation with bankruptcy, bloodletting, spleen, despondency. Kantism and positivism have crushed romantic naïveté, and with it much of France's idealism. Science and psychology have developed along utilitarian lines, and the monied bourgeoisie has no sympathy for its artists and philosophers. In 1850 Raudot, a member of the Assemblée Législative, writes *De la Décadence de la France,* in which he shows how France has fallen behind the other great European powers in territory, population, industry, military forces. He points to over-centralization, the decay of agriculture, the collapse of family life, and a mysterious but real loss of "spirit" as central factors in a national decadence. The terrible *débâcle* of 1870 intensifies a general pessimism. In "Mauvais sang" from *Une Saison en enfer* Rimbaud reflects the fatalistic thinking of countless young Frenchmen on the "inferiority" of their race. And this occurs a generation after Napoleon!

The French decadent world is indeed bleak, as the American historian Wolf points out:[24]

With the exception of a few years under the government of Louis Napoléon, the entire period since Waterloo has seen the progressive failure of the French to adjust their development to the process in the other advanced countries of Europe. In the period before the Revolution, France was a leader, perhaps *the* leader, in Europe; her curve of development set the standard for Western society. A cursory glance at the history of France in the last three centuries will give the evidence we need.

The decline is starkly evident. France has lost her *élan vital* which once spurred her on to incredible accomplishments. Thus Wolf concludes, as the decadents agree, that French society of the nineteenth century is truly "decadent":[25]

The differences that appear in the course of the nineteenth century are fundamental; they imply a wide diversity of social and political goals and, indeed, mutually exclusive conceptions of God. Furthermore, the process of fragmentation was progressive; by the end of the century there were three major mythologies clamoring vehemently for supremacy, and within each of the major divisions cults were beginning to appear further to atomize the national will.

To be healthy, he believes, like the decadent writers, that a nation must have a common mythology, i.e., a catholic set of ideals activated by an *élan vital*. Now, this position is of course highly debatable, and its thesis may be accepted, rejected, or at least qualified. But historical truth, at this point, is not our concern. What is important is that the French decadent writers share this vision of a decaying world, *and hence it is true for them*. A pre-Spenglerian nightmare of doom and death permeates their work.

French writers react quickly to this vision of society. In the early 1880s, when decadents and symbolists are still confused with one another by the public, they not only have an explicit understanding of France as a moribund society, crystallized in its decadent literature, but have also formulated an awareness of their peculiar role within this context: [26]

By this time decadence seemed to signify a kind of moral solitude of an artist, coupled with an exasperated and perverse form of mysticism. In many ways it was the familiar moral and physical drama of the young of all periods, but the generation of 1885, even more than that of 1820 with which it had traits in common, felt depression and defeat more poignantly, more tragically than others. The fashion of decadence was their way of steeling themselves against bourgeoisism and triviality (*la vie quotidienne* of Laforgue), against industrialism and naturalism. It concealed their deepest aspirations, because in their feeling that reality was something other than the real world (*la vraie vie est absente*, Rimbaud had said), they touched on a new sense of mystery or mysticism of which Mallarmé was the most subtle and persuasive exponent.

The keywords that reflect the prevailing spirit of the times are defeat and depression. Decadence is, in fact, a mood which both reflects and activates French social decay. There is no better way to describe it than as the loss of the vital urge of life, the last stage of biological process as the social organism withers away. The sap of a people, too, the decadents believe, dries up with the approaching winter of old age and inevitable death. Time has enervated the decadent nation. France shall die. It is from this biological principle that Brooks Adams, who is truly the mouthpiece of the French decadents, formulates his fatalistic law of civilization and decay: [27]

Such uniformity of development in the most distant times, and among the most divergent peoples, points to a progressive law of civilization, each stage of progress being marked by certain intellectual, moral and physical changes. As the attack in war masters the defence, and the combative instinct becomes unnecessary to the preservation of life, the economic supersedes the martial mind, being superior in bread-winning. As velocity augments and competition intensifies, nature begins to sift the economic minds themselves, culling a favoured aristocracy of the craftiest and subtlest types; choosing, for example, the Armenian in Byzantium, the Marwari in India, and the Jew in London. Conversely, as the costly nervous system of the soldier becomes an encumbrance, organisms, which can exist on less, successively supplant each other, until the limit of endurance is reached. Thus the Slavs exterminated the Greeks in Thrace and Macedonia, the Mahrattas and the Moslems dwindle before the low caste tribes of India, and the instinct of self-preservation has taught white races to resist an influx of Chinese. When nature has finished this double task, civilization has reached its zenith. Humanity can ascend no higher.

The eagerness with which France accepts Adams, at the close of the century, indicates a spiritual kinship. With Montesquieu and cyclical theories of history in mind, the decadent writers face the future with the grim conviction that they are the last men of an expiring fatherland.

And certainly Adams' law applies to French decadent literature. From Balzac on the French realists, as writers, portray the progressive triumph of money in an over-centralized capitalist society. Greed, the lust for money, is nationalized, so to speak, and ceases to be the miser's peculiar mania. The whole nation is mad for gold. New types of men spawn in the economic jungle of Balzac, Zola, and the Goncourts. The wellsprings of their idealism have dried up, and the inevitable result, as in *Peau de chagrin,* is the irreparable loss of *élan vital.* The heroes of decadent literature are unthinkable in the eighteenth century or, for that matter, in much of romanticism. It is only with the genius of Stendhal, with Julien Sorel, that the new hero emerges in triumph. Nineteenth century heroes are psychical mutations, actual changes of type, as single-minded and ambitious men emerge throughout decadent fiction. They are a new breed, a foreign race; gone forever is the *honnête homme* with, as the decadent would say, his ridiculous sense of decorum. This vital change is, in fact, what Gobineau really has in mind when he writes about race: [28]

Je pense que le mot *dégénéré*, s'appliquant à un peuple, doit signifier et signifie que ce peuple n'a plus la valeur intrinsèque qu'autrefois il possédait, parce qu'il n'a plus dans ses veines le même sang, dont des alliages successifs ont graduellement modifié la valeur; autrement dit, qu'avec le même nom il n'a pas conservé la même race que ses fondateurs; enfin, que l'homme de la décadence, celui qu'on appelle l'homme *dégénéré* est un produit différent, au point de vue ethnique, du héros des grandes époques.

There could be no clearer exposition of the theory of mutation, and the idea, with slight modifications, well fits into the work of Zola and the Goncourts. Decadence is pathological degeneracy.This is the inevitable result of the cause of the mutation, the fatal loss of the precious *élan vital*. Decadence is senility in the shadow of death.

Decadence seems bleakly Nordic, not typically Gallic. If their world is so despicable, moreover, then what are the decadents to write about, and why? The answer is clear. They must depict their own society, for they have none other, and they do so in fascinated awe: [29]

The decadents had to deal with the old dilemma that had troubled Gautier, Baudelaire, and Huysmans—a professed love of the modern and a hatred of most of its characteristic manifestations. As artists of a decadent age they wanted to write about it, and at the same time they detested its materialism and its progressivism. They tried to solve the problem by aligning themselves not only against Romanticism, but against Zola's Naturalism ("les purulences fétides issant des exutoires," as Baju defined it on January 5, 1888); they took refuge, now in an exaggerated *préciosité*, now in a careful description of the dance-hall, night-club scenery which had fascinated Baudelaire and the Goncourts. They practised, in short, what Hennequin had called both a *délicat* and a *populaire* style. Concerning the former, Verlaine wrote that *Décadisme*, while it was the literature of a decadent age, was not necessarily decadent itself: in reaction against its period, it sought "le délicat, le raffiné, l'élevé . . . contre les platitudes et les turpitudes ambiantes."

Many decadents, in short, despise their subject matter, and Verlaine even argues that while their content is "decadent," their purpose is not. In a sense they have a didactic purpose: to warn the world of impending doom. Most writers feel this in their blood; unlike Péladan they express it implicitly and confusedly. Writers are, after all, notoriously illogical, and rarely speculative philosophers like Adams. But the themes are nonetheless present in decadent literature. And as Verlaine claims, the decadent style, which has been so maligned, is no more than the means necessary for portraying the social rot.

Thus the decadents are greatly preoccupied with the social scene. They do not shrink from it, as some critics suppose, like an ostrich with its head in the sand. Their interest even becomes an obsession which, explicit or implicit, links them in a common bond that transcends the artificial boundaries of literary schools. Even the realists, for example, share much in common with the decadents:[30]

Les décadents ne sont point du tout hostiles au naturalisme. Les naturalistes, eux aussi, croient à la décadence de la société moderne et ils la peignent avec plaisir, telle qu'elle est; au nom du positivisme, ils nient les affirmations d'une "morale publique et religieuse"; ils décrivent minutieusement les instincts de l'homme; ils s'attachent surtout à peindre sans préjugés ce que la littérature appelle "amour", et que, eux, ils nomment instinct sexuel. Tout aussi logique que la rage naturaliste d'affirmer les "laideurs" de la vie est une volonté de nier les conditions mauvaises de cette vie, de se révolter contre l'instinct d'échapper à la grande tromperie de l'existence.

Hence the realists and naturalists, the parnassians, decadents, and symbolists all portray a decadent society. This is, in differing degree, their common concern. They differ from one another primarily in what they feel can be done about this social, aesthetic, religious decay, and in their manner of depicting it, their style. Yet the idea of decadence is catholic, and to this extent they are all "decadents."

The parnassians exemplify this point. Leconte de Lisle and Heredia paint great Wagnerian scenes of decline and fall, all based on a notion of cultural decadence. This is their greatest theme, almost their only theme. Leconte de Lisle is a kind of positivist and naturalist as he carves out fatalistic messages in restrained though not impersonal verse. The philosopher Charleton assesses him more accurately than the literary critics:[31]

However reluctantly, he is forced to adopt a wholly naturalistic philosophy. When he praises Greek polytheism, it is for its moral code, its respect for human dignity, its love of beauty, and its social and political consequences—not, significantly, for any supernatural element. And when he turns to Buddhism for consolation, it is to "une manière de bouddhisme scientifique" in which even 'Nirvana' is shorn of any transcendental meaning. He excludes the more mystical doctrines of orthodox Buddhism —the conception of the Supreme Being, Brahma, into whom the believer may be absorbed, the 'paradise' of 'Lower Buddhism', the 'Nirvana' or 'Higher Buddhism'. Here his outlook is close to positivism.

And here his outlook, it must be added, is essentially decadent. His poems portray the classical periods of fallen civilizations in didactic warnings of final decay. He addresses the contemporary scene in France through his concern with the past, for in his cyclical theory of history the same stages of civilization recur eternally. Decadence is his focal concern, his motor force, in "Le Soir d'une bataille," "Fiat nox," "Hypatie"; and his persona of impersonality falls away as he addresses France in "Aux Modernes." Decadence is more implicit in Heredia's Les Trophées, but nonetheless present, as evidenced by "A un Triomphateur" and "Sur un marbre brisé."

Symbolism has rarely been considered as a social commentary, but in fact many symbolist writers have an overt concern. Verlaine's "Je suis l'Empire à la fin de la décadence" states explicitly what is implicit in much symbolist writing. There are traces in even such unlikely poems as "Lassitude" from Maeterlinck's Serres chaudes. The symbolists simply despair of the social decadence, and hence many of them turn to art as a kind of Schopenhauerean consolation. Others, like Mallarmé in *Un Coup de dés,* turn to a type of cosmic pessimism. Real social concern, so evident in Rimbaud, is poignant. Indeed, some critics believe that the idea of decadence touches off their vision of the world—their eschatology:[32]

La poésie n'avait plus désormais qu'un programme: exprimer le mystère auquel l'homme finissait toujours par se heurter. Le poète devait redevenir le *vates,* au sens où l'entendait l'antiquité. Il écouterait vibrer son coeur sous les ondes émanées du grand inconscient.

To see the symbolist poet as a continuation of the romantic poet-prophet may seem extreme. But however true that is, the symbolists are obviously concerned with society. Even the symbolists identified most closely with art for art's sake have social depths. Thus André Barre observes in this connection that the symbolist "synthétisme d'inspiration a préservé notre littérature d'un suicide dans les marais scatologiques"[33] and that "le symbolisme a donc été une école d'espérance et de liberté, nullement un atelier de technique."[34]

It is apparent, then, that all the so-called literary schools, in varying degrees, are unified by a common preoccupation with decadence.

Towards a Definition of French Decadence

Historically, the word "decadence" has been used both denotatively and connotatively. The pejorative meanings must be dismissed immediately. Even some of the so-called denotative uses of the term are highly exaggerated if not outright confusing. In *La Poésie décadente devant la science psychiatrique* in 1897, for instance, Dr. Emile Laurent, a physician, dismisses these writers rather curtly as pathological. He proves his thesis, he believes, by dissecting their "perverted vocabulary" and the peculiar rhythms of decadence, by analyzing their elation and depression, their melancholia and mysticism, their moral blindness, egomania, and antisocial nature. Max Nordau epitomizes this position more than any other commentator. He writes:[35]

Under the influence of an obsession, a degenerate mind promulgates some doctrine or other—realism, pornography, mysticism, symbolism, diabolism. He does this with vehement penetrating eloquence, with eagerness and fiery heedlessness. Other degenerate, hysterical, neurasthenical minds flock around him, receive from his lips the new doctrine, and live thenceforth only to propagate it. They act as, in consequence of the diseased constitution of their brain and nervous system, they are compelled to act.

This deterministic and "psychological" understanding of decadence is a convenient way to dismiss the movement. But today the judgment stands as a medical curiosity. It affords no understanding whatsoever of the phenomenon of decadence.

The term "decadence," then, describes a style or a social state reflected in literature, or both at once. The "decadent" is either the writer or his supposed projection, the hero. Although most critics have understood decadence as style, this approach is ultimately confusing and inaccurate. The parnassians, symbolists, and the "decadents" proper are, for a brief span, an identical group, while at the same time they are all promulgating different styles.

Style is too inexact a way of defining decadence. What about the style of the early and the late Huysmans? What about Pierre Louÿs, a decadent with a classical style? What about the realists, who share a decadent worldview but not a decadent style, or the Goncourt brothers with their impressionistic style? How can one include Mendès, Bourges, Rachilde, Péladan, Lorrain, Lombard, Gourmont, Mirbeau, Villiers de l'Isle-Adam, Barbey d'Aurevilly, Mallarmé, Rimbaud, Verlaine, not to say Leconte de Lisle, Heredia, or Zola and the Goncourts, all under a discussion of a peculiar style called "decadent"? One cannot. The dissimilarities are too great. There is certainly a decadent fascination with syntax, as various critics have pointed out. But there is no general decadent style. The minor writings of *Le Décadent* or *Le Chat noir* are intellectual feats that skirt the basic issues of decadence. To take them seriously is like trying to understand modern existentialism by way of beatnikism. Style is only a medium of expression. The real question is not how the decadents expressed themselves, for they did so in a variety of manners, but what, rather, they were trying to say.

Decadence is a worldview: the particular vision of the world held by French writers around 1850 to 1900, or the outbreak of World War I—a society conceived in terms of decay. The decadents portray their world in many ways. As individuals no less than as groups they respond to their society. But the cardinal idea of their society as decadent is a unifying concern. *Thus French decadence is simply the literature of this period which implicitly or explicitly reflects the general obsession with social, political, moral decadence.* This is tantamount to saying that French decadence is simply itself, and that to define it we must learn only to recognize it.

Such a definition does not explain decadence; it merely points to the phenomenon. This is precisely the function of the denotative definition. Hence it only opens a discussion of the problem, in which many ambiguities will soon become apparent.

Is it true, for example, that the decadents neglect the essentials of civilization and prize only its vanities which have no survival value? Yet these vanities are necessary for the decadent's own survival. He, at least, cannot live without them. Decadence may well be the history of a vanity becoming a necessity, as man, appearing in literature as the hero, evolves different ideas of what is necessary and what is not. And does the decadent not have an ethical justification for his anti-naturalism? If nature is hostile to the mind, if it prefers its amoral, beastlike barbarians, men of blood and the soil, then few modern readers can fail to sympathize with the sensitive decadent in his love of beauty and an intellectualized truth. The heroes of decadent literature will pose, and attempt to resolve, these and many other ambiguous questions.

Perhaps decadence is even noble. Perhaps it is a kind of growth. While the decadent's organs of survival are pitiably atrophied from the barbarian's standpoint, his organs of perception are certainly raised to incredible pitches. This enables him to perceive beauty in manifold new guises. And perhaps the decadent, like a true hero, is even willing to die for the benefit of his race: he will commit suicide. Renato Poggioli is to pose this question, and resolve it to the decadent's satisfaction, in *The Autumn of Ideas*:[36]

Such a civilization falls defenseless before the onslaught of barbarism precisely because it envisages that scourge not only as a moral retribution, but also as the only possible biological alternative.

When the hour of decision comes, he discovers all too late that history has reverted to nature; and that the barbarian, being nature's child, is now becoming history's agent. At this point the decadent recognizes that he is left no alternative but to play a passive, and yet theatrical, role on history's stage. That role is that of scapegoat or sacrificial victim; and it is by accepting that part, and acting it well, that he seals in blood the strange brotherhood of decadence and barbarism.

The decadent, in short, welcomes destruction at the hands of the barbarians. He knows, ironically, that he has no further purpose and that nature must replace him. He runs to accept nature's verdict. Is it masochism that impels him to seek death under the barbarian sword? Or is it rather nobility— the reasoned thinking that it is best for him to die? The decadent poses a thorny problem worthy of all heroes. It leads to other fascinating questions which, regrettably, do not concern us here. The problem of decadence, with all its psychological and ethical aspects, only begins to come into focus once the slippery term "decadence" has been defined.

For the moment, as we prepare to examine the decadent hero, we must keep two propositions in mind. Both are from Anatole Baju, a poor decadent writer but an astute observer. He argues: "La littérature décadente synthétise l'esprit de notre époque, c'est-à-dire celui de l'élite intellectuelle de la société moderne."[37] And he further states: "La littérature décadente se propose de refléter l'image de ce monde spleenétique."[38] Baju is correct on both counts. Decadent literature is truly a synthesis of different responses to a common problem. And the focal point of this literature, which reflects life, is man himself through his literary projection, the decadent hero.

TWO

THE DECADENT IN HIS WORLDVIEW

WRITERS of the French de-
cadence visualize their society in bleak images: It is in a
decline and it will fall. Some perceive it going out with a
crescendo of doom and damnation while others personify
it as a cerebral hero giving a last pitiable whimper. There
is much difference of mood. Their images may recall the
barbarians sacking Rome, like Leconte de Lisle's poems; or
a neurotic aesthete studying his own collapse, like Huysmans'
Des Esseintes; or a grandiose *Götterdämmerung,* like Bourges'
Le Crépuscule des dieux. The decadent hero is the somber
protagonist of this Wagnerian literature.

But while they differ on the way their world will fall, the
decadent writers generally agree as to why it is declining.
This is not to say that they subscribe to a common philosophy. But explicitly or implicitly certain key ideas are prev-
alent. Hence there is a decadent worldview.

There are different aspects to this worldview and to the
decadent as he reacts to it.

First, the city as the great megalopolis emerges as an overpowering symbol. It is evil because it divorces men from
nature and conditions them to the artificial stimuli of city-
living. Men lose their *élan vital* with the emasculating tri-

umph of money. The decadent is often ambivalent in his attitude towards the city, as indeed towards civilization. A decadent hero like Pierre Froment can contemplate Paris, from the heights of Montmartre, in Zola's *Paris,* as the source of twentieth century progress. But at the same time, throughout decadent literature, the protagonist hates his city as he hates civilization, for all its vices and impurities. This fundamental ambivalence is expressed more in terms of wonder and admiration in the realists and some of the late romantics. But in the decadence proper the megalopolis is the modern Babylon—an object of profound and abiding distrust and hatred.

Second, modern man, by nature, ceases to be active. He is, to be sure, concerned with making money, enjoying mistresses, cheating his competitors in the business world. But in a city-world, as opposed to an agricultural society, his activities naturally tend to be mental. Hence the decadent hero becomes cerebral. He is, in time, an aesthete, a decadent pervert, who lusts after the ephemeral allurements of the painted city in a frantic search for pleasure.

Third, modern woman emerges in a strange reversal of natural function. She is masculinized. She is no longer the wife, mother, or earth-woman. She becomes the *femme fatale,* the vampire, the tempting object of man's vanity. She is a kind of Nana, the Scarlet Woman reigning in Babylon, or a type of Marthe Demailly intent on destroying her man.

Fourth, the androgyne appears as a sexless creature. At once male and female, the androgyne is not usually homosexual. It is simply woman hardened and man gone soft. Though it has the attributes of both sexes, it often has the function of neither. The androgyne is asexual and it symbolizes sterility. It is born, ultimately, from nature's rebellion against the artificial life of the megalopolis. Now, the androgyne, as a pervert, frequently wallows in a sexual miasma. But since it cannot reproduce itself, nature halts further development of the decadent and ends the corrupt and dying civilization. This is nature's purpose in bearing the androgyne.

Fifth, an extension of this idea, the civilized man is inevitably bored with life as the tinsel of the city ceases to excite him. He no longer wants to live. A wish to die—a metaphysical deathwish—motivates the decadent, who may then kill himself in a jaded search for the supreme sensation, or who, theatrically, may choose to sacrifice himself at the altar of nature. The decadent may open the gates of his city to the barbarians, though he knows they will kill him. Even when his deathwish is unconscious, the decadent aesthete no longer has the will to live. The romantic hero is typically a man of energy, but the decadent is most often the hero of supreme lassitude. The cerebral decadent welcomes death as the quietus of life. The boring drama of adolescence, maturity, and age is ended, and the tedious cycle of life complete. Death is his aesthetic solution to the riddle of life: death is ultimately necessary because life has no further artistic interest. Death is the finis of a work of art.

This, in essence, is the decadent worldview. A few writers depict it schematically, like Péladan in the many novels of *La Décadence latine,* his decadent epic. Most writers, however, tend to be explicit about only two or three themes, which they develop in their work, while the broad worldview remains implicit. Writers are, after all, not speculative thinkers, and some of them are surprisingly obtuse. One cannot always expect intellect in art. But this vision of society is nonetheless evident, and the decadent worldview may be abstracted, rather precisely, from the body of decadent literature. Then the decadent hero fits more neatly into the total picture.

THE MEGALOPOLIS

The great city, while attractive, is at once evil and destructive. This is the fundamental tenet of the decadent worldview. The idea of the city as Babylon recurs from Montesquieu and Rousseau throughout the nineteenth century, and numberless authors embody it in poem, story, novel. But, again, writers are not logicians, and they rarely schematize. It remains for a German philosopher, who inherits these French decadent ideas, to incarnate a terrifying portrayal of the megalopolis with which they would all agree:[1]

Finally, there arises the monstrous symbol and vessel of the completely emancipated intellect, the world-city, the centre in which the course of a world-history ends by winding itself up. A handful of gigantic places in each Civilization disfranchises and disvalues the entire motherland of its own Culture under the contemptuous name of the "provinces." The "provinces" are now everything whatsoever—land, town, *and* city—except these two or three points. There are no longer noblesse and bourgeoisie, freemen and slaves, Hellenes and Barbarians, believers and unbelievers, *but only cosmopolitans and provincials*. All other contrasts pale before this one, which dominates all events, all habits of life, all views of the world.

The megalopolis is an octopus reaching out with giant tentacles to engulf the surrounding countryside. The great city, Babylon, destroys its last rootless men, the decadents. From Balzac on, Paris is an open sewer which drowns in incredible filth the healthy provincials who are lured to it by visions of fame and money.

References to the cosmopolitan decadent in his city are numerous. In *Les Vingt et un jours d'un neurasthénique* Octave Mirbeau exclaims baldly: "La France est foutue, nom de Dieu! La France est dans les griffes des cosmopolites!"[2] And he develops the theme. Zola's *Paris* recalls Rastignac's apostrophe to the city at the conclusion of *Le Père Goriot*. One critic typifies its spirit to perfection:[3]

Paris, tout entier; Paris avec toutes ses splendeurs, avec toutes ses épouvantes, avec tous ses vices; Paris éblouissant de lumières, et Paris noir; le Paris qui fait la fête, et le Paris qui souffre; tous les bruits de Paris: rires éclatants, paroles sereines, grincements de dents, sanglots . . . le Paris des trousseurs de jupes; le Paris des remueurs d'idées; le Paris qui rampe, pieds nus dans la fange. . . .

Paris, in brief, is fatal and irresistibly tempting. This will be an omnipresent theme.

The Goncourts show the hideous city destroying healthy peasants, like Germinie Lacerteux, who are seduced to it:[4]

O Paris! tu es le coeur du monde, tu es la grande ville humaine, la grande ville charitable et fraternelle! Tu as des douceurs d'esprit, de vieilles miséricordes de moeurs, des spectacles qui font l'aumône! Le pauvre est ton citoyen comme le riche. Tes églises parlent de Jésus-Christ; tes lois parlent d'égalité; tes journaux parlent de progrès; tous tes gouvernements parlent du peuple; et voilà où tu jettes ceux qui meurent à te servir, ceux qui se tuent à créer ton luxe, ceux qui périssent du mal de tes industries, ceux qui ont sué leur vie à travailler pour toi, à te donner ton bien-être, tes plaisirs, tes splendeurs, ceux qui ont fait ton animation, ton bruit, ceux qui ont mis la chaîne de leurs existences dans ta durée de capitale, ceux qui ont été la foule de tes rues et le peuple de ta grandeur!

The Goncourt brothers loathe the city. In this passage they are explicitly critical; in others they speak through *porte-paroles*. They express their hatred subtly, for instance, by describing Jupillon in relationship to the city:[5]

Le sourire, cet esprit et cette malice de la physionomie parisienne, était toujours chez lui moqueur, impertinent. Jupillon avait la gaieté de la bouche méchante, presque de la cruauté aux deux coins des lèvres retroussées et tressaillantes de mouvements nerveux.

The decadent writers hate Paris because the city is corrupting.

They also hate the megalopolis because it is enervating. It destroys the souls of its people and leaves them exposed, rootless, like Barrès' *Déracinés*. Charles Demailly, in the Goncourt novel of the same name, refers to his loss of *élan vital*. He exclaims desperately, futilely: "Il y avait une vitalité que nous avons perdue!"[6] He knows that megalopolitan man is the mirror of himself, bored, lethargic, and diseased. Demailly's physician, a sage observer, speaks for the Goncourt brothers in this novel. He diagnoses the psychosomatic disease of the megalopolis in the following guise:[7]

La vie moderne va du plein air de la vie agricole à la vie concentrée, à la vie assise, à la vie au gaz du charbon de terre, à la vie au gaz des lampes, à la vie nourrie par une alimentation falsifiée, sophistiquée, trompeuse, à tous les renversements des conditions normales de l'être physique.

The diagnosis is a central document in the decadence. It is also important because it emphasizes the peculiar relation-

ship of the novelist, like the Goncourts, to the decadent
philosopher, like Adams or Spengler. The Goncourt brothers
write about centralization much as Adams does, later, in
The Law of Civilization and Decay. They foreshadow the
monumental Spengler in *The Decline of the West* as, at the
outbreak of World War I, he attempts to synthesize the cur-
rents swirling about him from the nineteenth century.

The megalopolis is a great destructive machine which
grinds men down as surely as movable parts. Its frenetic
speed simply burns out people. The Goncourts write again:[8]

Un fier balayage de fortunes—ce Paris!—et la mort aux jeunes
gens! et si vite, et avec si peu d'aventures, si peu de bruit! Ah!
le boulevard en mange diablement de ces caracoleurs, de ces
viveurs! un an, deux ans au plus,—et brûlés!

They underscore the fact that this wear and tear is the
natural consequence of the *machinery* of the capitalist society. The wheels move as fatally as the gods. Laborers, bourgeois, aristocrats, unspoiled provincials, and decadent boule-
vardiers, all perish under the constant grind of the great
machine.

The cosmopolitan, or inhabitant of the great city, is, then,
not merely the smartly dressed dandy one might imagine. In
the decadent sense the cosmopolitan, stripped of his connotations with wealth and fashion, is simply decadent man in the
megalopolis. Of course there are decadents of the *haut
monde.* Bourget, in particular, is concerned with the decadent scions of a corrupt aristocracy. In *Cosmopolis* he observes:[9]

L'existence du Cosmopolite peut tout cacher sous la luxueuse
banalité de ses fantaisies, depuis le snobisme en quête de relations plus hautes jusqu'à l'escroquerie en quête de vols plus
faciles. . . .

But while decadent writers may portray a fashionable society,
this is not their exclusive or even main concern in the idea
of the cosmopolitan. Their point is simple. The cosmopolitan
is a city-man, whether from the Madeleine or the streets.
And the cosmopolitan life, as Bourget notes, is superficial,
hypocritical, empty. It is the world which Catulle Mendès,

among others, evokes in *Monstres parisiens,* stories about the moral derelicts, rich and poor, of the great Babylon. The attitude of Mendès is typical. He summarizes the decadent idea of the megalopolis by bitterly exclaiming:[10]

Ah! votre nom de Dieu de Paris! comme il étiole et comme il dévirilise. C'est la ville femme, la femelle de l'Europe, et quelle femelle! ni chair, ni sang, ni os; du maquillage, rien dessous.

Megalopolitan life is stultifying. The decadents, their energy sapped by its artificiality and grind, become zombies in a monstrous sepulchre. They are shells of men divorced from nature. The decadent message is that such men cannot and will not maintain their great city. They will not even survive.

MODERN MAN AS DECADENT

The son of the megalopolis is the decadent, i.e., modern man, particularly the one who is sensitive to the social decay around him. As artificial as a hot-house plant, he is the son of the pounding streets and the daily newspaper. He is so habituated to a constant flow of stimuli that he is unable to act without stimulus. Modern man is one who must be constantly titillated, then satisfied.

The decadent is not a happy man. His quest of pleasure is infrequently realized and never satisfied. Yet he cannot live without the luxuries of his city. He is an addict of the senses. Spengler is again instructive as he summarizes for the decadent writers the decadent hero's dissatisfaction and unhappiness:[11]

What makes the man of the world-cities incapable of living on any but this artificial footing is that the cosmic beat in his being is ever decreasing, while the tensions of his waking-consciousness become more and more dangerous. Tension without cosmic pulsation to animate it is the transition to nothingness. But Civilization is nothing but tension. The head, in all the outstanding men of the Civilizations, is dominated exclusively by an expression of extreme tension. Intelligence is only the capacity for understanding at high tension, and in every Culture these heads are the types of its final men.

This is an accurate picture of the decadent, who is as unhappy with his city as a spoiled child with a discarded toy. Spengler's language is mystical to a point, as the decadent writers themselves frequently are, but he really understands the decadent in psychological terms. He argues, like Zola, Péladan, indeed any one of a great number, that modern man is separated from nature, that the city alienates him from the soil and the old virtues of home, that his roots have been exposed. Man is a robot, a part of the great machine—moving but essentially unalive. His *élan vital* has dried up. In modern terms he is conditioned by the mass-culture of the newspaper world, as the French decadence chooses to name it. The decadent is helplessly manipulated, a cog in the perpetual motion of the machine. He is stimulated, satisfied, and the procedure is endlessly repeated. The decadent is contemporary man, a consumer and pleasure-seeker in the labyrinth of the great city.

The decadent hero as modern man is also lethargic. Overwhelmed by abulia in the tedium of life, he must force himself to act. He is a cerebral hero like, for instance, the vacillating writer of Marcel Schwob's *Le Livre de Monelle*. This weak, introspective type recurs in Schwob's *Coeur double,* where the author carefully distinguishes between "le monde extérieur" and "le monde intérieur." The decadent inhabits the latter world. It is one of sense perception and sensation, not of action. In such guise Frédéric Moreau watches the world pass him by in Flaubert's *L'Education sentimentale*. Démétrios rejects life for a dream in Louÿs's *Aphrodite*. Mateo Diaz watches his ideals vanish, powerless to act, as Conchita cuckolds him in Louÿs's *La Femme et le pantin*. All these decadents are typically ineffectual and static as life crushes them.

Maurice Barrès formulates a decadent "culte du moi." Philippe is an inept young man who analyzes himself through *Sous l'oeil des barbares* and *Un Homme libre*. He tries to cure his lethargy through "moral mechanics," but he never really acts. In *Le Jardin de Bérénice* he attempts to go into politics, as a last resort. Yet his life continues to be introspective, abortive. A mere wish for *énergie* cannot replace a lost *élan vital.* Entragues, in Gourmont's *Sixtine,* cannot control the woman he loves. He sadly watches her run away with her masterful Russian lover. There is no escape from the paralysis of modern man. In *Les Vingt et un jours d'un neurasthénique* Georges Vasseur travels to a spa in an effort to find health. But there, too, he runs across the debilitated wrecks of a paralyzing megalopolis. Modern man is invariably neurasthenic.

The decadent turns his vision inward to introspection rather than outward to action. Nearly every hero is an example. In *Les Chevaux de Diomède* the hero observes:[12]

Seul? Oui, je suis seul. Toute causerie me laisse seul, toute intimité me laisse seul. Je suis seul quand je touche la main d'un ami ou les genoux d'une femme, seul quand je parle, seul quand j'écoute et seul quand je crie. C'est vrai, mais qui donc, s'il pense, ne vit pas dans l'éternelle solitude?

All megalopolitans suffer from this deadly lethargy. The decadent hero, unlike the herdman, realizes that his society is decadent, but he cannot change matters. He is overwhelmed. It is thought, cerebralism, which makes him a decadent hero. He writhes neurotically in his abulia, like Sandy Rose in Gourmont's *Une Nuit au Luxembourg,* and dies of cerebral excesses. As a megalopolitan he is too conditioned to city stimulation and satisfaction to act on his own as *a natural man.* This inertia is what Grancey, in *Charles Demailly,* terms the moral disease of the age, as he exclaims: "Il y a des maladies de l'humanité comme il y a des maladies de la terre, un *oïdium* moral."[13]

In his despair modern man may decay morally. The decadent turns to sensualism as a form of action, but even that is abortive and unsatisfactory. In Lorrain's *Monsieur de Phocas,* a typical novel of the decadence proper, lesbianism, incest, and drug-addiction are rampant. A catalog of crimes, like Praz's *Romantic Agony,* might be compiled on this erotic current in decadent literature. Cerebralism, lethargy, and hypersexuality lead to severe neurosis. Many decadents reflect an unholy aura:[14]

Oui, un Démon me torture et me hante, et cela depuis mon adolescence. Qui sait? peut-être était-il déjà en moi quand je n'étais qu'un enfant, car, dussé-je vous paraître halluciné, monsieur, voilà des années que je souffre d'une chose bleue et verte.

Neurotic obsessions, *choses bleues et vertes,* afflict innumerable decadents and make deviates of many. The list of perverts is extensive. In Rachilde's *Les Hors nature* Jacques Reutler de Fertzen has a homosexual attachment for his young brother. Neurotic deviates recur throughout Lorrain, Péladan, Lombard, Mendès. *Buveurs d'âmes,* a typical work, is "une étude très curieuse et très creusée d'un caractère d'homme amoureux de la souffrance."[15] Cerebralism starts in lethargy and ends, say, in masochism.

The decadent portait of modern man is not very flattering. One shudders from Villiers de l'Isle-Adam's *Isis* and *Derniers contes.* Péladan's *La Décadence latine* is a modern epic about demoniacs, deviates, mystics, maniacs. There is no need to multiply examples. The point is that the decadent illness, in consensus, arises from modern man's isolation from nature. It prevents him from acting and causes him to suffer from introspection, abulia, hypersensibility. The decadent writers are specific on this:[16]

La vie rétrospective, cette habitude des intelligences décadentes, ce paradis artificiel qui consiste à se créer une entité dans le temps défunt et à vivre des heures de rêve dans les civilisations mortes pour échapper au nauséeux présent; tel fut son unique plaisir.

By turning from reality, i.e., realizable aims and aspirations, the decadent is exposed to a nightmare world of perversions.

Modern man is, morally, a leper. He commits all crimes for power and egotistic satisfaction. The decadents create the world of Bourges' *Le Crépuscule des dieux,* as Lebois hastens to point out:[17]

Les conclusions à tirer du *Crépuscule* sont diverses. La noblesse d'Europe, qui incarna si longtemps la civilisation, est à l'agonie: intuition en 1880, certitude aujourd'hui. Rongée par ses propres tares, son inaptitude à évoluer, elle est en outre minée par l'hostilité de ses sujets. . . . Bourges brosse un saisissant tableau de l'Europe capitaliste, celle qui, pour tenter de survivre, précipitera le monde, trente ans plus tard et pour combien de décades? dans la guerre: marchands de canons, futurs fournisseurs de godillots ou de caleçons aux armées, gendres de Grévy et petits sucriers, tribuns tombeurs de ministères ou manoeuvriers de couloirs dans des Parlements ou des Reichstags; leurs compagnes: snobinettes de luxe ou de luxure, cocaïnomanes ou nymphomanes; et les plumitifs mérités par ces parvenus: romanciers mondains, chroniqueurs faisandés, larbins et cireurs. Par-delà le Crépuscule des gentes, le Crépuscule de l'Europe.

Decadents people this society terminated by the Great War, described in the fiction of the epoch, schematized by Spengler at the eve of the actual cataclysm. Their vices, decadent writers claim, are responsible for the catastrophe. The nightmarish world of gothicism, overflowing with perverts and deviates, cannot endure. The decadents arise from the megalopolis, the epitome of artificiality, as aesthetes, cosmopolitans, lethargic protagonists. But regardless of guise modern man is always a cerebral hero given to reflection rather than action. When on occasion he happens to act, he strikes out blindly, meaninglessly, like Hamlet against Polonius: the aim of action is never realized. The decadent plays his theatrical role on the stage of history before nature finally rebels and cuts him down.

THE MODERN WOMAN

The decadent, unlike the romantic hero, is passive by nature. He inhabits a static, intellectual world of emotion and sensation. In a reversal of function the decadent woman is active and masculinized. She is a prototype of the man-consuming *femme fatale*. But to see her only as the vampire is to misunderstand her role. The term "modern woman" more aptly describes her place in the decadent worldview. For it is all women of the civilization, not merely the *femmes fatales*, who are destructive. Whether a seductive temptress or sedate housewife, modern woman destroys the decadent man.

The novelists portray the fact that philosophers comment upon at the end of the century. Brooks Adams, in this connection, notes that the decline of woman is implicit with the rise of economic man. The woman as wife and mother disappears, and with her the value which nature gives her. The new woman is a beautiful parasite. This is one of the great decadent themes.

Since writers must express their ideas in the form of fiction, they analyze the modern woman vis-à-vis a particular thing. The Goncourt brothers, for instance, talk about modern woman in relationship to the novel which is so greatly concerned with her. The comment is devastating:[18]

... En sorte que tout homme de ce siècle, sachant lire et sachant voir, a été dûment édifié et apitoyé sur cette maladie organique de la femme moderne, maladie inconnue avant la mise des nuages en bouteilles et la découverte de certains mots: ce long crucifiement d'une âme d'épouse, délicate, élancée, sensitive et frissonnante, accouplée à un mari qui mange une pomme sans la peler, chante au dessert des dîners de noces, aime comme il digère, à ce mari enfin, "le gros homme" du roman, et de tous les romans.

In this particular novel it is Marthe, a beautiful actress and modern woman, who drives her husband insane—Charles Demailly. On the modern scene woman is always destructive. Mendès concurs. He notes:[19]

Or, puisque selon la mode elle est tombée du sentiment à la sensation, de la passion à la névrose, c'est sa chair et ses muscles et ses nerfs qu'elle avoue, véridiquement ou non.

Mendès is typically obsessed with the problem of the modern woman. Whereas his fiction, like that of many a decadent, is a covert attack, his persona falls at times and he is quite overt. In the preface to *La Première maitresse* he writes scathingly:[20]

... La femme est la cause la plus active des énervements de la volonté, des déviations de la pensée, des abandonnements de la conscience, des vraies fonctions non remplies, du but non atteint, et, finalement, du mécontentement de soi-même, qui est la pire des angoisses.

Megalopolitan woman is, to say the least, no longer man's helpmeet. She is his adversary in a battle of the sexes—a battle which, because of his cerebralism, he cannot win.

The *femme fatale* is the most striking category of "modern woman" in French decadent literature. Praz enumerates a large number in *The Romantic Agony*. The classic *femme fatale* is probably Clara in Mirbeau's *Le Jardin des supplices*. As a sadistic Englishwoman, she incarnates a type from Lady Dudley of Balzac's *Le Lys dans la vallée* to modern English-women in Gide's *Les Faux-monnayeurs* and Hemingway's *The Sun Also Rises*. She has neither goodness nor frailty. Her evil is titanic as she uses both men and women as objects of her insatiable lust in the Chinese torture gardens. Salammbô, in Flaubert's novel, is a *femme fatale* with romantic vestiges. Hyacinthe Chantelouve, in Huysmans' *Là-Bas*, is a succubus who consumes men with her passion. Stéphana, in Mendès' *Zo'har*, is diabolical as she seduces her brother. The carnality of Sara in Villiers' *Axël*, while subdued, is a real trait, and indeed describes all fatal women of the decadence.

Modern man despises yet fears modern woman while at the same time she bewitches him. Louÿs's Conchita, in *La Femme et le pantin*, is a beautiful seductress whom the author sardonically describes:[21]

Elle est même, en somme, honnête femme. Elle n'a pas eu plus de quatre ou cinq amants. A l'époque où nous vivons, c'est une chasteté.

For two years Conchita toys with Don Mateo Diaz, a middle-aged decadent, by promising but refusing herself. As a modern woman she takes his money while she taunts him. Money always replaces love in the decadence. Lust, sense pleasure, is a different theme. Conchita respects him—a vestige of the natural role of man and woman—only when he dominates her. Then she exclaims in her rare moment of truth:[22]

Pour que tu me battes, Mateo. Quand je sens ta force, je t'aime.

She uses sex to torture Don Diaz. She tells him of her many

assignations with her lovers, then welcomes his chastisement. Sadism is the modern woman's most salient trait.

In Louÿs's *Aphrodite* the courtesan, Chrysis, tries to destroy Démétrios, the great sculptor and queen's lover. She tells him that, though she has given herself to all others, he cannot have her: he must commit three enormous crimes. As a jaded decadent Démétrios is momentarily whetted by a desire he cannot instantly gratify. He perpetrates the crimes. At the end of the novel, however, when he spurns Chrysis, Démétrios explains what the cerebral decadent realizes but never acts upon:[23]

Vous n'avez toutes qu'un seul rêve, qu'une seule idée au cerveau: faire que votre faiblesse rompe la force de l'homme et que votre futilité gouverne son intelligence!

Modern woman's love for the decadent, if such it may be called, is sado masochistic. This is at the heart of decadent psychology. She loves him only when he forces her, and even then with a sensuality which often shocks him. She is more masculine, demanding, than he.

Modern woman is corrupt. *La pourriture de la chair femelle* is a constant theme. Péladan writes, for instance, about the seductive Léonora d'Este in *Le Vice suprême*: [24]

Idole comme Shiva, son culte c'est l'hécatombe. Cléopâtre a fui, à Actium, afin de voir son amant abandonner le combat et l'empire du monde pour suivre sa galère. Toutes les femmes, dans la mesure de leur destinée, essayent la fuite de Cléopâtre, et celui qui ne leur fait pas litière de tout, est un monstre.

It is a striking and recurrent image. Modern woman uses her weak lover, tires of him, destroys him. In the following verses Verlaine tells a similar story of the decadent and the modern woman:[25]

> Je fus mystique et je ne le suis plus,
> (La femme m'aura tout repris tout entier)
> Non sans garder des respects absolus
> Pour l'idéal qu'il fallut renier.
>
> Mais la femme m'a repris tout entier!

J'allais priant le Dieu de mon enfance
(Aujourd'hui c'est toi qui m'as à genoux)
J'étais plein de foi, de pleine espérance,
De charité sainte aux purs feux si doux.

Mais aujourd'hui tu m'as à tes genoux.

La Femme, par toi, redevient LE maître,
Un maître tout puissant et tyrannique,
Mais qu'insidieux! feignant de tout permettre
Pour en arriver à tel but satanique . . .

O le temps béni quand j'étais ce mystique!

The message is plain. Modern woman, like a vampire, sucks man's blood and grows strong as he weakens. She dominates him.

There is another current of modern women in decadent literature. It is the neurotic. The *femme fatale* is strong, self-possessed, brutal. The neurotic, on the other hand, loses her self-control even while she remains destructive. There are numerous neurotic women in the decadence: Mme Istar Capimont (Péladan, *Istar*), Paule Riazan (Péladan, *Curieuse!*), Liliane Forli (Mendès, *La Femme-Enfant*), Soeur Philomène (the Goncourt brothers), Germinie Lacerteux (the Goncourts), Célestine (Mirbeau, *Le Journal d'une femme de chambre*). Their neuroses assume many forms—neurasthenia, hysteria, nymphomania, perversion. Modern woman as a lesbian particularly fascinates Verlaine. In "Sur le balcon" he writes with an embarrassing sensuality:[26]

Toutes deux regardaient s'enfuir les hirondelles:
L'une pâle aux cheveux de jais et l'autre blonde
Et rose, et leurs peignoires légers de vieille blonde
Vaguement serpentaient, nuages, autour d'elles.

Et toutes deux, avec des langueurs d'asphodèles,
Tandis qu'au ciel montait la lune molle et ronde,
Savouraient à longs traits l'émotion profonde
Du soir, et le bonheur triste des coeurs fidèles.

Telles, leurs bras pressant, moites, leurs tailles souples,
Couple étrange qui prend pitié des autres couples,
Telles, sur le balcon, rêvaient les jeunes femmes.

> Derrière elles, au fond du retrait riche et sombre,
> Emphatique comme un trône de mélodrames
> Et plein d'odeurs, le Lit, défait, s'ouvrait dans l'ombre.

Decadent women are psychopathic. Salammbô has a fertility rite with a snake and Laure Lordès (Rachilde, *L'Animale*) fondles a cat. Clara, Hyacinthe Chantelouve, Germinie Lacerteux, and Mme Honorine d'Arlement (Mendès, *La Première maîtresse*) are nymphomaniacs. Péladan's Néobelle and Paule Riazan are frigid, but delight in enticing men. Liliane Forli is a young Lolita in a novel of infantilism. The list is interminable.

The women of Rougon-Macquart, in Zola's epic, are all neurotic. Indeed Zola considers the failure of modern woman to be the matrix of decadence: The race would be purged through its women, as he writes of Félicité. With the mother begins the initial *faute* transmitted through the women of the family. Zola notes with cold precision:[27]

Je veux expliquer comment une famille, un petit groupe d'êtres, se comporte dans une société, en s'épanouissant pour donner naissance à dix, à vingt individus, qui paraissent, au premier coup d'oeil, profondément dissemblables, mais que l'analyse montre intimement liés les uns aux autres. Historiquement, ils partent du peuple, ils s'irradient dans toute la société contemporaine, ils montent à toutes les situations, par cette impulsion essentiellement moderne que reçoivent les basses classes en marche à travers le corps social, et ils racontent ainsi le Second Empire, à l'aide de leurs drames individuels, du guet-apens du coup d' Etat à la trahison de Sedan.

Thus Zola goes so far as to link modern woman's neurosis, *la faute initiale,* to the general social decadence of the period. Decadent literature has even political repercussions: Sedan is the inevitable result of modern woman's separation from nature and her unbalance.

The attributes of the modern woman are well summarized in a little-known heroine of the decadence, Mme Honorine d'Arlement in Mendès, *La Première maîtresse.* She is a widow in her early thirties. She has already killed a husband and consumed a series of lovers through her sexual excesses, though faithful to each in his turn. She looks like a good bourgeoise and indeed accepts all the middle-class values. But she is neurotic and insatiable. Love is her way of draining a man's energy, his life, and leaving him an empty husk. She seduces the seventeen-year-old Evelin Gerbier, who asks himself in amazement:[28]

Comment! cette femme, si paisible, s'exprimant avec la politesse banale usitée dans les visites, c'était celle qui l'avait pris, enlevé, dévêtu, et tenu, palpitant et sanglotant, dans l'ombre, sous ses lèvres acharnées,—qui lui avait bu le souffle et l'âme?

It is this calm bourgeoise who caresses Evelin at the foot of his dead mother's bed after she has faithfully cared for the old woman. And later the decadent and the modern woman stroll through the streets of Paris, at night, in search of new companions in their frantic quest of pleasure.

It is interesting that *La Première maîtresse* portrays a tranquil, bourgeois widow as the "modern woman." She is bovine rather than fatal. Her crimes, however, seem all the greater for her domesticity. With Clara or Hyacinthe Chantelouve, fatal women in the grand style, the reader anticipates sexual horrors. But with an even-tempered housewife like Honorine the reader is shaken. This is what Mendès wishes. In modern society even the bourgeoise, he says, has become a fatal woman. By being typical Honorine d'Arlement is a devastating comment upon the disturbance of the times.

THE ANDROGYNE

A third sex emerges in decadent literature. It is the androgyne, which may be a man with feminine characteristics or a woman with masculine traits. In Péladan the androgyne is nearly always a woman, in Lombard and Lorrain a man. The androgyne may be a transvestite, a pervert, or asexual, but the sexual activity is unimportant in the decadent worldview. The decadent writers stress the androgyne's biological sterility: it incarnates what is anti-natural in its most obvious form, and it is thus a refutation of sex, love, life. The androgyne is an extreme instance of the decadent or modern woman.

The androgyne is often hypersexual. In Mendès' *Méphistophéla,* for instance, the Baroness Sophor d'Hermelinge has a homosexual attachment for her husband's sister. She is a notorious lesbian who falls in love with her own daughter, Carola, who is also an androgyne. This flamboyant sex-novel is typical of the decadence proper.

There are sexual overtones throughout the decadence. In *Les Névroses* Maurice Rollinat pens his verses on psychiatric cases of the androgyne; there is a plethora of perverts and transvestites. In Péladan's *Le Vice suprême,* a cardinal novel of the decadence, Claire (La Nine) is a sadistic androgyne who maintains her own as a man in a circle of fifteen atheists. Péladan describes her peculiar charm:[29]

La Nine n'avait pas de hanches; la Nine n'avait pas de gorge: la ligne de sa taille se continuait verticale à ses cuisses étroites, ses reins n'étaient que des pectoraux abaissés. De son sexe, ni les flancs larges de la fécondité, ni les saillantes mamelles de la maternité, mais le charme de chatte et la grâce du mouvement félin. Elle était, consciemment l'androgyne pâle, le vampire suprême des civilisations vieillies, dernier monstre avant le feu du ciel.

The types of the androgyne and the *femme fatale* merge in La Nine as they do in so many decadent heroines. Her hypersexuality is psychopathic. She is masculine in appearance and intellect—an abnormality which enflames the decadent's lust. This explains why Des Esseintes in *A Rebours,* for example, succumbs to the American acrobat, Miss Urania:[30]

Peu à peu, en même temps qu'il l'observait, de singulières conceptions naquirent; à mesure qu'il admirait sa souplesse et sa force, il voyait un artificiel changement de sexe se produire en elle; ses singeries gracieuses, ses mièvreries de femelle s'effaçaient de plus en plus, tandis que se développaient, à leur place, les charmes agiles et puissants d'un mâle; en un mot, après avoir tout d'abord été femme, puis, après avoir hésité, après avoir avoisiné l'androgyne, elle semblait se résoudre, se préciser, devenir complètement un homme.

The obverse happens simultaneously. Des Esseintes, a pliable decadent, becomes progressively effeminate as he responds to her masculinity. They change sexes. Huysmans notes that "cet échange de sexe entre Miss Urania et lui, l'avait exalté."[31] The sexual fascination exercised by the androgynous woman over the decadent male is fatal.

Lesbianism and tranvestism, which are sub-themes of androgynism, are frequent motifs. Léonora, a *femme fatale* and *monstre métaphysique,* as Péladan calls her, listens to the call of perverted love. She almost succumbs:[32]

Peut-être Léonora eût-elle risqué les caresses de Bianca: mais la suprême recommandation du P. François la maintint en face d'une tentation qui n'osait pas. En cette rencontre, elle eut la haute volupté qui s'éprouve au perpétuel coudoiement d'un péché intense, facile, secret et refusé.

and again:

Betty, viennoise, selon la formule de Gozzi, mélancoliquement timide, et d'une mignonne gaucherie à la Schoorel, couvait Léonora de regards troublés, en une adoration qui la faisait lécher de baisers les mains de la princesse, avec une animalité douce dans la caresse.

Léonora feels the impulse strongly, but though an androgyne she is not a lesbian.

Many androgynes are asexual although they feel a perverse pleasure in transvestism. In Villiers' *Isis* Tullia Fabriana disguises herself as a man for her many adventures. Gautier's *Mademoiselle de Maupin* is permeated with transvestism. The heroine even describes herself as an androgyne:[33]

Beaucoup d'hommes sont plus femmes que moi.—Je n'ai guère d'une femme que la gorge, quelques lignes plus rondes, et des mains plus délicates; la jupe est sur mes hanches et non dans mon esprit. Il arrive souvent que le sexe de l'âme ne soit point pareil à celui du corps, et c'est une contradiction qui ne peut manquer de produire beaucoup de désordre.

Mlle de Maupin is a transvestite who often travels in a man's guise. She ultimately falls in love with Albert, and although he suspects that she is a woman, he loves her whether she is or not. Homosexuality is a latent theme. In her disguise Mlle de Maupin comes to say:[34]

Je perdais insensiblement l'idée de mon sexe, et je me souvenais à peine, de loin en loin, que j'étais femme; dans les commencements, il m'échappait souvent de dire, sans y songer, quelque chose comme cela qui n'était pas congruent avec l'habit que je portais.

In the dénouement she has relations with Albert, but she leaves him the next morning. She explains that she does not wish to destroy their beautiful dream by having a vulgar reality replace it. The real reason for her departure, nevertheless, is that to the end she retains a man's soul in a woman's body. She does want to surrender her androgyny.

Even when lesbianism and transvestism are not rampant, an androgynous mood permeates decadent literature. This is true, for example, of Lorrain's *Princesses d'ivoire et d'ivresse*:[35]

De tous les contes entendus, lus et feuilletés dans mon enfance sont nées ces princesses d'ivoire et d'ivresse: elles sont faites d'extase, de songe et de souvenirs. Il en est d'ensoleillées, plus précises et plus vivantes, princesses d'ambre et d'Italie.

It is sex without sexuality, as in his later book, *Pelléastres*. Lust is subdued. In Péladan's *Curieuse!* Princess Paule Riazan is the androgyne who, though virtuous, has a morbid curiosity about Parisian night life. Nébo Mérodack is her escort through miasmas of depravation. The author describes her pointedly:[36]

La beauté de la princesse étant mi-partie d'un jeune homme et d'une jeune fille, elle doit avoir dans l'âme la même dualité; j'ai salué en elle, l'être complet, possédant le double charme féminin et viril . . . l'androgyne se suffisant à lui-même et n'aimant pas.

He stresses here, as elsewhere, the androgyne's basic sterility. In *Finis latinorum* Péladan relates the androgyne to the modern woman. He says:[37]

L'androgyne—répond-il à un regard qui l'interrogeait—est cet être qui n'existe plus physiquement chez l'homme dans nos races.

The androgyne is certainly an omnipresent theme.

Sexuality is so prominent in the decadence that the entire movement is identified with it. Sexuality seems to be the decadent's *raison d'être*. A. E. Carter observes in this connection:[38]

Sexual perversions, in fact, are the chief ingredients of all these works—usually appearing as androgynism and Lesbianism, both described as symptoms of decadence. By the eighties, Romanticism's *mal du siècle* had become androgynism: "A quels cultes mystérieux vont-ils donc se vouer, ces hommes et ces femmes que *l'amour de soi* écarte l'un de l'autre?" asked Maurice Barrès in a preface he wrote for *Monsieur Vénus*. "La maladie du siècle . . . est faite en effet d'une fatigue nerveuse, excessive" which leads to "le dégoût de la femme" and "la haine de la force mâle," so that certain minds "rêvent d'un être insexué"—the androgyne.

The androgyne, despite its Imperial Roman parallels, is the logical extension of the ideas of artificiality and dandyism. A new state of mind produces the androgyne, just as social changes produce the new attitudes. Thus A. E. Carter chooses to understand the decadent movement in psychological terms. His approach is of course correct.

Yet there is a deeper layer of meaning. The philosophical significance of the androgyne, and indeed of decadent sexuality, should not be forgotten. The androgyne, essentially, is the last stage of development in modern man. It is the epitome of the anti-natural, which arises when the natural can evolve no further. Perversion and asexuality have philosophical as well as psychological meaning. The androgyne is perverted, true, but what is perversion but sterility? The androgyne cannot reproduce itself. Hence the decadent civilization which bears and nurtures it is destined to end. The androgyne, in this sense, is the last form of decadent man or woman, in whom the destiny of a whole civilization is fulfilled and comes to an abrupt end. After the androgyne, the déluge; after sterility, nothingness.

THE DEATHWISH

The impact of the decadent worldview is terrifying. The events that produce this worldview are linked together in the following way: The megalopolis destroys man's soul, i.e., his *élan vital,* by alienating him from nature. Then modern man becomes weak and effeminate, a cerebral decadent, an impractical aesthete, while the masculinized modern woman usurps his place. Finally the androgyne emerges as nature's rebellion against the artificialities of Babylon. Nature herself causes this reversal of the sexes in order to impose sterility upon the decadent civilization. Weak and unable to reproduce itself, the world comes to a cataclysmic end. The barbarians, men of nature, will come as the springtime of a new age in a spirit of rejuvenation.

The decadent no longer wants to live. His retreat signifies a metaphysical turn towards death. This deathwish, as it is best called, permeates nineteenth century literature. Spengler schematizes it for the decadent writers. He describes the decadent hero as megalopolitan man, as decadent writers certainly confirm, in the following light:[39]

And then, when Being is sufficiently uprooted and Waking-Being sufficiently strained, there suddenly emerges into the bright light of history a phenomenon that has long been preparing itself underground and now steps forward to make an end of the drama—*the sterility of civilized man.* This is not something that can be grasped as a plain matter of Causality (as modern science naturally enough has tried to grasp it); it is to be understood as an essentially *metaphysical* turn towards death. The last man of the world-city no longer *wants* to live—he may cling to life as an individual, but as a type, as an aggregate, no, for it is a characteristic of this collective existence that it eliminates the terror of death.

This philosophical understanding of the deathwish is inherent in the decadent writers themselves. It is the deepest stratum of the layers comprising the decadent worldview, lying far below decadent psychology.

The deathwish is an act of historical necessity for the

decadent. Smith diagnoses the decadent symptom. "Nihilism reflected the conviction that things had to get worse before they could get better, that out of the destruction of the old a new and better structure might arise."[40] The decadent's life is a slow death if he resists the temptation of suicide, and being sterile he will not reproduce himself. From his ashes will arise, like the phoenix, the new man. Hence contemporary life must perish if life itself is to continue. But the decadent, above all, is a man who looks backward. He is the antithesis to progress, i.e., movement towards a goal, unless that goal is understood as death. While he may glimpse the future, while he certainly feels history at his heels, the decadent never perceives clearly things to come. The present, and particularly the past, is his own domain. And it is incurably ill, slowly dying.

The decadent is profoundly disgusted with life. Baju exclaims what a multitudinous chorus of writers echoes: "Notre époque n'est point malade; elle est fatiguée, elle est écoeurée surtout."[41] But decadents play with words, for their *Weltschmerz* is an illness. In his spleen the decadent hero yearns for death. Baju again speaks for the decadent writers by noting:[42]

Oh! ce spleen n'est point celui des empereurs blasés de pouvoir, de femmes et d'orgies; il est plus noir, plus intense, plus irrémédiable, puisqu'il porte à maudire l'existence, appeler la Mort et souhaiter le Néant.

The deathwish is not simply a passive retreat from life; it is an active yearning for death. Never has a worldview been more intensely bleak. Victory is impossible for the decadent. He can look forward only to frustration, despair, and defeat, and, as his solace, the annihilation of sense-perceptions through death.

At this point in the decadent worldview value judgments must be carefully stated. Then, if they have any meaning, the decadent may be accounted a noble man. The statement is paradoxical. What it means is simply this: The decadent may be the hero who attempts anything, in his psychic meanderings, to justify an idea of life. He will even search out death.

In this sense there is a hopeful note in the somber decadent worldview. While the decadent will die, as he knows, and while he welcomes death, at least the race will survive—will indeed move to a new classicism of health and sanity. This is the basic enigma of the decadent worldview. Many critics have sensed it, a few have stated it, and Renato Poggioli formulates an hypothesis:[43]

The problem of decadence is to be seen in its inability to resolve its own dialectic, in its eagerness to see its own Gordian knot brutally cut by the barbarian sword. The very notion of decadence, at least in its modern version, is practically inconceivable without this psychological compulsion, on the part either of the individual or the group, to become the passive accomplice and willing victim of barbarism.

Thus the decadent will remove himself from the megalopolis. He will commit suicide in some form, in order to give his place to the barbarian knocking rudely at the gate. This is what may be called the strange brotherhood of the decadent and the barbarian:[44]

Being left with no other alternative than that of serving as the passive victim of the tragedy of history, the decadent pretends to contribute to its cruel poetic justice by doing more than merely waiting behind the closed walls of the citadel of culture. He thus often chooses to open the gates of the city to its barbaric besiegers, who will be its destroyers, as well as his executioners. Decadence may well be another name for civilization's self-betrayal.

So the decadent destroys himself. Whether his suicide is a noble sacrifice, as in one scheme of values, or a dastardly self-betrayal, as in another, is of course a question of judgment. But the fact of the historical necessity for his death is clear enough, at least if the startling premises of the decadent worldview be granted. The deathwish, as a final impetus, leads the decadent to search for death as the tragic dénouement in his dark drama.

THREE

THE DECADENT:
A METAPHYSICAL HERO

A DIFFERENT kind of hero, or ideal man, emerges from the pages of decadent fiction. He is a peculiar introvert—dreamy, listless, sophisticated, his face etched with sad knowledge of life and the world. Superficially he resembles the romantic hero, but there is a basic difference. Decadent world-weariness is much deeper than romantic ennui. The decadent hero is a man who has lived too much and who no longer has either the energy or desire to act. He is, in short, a cerebral hero *par excellence*. Unlike the dynamic romantic hero, the decadent is the ideal man of passivity and inactivity.

There are ramifications to decadent cerebralism. As a victim of abulia, the hero may or may not be aesthetically oriented. Decadent aesthetics, contrary to popular criticism, is by no means the *sine qua non*, or even the fundamental article, of the decadent credo. It is merely a possibility. Again, the decadent may be a cosmopolitan, a cold and self-possessed man of the world. He may be a sensualist, hedonist, or, as often happens, a pervert. Above all, there is a metaphysical aspect to the decadent. This trait, regrettably, is often ignored.

The decadent is the scion of the romantic dandy. As a

matter of fact, this is almost his exclusive lineage directly from romanticism. He shares little with other types of the romantic hero. The decadent, for example, is not a romantic seeker, i.e., a man engaged on desperate pursuits of lost horizons. Idealistic quests are too juvenile to fit into decadent philosophy. Nor is the decadent really a man of fate, someone emprisoned in a social and cosmic context, destroying either himself and/or others as he writhes in anguish. As far as fatality is concerned, the decadent is like the dandy: he refuses to be embroiled in human relationships, and he lacks the man of fate's capacity for social and cosmic feeling.

Certainly the decadent is not a rebel; he feels no need for rebellion, which he regards as childish. Although he finds the world imperfect and substitutes artificiality for nature in an attempt to make it more livable, the decadent regards insurrection as nonsense. The idea of rebellion elicits a wry smile. Neither is the decadent a "pathological hero," as an idea of the romantic hero subsumes the term. He is far too removed from ordinary responses for the term to apply. The decadent would be the first to admit that, from the world's standpoint, he is "pathological." He would even gloat, mildly, over the fact: but his cold, blasé smile precludes all serious application of the term. Every decadent is "pathological" by modern norms, but the concept is simply not important in the decadent worldview. It is superfluous, meaningless. Finally, the decadent is not a romantic poet-prophet. He has no goal in life, no wishes to lead his people, like a Moses-prototype, through the wilderness to the New Canaan. The decadent discounts idealism as naïve.

There is in the French decadence an archetypal hero who incarnates all these traits. It is Duke Jean des Esseintes in Huysmans' *A Rebours,* published in 1884. He towers above all other heroes of the decadence. As Barbey d'Aurevilly said and as Huysmans himself sensed, this novel, if such it may be called, carried the idea of decadence to the point of no return. After it there was nothing new to add, the subject was at its philosophical end, and later work would necessarily be a valedictory. *A Rebours* is the central work of decadent literature. Its hero—a metaphysical hero—typifies the decadent soul.

Against the Grain—the very title summates the cult of artificiality which is not only basic to decadent aesthetics but is also fundamental in the decadent order of things. The decadent hero is immediately characterized as unnatural, i.e., the man of anti-nature. Though this fact is obvious, it must not be glossed over. Just as decadent style and predilections in art and literature are twisted and involuted, so too (for deeper reasons) the blood of the decadent is tainted. Or as Spengler would say, his cosmic beat is discordant with the rhythms of nature. The image is one which decadent writers would approve.

The story is instructive. Jean des Esseintes is an effete young man, independently wealthy, who has devoted his life to the pursuit of pleasure. He has no other interest. Yet his sensual experiences leave him the bitter dregs of satiety and ennui. He remains unsatisfied. In a desperate attempt to key up his failing senses, he retires to a country house at Fontenay. He fits it out like a monastery, served only by two faithful domestics, and enters his aesthetic paradise. He withdraws from society, however, not to retire from luxury but to find again the sensual pleasures dulled by his excesses in Paris. They alone make his life bearable. Des Esseintes interprets life always in sensual terms. He is an organism with acute antennae responding to subtle stimuli. Beyond this he has neither aim nor *raison d'être*. Once pleasure inures his senses, he is faced with an enigma: He must either find new avenues to excitement, or he withers upon the vine. Thus Fontenay is at once his pleasure house and his last resort.

The life he builds for himself is curious. He devotes himself to literature, though of course not to classical writing with its emphasis on sanity, balance, wholeness. He rather shows a predilection for Latin authors of the decadence—Lucan, Petronius, Apuleius—and for certain strange Church fathers and for the discordant barbarities of the Anglo-Saxon writers. Then comes the gulf. Nothing interests him until he encounters Villon, D'Aubigné, Bossuet, Bourdaloue, Ni-

cole. His special favorite is Pascal. Among the moderns he
is fascinated by Baudelaire, Barbey d'Aurevilly, Verlaine,
Mallarmé, Poe, Villiers de l'Isle-Adam. He even has Barbey's
Les Diaboliques exquisitely printed on fine vellum. His attitude typifies the decadent: he is either enthusiastic or
bored, for there can be no middle ground. He either responds or not. Literature is a source of sensual satisfaction,
not a disinterested, scholarly pursuit. His preoccupation with
letters is that of *l'art pour l'art*. He gleans sense-impressions.

Des Esseintes deliberately cultivates his senses to the highest possible sensitivity. He redecorates his monastic retreat,
papers his walls with exotic colors (orange his favorite), relishes the fine details of expensive rugs and costly *objets d'art*.
He has a tortoise beautifully inlaid with jewels so that it
creates a sparkling pattern as it moves, stones glittering,
across the deep rugs of subdued colors. He is sensitive to
brilliantly colored exotic plants that exude delicate odors.
The paintings of Gustave Moreau and the engravings of
Luyken fascinate him. He likes the violent passion and grandiose orgy of artistic representations of the Roman decadence. His sense of smell is acute. He blends subtle shades
of liqueurs and daily experiments with a large array of per-
fumes. Scent is overpowering, taste distracting and intoxicat-
ing. He sketches pictures in the air with his perfume atom-
izers, and his liqueur library must concoct ever rarer and
headier beverages. In the meantime his isolation is complete.
He shuts himself away from the world in order to focus his
egocentric sensualism as sharply as possible. Then he stimulates and mechanically gratifies his own sense-organs. The
world has no further meaning in itself, for it no longer has
an artistic justification. It does not hold his interest.

Memories remain of course, and since they elicit response,
he lends himself to dreamy introspection. From these memories, with sight succeeding sound and odors and tastes
commingling, the past is recreated or rather, as in Proust,
reborn. It comes alive again with all the poignancy of detail
which it had in actuality. Thus Des Esseintes recalls the
street boy, Auguste Langlois, whom he corrupted and tried

to make into a murderer. His design was devilishly simple. He furnished the lad money and took him to Mme Laure's brothel. He intended to habituate him to tastes which his purse could not afford. Then, to satisfy the narcotic demands of wine and women, the boy, he thought, would surely become a criminal who would steal, even kill, to get the money necessary for his pleasures. And Des Esseintes would thereby have gratified his metaphysical desire to flout nature and attack society. As memory dissolves he regrets that he has never discovered whether his design bore fruit.

The bitter-sweet memory of Miss Urania arises from the past. He has known many women and perverse pleasures. But she was especially a source of heady excitement. An American acrobat with a lithe, masculine body, though mediocre mind, she soon became an obsession. In the perverted delicacy of their love-play it seemed that he was slowly metamorphosed into a woman while, before his very eyes, she gradually became a man, roughly making demands upon his pliant body. He wanted her like a woman, and she possessed him like a man. But in time even she failed to whet his appetite. Ecstasy could not be indefinitely maintained. Joys, when repeated, became elusive and finally vanished. His sensualism craved new sensations, new experiences.

Yet what remained? He had exhausted the range of human possibility, he thought, and thus withdrew to Fontenay in an effort to reactivate his lethargic body and to awaken his dormant senses. In his pleasure house he continues to work upon his body, whipping it on, stimulating it like a homo-duplex, one part of his psyche watching the other half react. Reality, dream, memory become impossible to separate from one another in a tangled web of sensations. Once he starts to travel to England, a country he has always wanted to visit. But his senses create in his mind the impressions which England would undoubtedly elicit. Then the trip no longer has a justification; it is devoid of interest. In his mind's eye Des Esseintes has already *seen* England. To repeat the emotional experience would be tedious. He sinks back into deep lethargy. Finally his body surrenders, the senses fail to react, the spirit can go no more, and Des Esseintes has a physical collapse. The village physician, answering his call, is astounded by his decadent life—an existence metaphysically oriented *à rebours,* against the grain. He warns the young man against such luxurious living. Des Esseintes, having exhausted sensual possibilities, listens rather listlessly. He may return to Paris, to health and sanity. There seems to be no other choice. A doubt remains. The decadent still hesitates. He is unsatisfied and insatiable to the end.

It is apparent that the decadent hero, thus depicted, represents a new stage in the unfolding concept of the ideal man in the nineteenth century. Most obvious is his lack of energy and direction, which are cardinal traits of the romantic hero. The decadent is cerebral and passive. His aesthetic sensitivity seems to exclude action and participation. He is the supreme sophisticate who is lethargic rather than imperturbable. He is the prototype of the tired aristocrat, the last son of a dying family in an exhausted race.

To be sure, the decadent has one romantic antecedent— the dandy of whom he is the logical extension and conclusion. In theory at least, the dandy refuses to be enmeshed in social struggles or religious concerns. Though acutely sensitive to life, he cannot be reached in the core of his being. And since nothing ever penetrates the wall of his iron reserve, nothing can destroy him. His detachment is the first article in a code of decorum devised to protect himself against dangerous involvements with the world.

While the decadent resembles the dandy in some respects, he is qualitatively different. Both are egocentric figures, certainly, but they express their egomania in different ways. The dandy has a behavior code guiding his actions whereas the decadent does not, and the former punctiliously observes his laws of decorum. If he flouts social or ethical precepts in following them, the dandy is not aware of it. At least he is not concerned, for he remains a subject without an object. On the other hand, the decadent is simply unaware of the world except for its uncorrelated sense-impressions. In a word, he is philosophically heedless. He is bored with society, which offers little interest and less excitement, and looks upon it with dull ennui. Or when it momentarily stimulates him, he gladly surrenders to its transient allurement without cloaking himself in the dandy's protective detachment. The decadent wants to respond to stimuli, but usually he cannot. The dandy wants to enjoy the sensations of life, but he remains constantly on guard. Unlike the decadent, the dandy maintains a defensive pose. The decadent does not display the dandy's self-conscious awareness of himself vis-à-vis society and the cosmos.

There are several aspects to the decadent, as evidenced by Des Esseintes. First, he is a cerebral hero. Emprisoned in his abulia, he cannot act in even mundane matters. Second, he has a strong aesthetic penchant, characterized by *l'art pour l'art*. He turns to painting and literature for the sensations they afford. Third, the decadent is a cosmopolitan, often a traveler who has encountered the unusual and the exotic. But even when like Des Esseintes he has traveled little, he is still a man of the world. He is at his ease in society and can frequent the great salons. He typifies the cosmopolitan's relativism, for he has neither regional ties nor the personal beliefs engendered in space by time. He is not a man of the blood and the soil but one of the city. Fourth, the decadent is a kind of pervert. Certainly his tastes and inclinations are perverse in comparison with the norm. Des Esseintes typically enjoys his perversions. In his cult of artificiality he cultivates perversity in order to heighten excitement to its greatest pitch. Unlike the pathological hero in romanticism, however, the decadent is content with his perversities, and he usually maintains some control over himself: he deliberately chooses the paths of perversion, whereas the romantic's pathology is forced upon him by conflict from within or without.

Fifth, an extension of the four types mentioned, the decadent is a metaphysical hero. As a passive hero who has passed beyond activity, he is disenchanted with life. Thus he tends to become a negation of life, an imp of the perverse, as he strives to titillate his sleeping senses. His artistic sensitivity is much darker than the dandy's. He is *faisandé*, gamy, whereas the dandy retains a cold intellectual posture before life. Furthermore, the decadent reveals a metaphysical attraction to death which the dandy rarely displays. The dandy is willing, sometimes eager, to destroy others, but he does not often turn his destructive energy in upon himself. The decadent does. He has a deathwish working against the forces of creation and life in himself and in nature. He develops the cult of artificiality, then, to its completion: the purposeful violation of nature and natural process.

The decadent is therefore a metaphysical hero. His single-minded pursuit of sensation colors his worldview and predetermines his peculiar attitudes towards society, life, God. His religion is *l'art pour l'art*, sensualism, egocentrism. His amorality is complete and constitutes his metaphysical position. Reality, he believes, is only response to sense impressions. All else is illusion, indeed delusion. Hence the decadent is exclusively concerned with himself and totally isolated from his fellow creatures. He is glad because he has no regard for them. He inhabits a static universe where others move and writhe, caught in social and cosmic circumstance, but where he remains forever apart, concerned only with his pleasures. Even his chance actions as an imp of the perverse, such as Des Esseintes' attempt to corrupt Auguste Langlois, cannot long retain his interest. The decadent is no rebel. He is rather an incarnation of destructive forces that bring a dying civilization to an end—which he welcomes as a respite or a final titillation in a grand incarnation of the deathwish. But he rarely acts, and never acts meaningfully, since he is a cerebral hero. He merely is, he exists, and he does not lash out against the laws of God and man. His existence is itself negation. The decadent is catabolism.

Des Esseintes' ideas are reflected throughout the literature of the epoch.

The decadent as metaphysical hero, like Des Esseintes, has a worldview in which art subsumes the ideas of nature and life. A part of life, one aspect, becomes greater than the whole. The idea of totality is reformulated. This is essentially the theory of *l'art pour l'art,* which of course does not refer to a weak decadent fondling sunflowers in a blue vase. By epitomizing the anti-natural, art replaces nature and occupies the former role of life as totality. Form, structure, style are corollaries of this social and cosmic view of art, which gives rise to a new psychology.

The changed state of things demands a new man. This is what Schwob, among others, has in mind when he gropes for a definition of the spirit permeating the new literature:[1]

Depuis la grande renaissance romantique, la littérature a parcouru tous les moments de la période de relâchement du coeur, toutes les émotions lentes et passives. A cela devaient aboutir les descriptions de la vie psychologique et de la vie physiologique déterminées.

In short, art should not be a reflection of life, a bit of nature utilized by reason as nature's handmaiden. Art should be life. Decadent art (for this is what Schwob means) is necessarily descriptive. It is a novel of mental adventure, so to speak, whether it depicts the introspective "monde intérieur" or the sense-perceived "monde extérieur." By having art usurp nature, the decadent writer makes the most earnest claim ever voiced for literature: for the first time literature is life, not merely a reflection of life. It is the guiding purpose of life, an end in itself, and/or a kaleidoscope refracting all other interests. In this new fiction, the embodiment of *l'art pour l'art,* the decadent hero occupies a qualitatively different place. He is the supreme example of the metaphysical hero.

Des Esseintes' introspection is reflected by other decadent heroes. They all turn in upon themselves. Barrès, for example, has Philippe elaborately develop a cult of the ego. It is a philosophy of sensualism, i.e., bringing his sense-impressions into sharp focus:[2]

Il est, Simon, des hommes qui ont réuni un plus grande nombre de sensations que le commun des êtres. Echelonnés sur la voie des parfaits, ils approchent à des degrés divers du type le plus complet qu'on puisse concevoir; ils sont voisins de Dieu.

Classicism never makes such claims. It is for decadent literature, as stated, to make life of mere writing. The ego assuredly has a creative aspect: it remakes life. Decadent introspection, then, is not simply a refusal to communicate with the world, but also a self-preoccupied attempt to create another world through the cult of *sensationalism*. The decadent perceives his own world as surely as Kant does. Such a concept entails a social consequence.

The decadent becomes anti-social. This does not mean that he rebels against society, since insurrection, however attenuated, is foreign to his nature. But the decadent feels himself a *metaphysical* hero, an ideal man, emprisoned, like Barrès' Philippe, among the barbarians and the philistines. He is superior:[3]

Pour moi, dès mes premières réflexions d'enfant, j'ai redouté les barbares qui me reprochaient d'être différent; j'avais le culte de ce qui est en moi d'éternel, et cela m'amena à me faire une méthode pour jouir de mille parcelles de mon idéal. C'était me donner mille âmes successives; pour qu'une naisse, il faut qu'une autre meure; je souffre de cet éparpillement.

One thing is obvious. The decadent's sensibility is infinitely finer than the herdman's. He is a creative spirit, albeit *à rebours,* and his social isolation is necessary in his view of things. His introspection, his preoccupation with his senses, alone make possible his creativity. The decadent's isolation, then, is not merely negative. As with Des Esseintes, it is the only way of shutting off the clamor of the world in order to savor undefiled his sense-impressions. His introspection is a way of living a thousand lives rather than one, as Barrès observes. It is a communion with self, an artistic adventure. Art passes over into life, it replaces life, it becomes life. The metaphysical metamorphosis is complete.

The psychology of sensualism, as with Des Esseintes, is at the heart of the cult of artificiality and the theory of *l'art pour l'art.* This idea of decadence cuts through literary boundaries. It includes naturalism, realism, the various movements of the epoch, as well as decadence proper. The decadent hero appears in many guises, but he turns to art for the same reason. Martino observes in this connection:[4]

Tout aussi logique que la rage naturaliste d'affirmer les "laideurs" de la vie est une volonté de nier les conditions mauvaises de cette vie, de se révolter contre l'instinct, d'échapper à la grande tromperie de l'existence. Plusieurs, parmi les décadents, affectent le mépris de la femme et vont vers les dérèglements de l'instinct, ou bien vers un mysticisme de chasteté.

Art is a magic realm where it is transmuted into nature, reality. It is a metaphysical message. The decadent turns to art, as Schopenhauer recommends, as a kind of mysticism. Like Des Esseintes he converts his sensual energy into a type of intellectual and aesthetic chastity. Schopenhauer is not by chance the favorite philosopher of Des Esseintes: the connection between pessimism and decadent art is unseverable. Martino further adds on decadence, developing the concept of realism:[5]

Au bout de peu de temps, le réalisme, plus simple et moins ambitieux, dont il voulait occuper la place, a repris sa marche, un peu assagi par les échecs de son cadet [le naturalisme], plus disposé à voir et à se représenter, sans parti pris d'aucune sorte, les aspects multiples de la vie moderne.

The decadent, whether an aesthete or naturalist, wants to see life in its totality, and he feels he can do so only through sense-impressions. The decadent is not necessarily a lecher, though he is partly this too, but also and more importantly a philosopher of the senses. Dumesnil correctly traces this current:[6]

. . . Le réalisme sort directement du romantisme, et tout ce qui, dans la nouvelle école, groupée autour du peintre Gustave Courbet, semble s'opposer radicalement aux théories jadis formulées par Victor Hugo dans la *Préface de Cromwell,* découle au contraire naturellement de ces principes.

This hope of embracing totality through art passes from romanticism to realism, parnassianism, and naturalism, all three movements of which join the decadence proper in a common concept. Decline and fall—whether conceived in grand poetic terms, as a social concern, or conceptualized with literary involutions—is their common ground. The decadent vision of the world results from a pragmatic philosophy of the senses. The decadent protagonist is to some extent the stepchild of David Hume. The decadent hero often revels in luxury, to be sure, but he has knowledge of self as a goal. Hence decadent art is not only an escape, an anti-natural bias, an ecstatic release, but also a form of knowledge. The fact that the decadent hero twists this knowledge beyond normal recognition is beside the point. This is the metaphysical aspect of art. The theory of *l'art pour l'art* is only superficially concerned with aesthetics. Form and style are clothing for the decadent worldview.

Des Esseintes typifies the decadent with his Schopenhauerian cynicism. He reflects a general idea of human nature which runs throughout decadent literature. Verlaine, for example, exclaims bitterly:[7]

> Je ris de l'Art, je ris de l'Homme aussi, des chants,
> Des vers, des temples grecs et des tours en spirales
> Qu'étirent dans le ciel vide les cathédrales
> Et je vois du même oeil les bons et les méchants.

> Je ne crois pas en Dieu, j'abjure et je renie
> Toute pensée, et quant à la vieille ironie,
> L'amour, je voudrais bien qu'on ne m'en parlât plus.

> Lasse de vivre, ayant peur de mourir, pareille
> Au brick perdu, jouet du flux et du reflux,
> Mon âme pour d'affreux naufrages appareille.

The biting decadent spirit moves through these lines. Baudelaire's "Le Voyage" is another statement of the theme. The metaphysical hero is once again victimized by abulia, and he looks upon life with a jaundiced eye. He is isolated. He has nothing in life but art as his consolation, and he ridicules even that as transient and imperfect. He cannot believe in God, love, man, nature, idealism. The final verse suggests the appeal of the omnipresent deathwish. The vacillating decadent appears fullblown as a nihilist. The power of destruction is a salient trait in his psychological constitution. A demonic glint fires the blasé hero's eyes for a moment before, subsiding, it changes into another fleeting mood.

A primary decadent concern, voiced by Des Esseintes, is with appearance and reality. Is appearance itself, as apprehended by sense-impressions, the only reality man can know? The matter is complex. But the point here is the decadents are preoccupied with the problem. It appears, for example, in Villiers de l'Isle-Adam's *L'Eve future*. The decadent hero, Lord Ewald, rejects the modern woman, Alicia Clary, who, though "an ideal held by three quarters of humanity," is destructive to man. Edison, the great inventor who appears in the novel, then proceeds to make an artificial woman who looks and acts exactly like Alicia. Although she emits an occasional electric spark, she does not have human vices. Edison explains to Ewald:[8]

C'est cette *ombre* seule que vous aimez: c'est pour elle que vous voulez mourir. C'est elle *seule* que vous reconnaissez, absolument, comme REELLE! Enfin, c'est cette vision, objectivée de votre esprit que vous appelez, que vous voyez, que vous CREEZ en votre vivante créature, *et qui n'est que votre âme dédoublée en elle*. Oui, voilà votre amour.—Il n'est, vous le voyez, qu'un perpétuel et toujours stérile essai de rédemption.

He draws a metaphysical distinction between appearance and reality. He concludes, in decadent guise, that appearance is reality: at least the only reality which man, with his sense-orientation, can perceive and know. This distinction differentiates the decadent from the romantic hero, who in his obsession with the problem would rather answer that appearance is delusion, and reality the unseen thing behind the mask of appearance. The decadent worldview remains pragmatic, and the decadent hero something of a positivist.

The materialist aspect of the decadent worldview is seen in its idea of heredity. Duke Jean des Esseintes has bad blood; he is the last survivor of a moribund family. There is a biological concept of decadence, or pathological degeneracy, that applies to many decadent heroes. The Goncourts, for instance, speak repeatedly of the transmission of unhealthy traits:[9]

Tout se transmet: le péché originel est un fait physique. La physiologie n'a pas assez creusé cette question de la transmission de la race; cette continuité, par voie de succession, non seulement d'une infirmité, mais d'une habitude, d'un caractère; un fils a le geste de son père; les historiens nous parlent du pied d'une famille, de l'esprit d'un autre.

The same idea is developed by Curel in *Les Fossiles*. Bad traits are transmitted from fathers to sons, as with Des Esseintes, until finally they create a degenerate monster whom nature must rise up to crush. A social view is implicit. Since bad people are transmitting unhealthy characteristics, most people in modern society are not only bad but getting worse. Hence the decadent writers are concerned with eschatological catastrophe: nature wreaks her vengeance against the unnatural race for its corruption. They accept this idea literally. In developing his theory of pathological degeneracy in *Les Rougon-Macquart,* Zola says baldly that Sedan is the inevitable result of social decay. Man is of course part of a social organism (which tends to reflect a cosmic order according to some decadents), whether he wishes or not. And when the part decays, the whole will rot. Even though the transmission of acquired characteristics is unfactual, as modern biologists state, the decadent writers maintain otherwise in a concrete system of metaphysics. They are interested in elements, things, not ideals, not the Platonic concepts of romanticism.

Just as Des Esseintes is an Epicurean prototype, so decadent literature overflows with sensualist philosophers. Mr. James Sandy Rose of Gourmont's *Une Nuit au Luxembourg* is such a decadent. He is the apostle of the philosophy of sensualism, of Epicureanism in its pristine form. As he is walking one day, he chances across a mysterious stranger, clearly a Christ figure, who engages him in a long dialogue. The stranger says explicitly that he, the decadent, should preach the religion of Epicurus and convert the new Athenians to sensualism.[10] The stranger reflects a classical cosmology, symbolized by the beauty and order of the Luxembourg gardens. He expounds a realistic philosophy of existence:[11]

Dieu est une rêverie charmante ou cruelle, utile ou dangereuse, selon les têtes où elle règne, mais ce n'est qu'une rêverie. Est-il nécessaire que je vous explique l'impossibilité de Dieu? Dieu, pour les hommes, n'est pas un raisonnement, mais un sentiment.

The typical decadent is not a mystic. He lives very much in a world of things. In the final scene "Lui," as the stranger is called, disappears. Rose takes home a girl named Elise, who had spoken with him that fatal night. For the mysterious stranger, or the god, she symbolizes a goddess, though men would look upon her as a streetwalker. Rose watches her sleep in animal tranquillity. She is for him more than a mere woman. She is nature. He has learned his lesson well.

Like Des Esseintes the decadent hero is a relativist. He lives in a world of sensually perceived phenomena of changing forms, not an immutable universe of eternal forms. In *Les Chevaux de Diomède* a metaphysical hero speaks about modern man, reality, and faith:[12]

C'est vraiment un bon spécimen de la crédulité scientifique, qui ne diffère pas des autres que par l'objet. Il y a deux siècles, il eût défendu la Bible contre Bayle. Aujourd'hui il défend la Science—encore contre Bayle, contre l'ironie, contre le sourire. Il est de la race des croyants, race éternelle et peut-être la vraie réserve du monde. L'homme honnête et simple croit; c'est sa fonction. Il croit en la vérité enseignée par les autorités de son âge; tour à tour et quelquefois en même temps il croit à la parole de M. de Condorcet et à celle de M. de Maistre. Avide, sa foi devance l'avenir; elle devance les miracles; elle s'affirme dans toutes les possibilités conformes aux principes permis. Ce fut la théologie; ce fut la philosophie; c'est la science. L'homme naît à genoux. Il faut qu'il adore. Quand ce n'est pas un ostensoir, c'est une cornue; quand ce n'est pas l'infini, c'est un ovule.

The decadent is such a materialist that, like any good positivist, he comes to question science itself. In the same novel Pascase asks Diomède what he is doing in life. The latter formulates the decadent creed in his succinct reply:[13]

—Je suis mon chemin. Je sais quelle serait ma réalisation.
—Quelle?
—L'ignorance totale, l'indifférence totale, l'indulgence totale. . . .

The three phrases summarize decadence. As a good positivist relying on his sense-impressions for his idea of reality, he knows only those impressions, *his impressions,* and thus not the world-in-itself. His sensibility responds to this idea of the world, leaves him with indifference, and leads him to indulgence. This is decadent reality.

Gourmont further develops his metaphysical position in *Sixtine.* The novel treats the decadent's fundamental concern with art and nature, and it reveals his concept of reality:[14]

La nature! mais c'est l'artiste qui la crée, la nature, et l'art n'est que la faculté d'objectiver en un simulacre la représentation individuelle du monde.

It is the aesthete speaking. In Schopenhauerean terms nature is one's own idea of it, and no more. Entragues, the hero, develops this position to its apogee:[15]

Ces sortes d'écrivains sont, ainsi que la plupart des hommes, que l'humanité entière, ou à peu près, victimes d'une illusion d'optique. Ils s'imaginent que le monde extérieur s'agite en dehors d'eux, c'est une transcendante sottise, mais dont ne s'engendre pas nécessairement leur esthétique spéciale. Le monde, c'est l'idée que j'en ai, et cette idée, les spéciales modulations de mon cerveau la déterminent: ils ont de laides cervelles, voilà tout. On pourrait ordonner d'amusantes esquisses ainsi conçues: le monde vu par un crabe, le monde vu par un porc, le monde vu par un helminthe.

Once again reality is not the thing-in-itself, which is unknowable, but the sense-impression of the thing. Moreover, it is the thing not as it exists eternally but as it changes constantly in time. One of the most philosophical of decadent writers, Villiers de L'Isle-Adam discusses this problem in *Histoires insolites, L'Amour suprême, Akédysséril,* and particularly in some of the *Derniers contes*.[16] *Axël* is a metaphysical drama on the same theme.

Des Esseintes voices a deathwish which other decadent heroes echo as the cessation of the *élan vital,* a titillation, or a catabolic yearning. In *Le Vice suprême* Péladan elaborates the position of the deathwish in his idea of decadence:[17]

L'étude passionnelle des décadences trouve, à peu près toujours, un déterminisme illogique, irrationnel, absurde aux phénomènes psychiques. A cette heure où une civilisation finit, le grand fait est un état nauséeux de l'âme et dans les hautes classes surtout une lassitude d'exister. Alors, sciemment, délibérément, on gâche sa vie, on émiette son intelligence, on aime le mal pour le mal, on le fait "pour le plaisir" et jusqu'à soi-même. Car de la décomposition générale des idées et des concepts, il résulte pour l'individu son haut vouloir et qui ne sait pas réagir contre le courant de l'époque, un phénomène formidable d'envoûtement.

Péladan refers to abulia as well as to the deathwish. Indeed abulia is a form of death. The metaphysical hero shrinks from life into extreme inactivity, a reflection of the nothingness and sensationlessness to come. The deathwish is inextricably tied to the knotty problem of art and nature. One decadent says explicitly:[18]

Hélas! pour le poète; hélas! pour son temps, s'écria Antar. Je suis décadent comme vous, comme tous. . . . C'est la fin de la poésie d'une race. La lyre latine tord ses cordes, sous l'inspiration de la folie et si ses accords sont si pénétrants, c'est qu'en elle la moitié, la meilleure du cerveau d'Occident se fêle et se détraque.

Art is the expression of a race. When the vital urge of a race's life perishes, then art too will wither away. In the decadent world of Péladan, capitalism, Protestantism, and corruption are synonymous. He is a royalist and Roman Catholic who hates Napoleon, Protestants, and Jews in descending order. Père Alta and Mérodack are his metaphysical mouthpieces, who watch their world-order decline and fall and its artistic expression vanish. There are other villains in the decadent worldview, depending on the writer's scheme of values. While many decadents do not share Péladan's pointed antipathies, they are all portraying an identical apocalypse.

The greatest *Götterdämmerung* in decadent literature may well be that described in Bourges' *Le Crépuscule des dieux*. Charles d'Este, Duke of Blankenbourg, characterizes himself at the end of this classic of decadent literature:[19]

Et lui-même, d'ailleurs, qu'avait-il été? Fils dénaturé, cruel père, mari terrible, maître détestable, jaloux, capricieux, inquiet sans relâche, quel bonheur avait-il goûté, quelle grandeur lui restait-il, à lui qui voulait tout mettre à ses pieds? Il se vit seul, plus que malheureux en famille, en frère, en oncle, et en enfants, déchiré au dedans par des catastrophes poignantes, sans consolation de personne, portant son front découronné, dans tous les hôtels de l'Europe, abandonné à deux ou trois valets, qui le gouvernaient despotiquement, ne faisant plus rien que pour eux, ayant donné à son bouffon, son goût, son jugement, ses oreilles, ses yeux; d'ailleurs, infirme et ridicule. La nuit montait autour de lui, les ténèbres s'épaississaient; ces temps cruels, hélas! avaient été le crépuscule de sa race.

It is a frightful judgment. All the familiar themes are present: bad heredity, nerve-storms, hypersensibility, perversion, luxury, sado-masochism. The social view of a society aflame and ascending in smoke is apparent. D'Este is a Wagnerian hero in the approaching night of civilization.

The metaphysical aspect of the decadent is implicit in Flaubert's *L'Education sentimentale*. It is the story of a decadent's *vie manquée,* not dissimilar to that of Des Esseintes. This is the life of two friends, Frédéric Moreau and Charles Deslauriers. Frédéric loves but never possesses Mme Arnoux, the faithful wife of a gambler and roué. He characterizes himself half-romantically: "Je suis de la race des déshérités."[20] But he is a metaphysical decadent at heart. He lives a fruitless, even unreal life, against the grain, and when he nears old age in 1867, he discusses his lost youth and his vanished aspirations with Charles:[21]

Et ils résumèrent leur vie.
Ils l'avaient manquée tous les deux, celui qui avait rêvé l'amour, celui qui avait rêvé le pouvoir. Quelle en était la raison?
—C'est peut-être le défaut de ligne droite, dit Frédéric.
—Pour toi, cela se peut. Moi, au contraire, j'ai péché par l'excès

de rectitude, sans tenir compte de mille choses secondaires, plus fortes que tout. J'avais trop de logique, et toi de sentiment. Puis ils accusèrent le hasard, les circonstances, l'époque où ils étaient nés.

They accuse society with a romantic vestige. In so doing they are correct and they are also decadent.

It is indeed society, in the decadent worldview, which catches men up in the grand sweep of history and necessity. The decadent is what he is because of his peculiar place in space and time, and the decadent is always aware of the theatrical role he plays. He is the creature of nerves and heredity, of society and the cosmos. He knows it all too well. His consciousness of space and time, unidealistically perceived through his acute sense-impressions, makes him a metaphysical hero. He is a pragmatist, even a positivist, who sometimes becomes a nihilist. His sophistication, like that of Des Esseintes, ultimately becomes inertia, a fatal indolence. He suffers from a moral and physical abulia that is overwhelming in face of his crumbling world. Destiny moves. He must move with it. The metaphysical hero can resist destiny, or nature, only by becoming anti-nature, by desperately grasping for something permanent—a happy moment dimly perceived—in the swirling onrush of time. And this he does.

FOUR

THE DECADENT:
A COSMOPOLITAN IN BABYLON

A GREAT theme in French literature of the decadence is its vision of Paris as a metropolis or as *any* metropolis. The seductive city is evil. It is Babylon.

Decadent literature reflects a romantic attitude towards the city. Whereas eighteenth century writers love the sophistication and ease of the great city and accept vice as inherent in the structure of things, romantics tend to reject the metropolis because it is fundamentally anti-natural. Yet they modify this Rousseauistic idea of nature and artificiality. There is an element of grandeur in the sprawling metropolis, as Balzac testifies in the dénouement to *Le Père Goriot*. As the century passes this concept becomes more ambivalent: while hating the city, modern man is awestruck by its majesty and by the excitement of its swirling movement and flashing colors. Nonetheless it is evil. From Balzac on in the nineteenth century, the metropolis entices healthy provincials with wild dreams of fast money and quick fame, only to grind them down, or raise them up for a moment, again to cast them out upon the crowded streets. Decadent literature shows a morbid preoccupation with the city and the problems of city-living.

In decadent writers the metropolis becomes a symbol. The profound distrust voiced for the actual city by political writers like Raudot, in *De la Décadence de la France* (1850), becomes a metaphysical concern. For Balzac the city means power, money, things. Realists and naturalists follow in this guise. Even poets change the direction of their inspiration because of the fact of the metropolis. In *Les Fleurs du mal,* for instance, Baudelaire, the first great poet of the modern city, writes a series of poems entitled "Tableaux Parisiens," e.g., "Paysage," "Le Crépuscule du matin," "Le Crépuscule du soir." Nature becomes a "petit îlot" in the metallic city. The poet's task is somehow to mold lasting beauty from the temporal sights and sounds of the hideous throngs of people. The city is indeed omnipresent in decadent writing.

Such ideas are often implicit since few writers are discursive thinkers. But an American and a German, at the close of the century, schematize concepts that had been foreshadowed by Montesquieu and Rousseau and incarnated by Balzac, Flaubert, Baudelaire, *et al.* In *The Law of Civilization and Decay,* for instance, Brooks Adams expresses the feelings of the decadent writers: the city is centralization, destructive velocity at ever faster tempos until its denizens become giddy, lose their *élan vital,* and, exhausted by the mad dance of life, succumb to the pavements. The city, he argues, signifies the end of culture. It masks death with superficial allurements. Men of blood and the soil, the barbarians, have become megalopolitans, soulless and weak denizens of the life-consuming city. Spengler, in *The Decline of the West,* goes further in giving philosophical form to the artistic depictions of the decadence. The world-city or megalopolis, as Spengler names it, is consuming. It simply burns men out, so that they no longer have the energy reservoir to carry on. The megalopolis, while fatally attractive, is not a creator of true culture. It is a huge museum of the past, a repository of the cultural creations which are now impossible. Thus Spengler characterizes the decadent megalopolitan with a voice of doom:[1]

The advance, too, from peasant wisdom—"slimness," mother wit, instinct, based as in other animals upon the sensed beat of life— through the city-spirit to the cosmopolitan intelligence . . . can be described as a steady diminution. . . . Intelligence is the replacement of unconscious living by exercise in thought, masterly, but bloodless and jejune.

This idea of man trapped in his megalopolis—of the decadent in Babylon—is sensed in romanticism. But it comes to fruition only in decadent literature. The dandy, buck, raffiné, élégant, cosmopolitan, or city bourgeois—all are decadents by definition: they are all inhabitants, each in his own way, of Babylon. Adams and Spengler, using hindsight not prophecy, give form to decadent literary themes in their philosophy of history.

The validity of the decadent thesis is unimportant here. This chapter simply describes the decadent vision of the city and exemplifies it through representative writing. Hence the portrait that emerges shows the decadent as a megalopolitan, the citizen of the great city, wandering through the Bazaars of Babylon, overwhelmed by its surging life, and bewildered by the profusion of incomprehensible voices emanating, so to speak, from the Tower of Babel.

The malady of city living is taken for granted. In L'Education sentimentale, for instance, Flaubert notes matter of factly a peculiar trait of Frédéric Moreau: "Une autre soif lui était venue, celle des femmes, du luxe et le tout ce que comporte l'existence parisienne."[2] The sentence evokes an entire society. It calls forth the hothouse world of wealth and vice that Catulle Mendès describes in his novels and stories. Mme de Ruremonde, Lise de Belvèlize, Valentin, he maintains, are typical Parisians in the great Babylon. Lesbia, Arc-en-ciel, Le Confessionnal, Rue des Filles-Dieu, 56, are testaments to the evil of megalopolitan life. La Messe rose is a typical collection of decadent stories. "La Messe rose et la messe noire" is the story of three lesbians named Jo, Lo, and Zo. In "Les Trois Valentines" three lesbians have all fallen in love with a scoundrel, Valentin. Lise de Belvèlize, in "Le Sac vide," lends her lover to a girl-friend, Madeleine. Her servant, Nonette, replaces her in bed for an assignation with an undesired but importunate lover in "Nonchalance." "Après le flagrant délit" is the story of a husband who discovers his wife's infidelity. He is charitable. Instead of killing her in anger, he makes her work in a house of prostitution. He loves his wife, he says, but as a Parisian his first love is money. These plots are ludicrous, of course, and elicit a smile from the modern reader. But Mendès and the innumerable writers of the decadence proper believe in the accuracy of their depictions.

Hence these decadent horrors give a new dimension to the image of Paris as the world-city: that of Babylon, the great harlot. Significantly Mendès entitles another collection of stories *Monstres Parisiens.* "Mademoiselle Laïs," a rich Parisian *hystérique,* is completely amoral. The husband of "Le Mari de Léo" sells the wife he adores as a common prostitute because, like all good Parisians, "il aime, autant qu'il aime sa femme, l'argent." Mme de Ruremonde is a prototype of the modern woman—cold, vain, sadistic. "Jeunes Mères" is the story of how Parisian mothers deform the most basic of loves:[3]

La Parisienne, irréconciliable ennemie du vrai, éprise des mensonges et des ruses au point qu'elle consentirait à se rendre laide plutôt que de rester soi-même, ne devait pas s'accommoder longtemps de l'instinct maternel, auguste et simple.

The horrors are multiplied. In "La Nouvelle Mariée" the young bride tells her middle-aged husband that of course she married him only for his money, and that if he does not allow her to entertain the young gallant waiting outside the nuptial door, she will publicly rather than privately disgrace him. The husband accepts because, like a good cosmopolitan, he treasures appearances. "L'Amoureux de Mademoiselle Massin" testifies to the cult of artificiality which characterizes Parisian life. A young man falls in love with Mlle Massin, an actress who, as Nana, appears ugly and distorted in the final act of the play version. He is heartbroken to discover that under the hideous makeup she is really beautiful. Mendès notes repeatedly: "Es-tu bien sûr, toi, Paris, qui es allé, en ce temps-là, durant cent soirées, applaudir la hideur et adorer la pourriture, es-tu bien sûr de ne pas avoir ressemblé à ce monstre?"[4] The apostrophe to Babylon makes explicit what is always implicit in Mendès' interminable novels and stories and, indeed, throughout decadent literature: Paris is a festering sore; its men and women are hopelessly corrupt, vicious, decadent; there is no salvation.

Jean Lorrain continues in the same vein. His novels all claim that the temptations of Babylon have seduced modern man, the decadent. His *Crime des riches,* for example, is a sordid study of Parisian aristocracy basking on the Riviera. In the dedication the author says bluntly:[5]

Je dédie ce *Crime des riches* qui pourrait être aussi le Crime d'être riche, car les caprices monstrueux, nés de la veulerie et de l'ennui des millions usurpés, entraînent physiquement et physiologiquement toutes les tares, et, si le Crime des riches échappe à la loi, protégé qu'il est par la lâcheté des gouvernements et des masses, la nature, elle, plus vraie que la société, donne l'exemple de l'anarchie en abandonnant les misérables forçats du capital à la folie et à la honte des pires aberrations.

These pious though perhaps absurd sentiments should convince the reader, if there still be a need, that decadent writers have a didactic purpose. Like numerous other authors, Lorrain repeats that Paris is indeed Babylon, sprawling and corrupt, where men prey upon one another in a mad quest for money, power, sense-satiation.

In *Curieuse!* Péladan describes the reputation of Paris:[6]

Une chose inédite, inavouée, dont tout le monde a conscience, c'est de considérer Paris, comme le grand mauvais lieu de l'Occident, le vilain quartier de toute l'Europe. En province, un indigène emblêmerait Paris sous les traits d'une femme de Grévin qui lève son verre et sa jambe; à l'étranger, on s'excuse toujours envers un Parisien de le convier à une orgie, si corsée qu'elle soit; même à Vienne, les noceurs autrichiens vous disent avec humilité: "Ne vous attendez pas à une noce de Paris!"

Péladan evidently believes that the nefarious reputation is justified in fact. He rambles on throughout *La Décadence latine* in tones of moral indignation. He abhors Paris for being anti-natural while contrasting Babylon with the healthy countryside. Pierre Louÿs, more indulgent than most decadents, has a vision of Paris as supremely corrupt. He agrees with the other decadent writers on this point. But he feels that such total moral disintegration is historically necessary. Babylon is inevitable. In that sense it is ridiculous to chastise the city for being what it is. One can only approve of Paris, Babylon, for being so frankly what it is. In the preface to *Aphrodite* he argues:[7]

Il semble que le génie des peuples, comme celui des individus, soit d'être, avant tout, sensuel. Toutes les villes qui ont régné sur le monde, Babylone, Alexandrie, Athènes, Rome, Venise, Paris, ont été par une loi générale, d'autant plus licencieuse qu'elles étaient plus puissantes, comme si leur dissolution était nécessaire à leur splendeur. Les cités où le législateur a prétendu implanter une vertu artificielle, étroite et improductive, se sont vues, dès le premier jour, condamnées à la mort totale.

The attitude of Louÿs is somewhat startling. He admires licentiousness, even feels that it is a legitimate expression of *élan vital*. In that sense Babylon is not decadent. But the ramifications of his idea are unclear. Such ambiguity, when pursued, can be found in other decadent writing. But the essential point, here as elsewhere, is that the decadent writer equates Babylon with licentiousness, greed, and evil. Whether these traits are unavoidably in the nature of the city, as Louÿs infers, is another question. The point is that the great megalopolis, despite value judgments, is consuming.

In *Cosmopolis* Paul Bourget reflects upon the strange denizen of city-life. He describes the cosmopolitan decadent in the following terms:[8]

L'existence du Cosmopolite peut tout cacher sous la luxueuse banalité de ses fantaisies, depuis le snobisme en quête de relations plus hautes jusqu'à l'escroquerie en quête de vols plus faciles, en passant par les brillantes frivolités du sport, les sombres intrigues de la politique,—ou la tristesse d'une destinée manquée.

His novels overflow with portraits of jaded aristocrats— monied cosmopolitans who, tiring of Babylon, retire to the

Riviera or a fashionable spa to bemoan themselves of the tensions of the megalopolis. But as in Octave Mirbeau's *Les Vingt et un jours d'un neurasthénique* Georges Vasseur, a modern cosmopolitan, discovers that his spa in the Pyrenees is only a microcosm of Paris with its derelicts and ills, so that there is no escape for the cosmopolitan. He carries his city with him, a psychic introjection, and his efforts at evasion are fruitless: "L'art est une corruption . . . la littérature un mensonge . . . la philosophie une mystification. . . . Je vais me rapprocher des hommes simples, des coeurs frustes et vierges."[9] But there are no unspoiled provincials along the beaches or in the mountains. They, too, are tainted. Babylon has sucked the countryside, like a leech, of its lifeblood, the peasantry. Nothing remains but the inevitable cataclysm.

The decadent cosmopolitan is not always, or even usually, a rich, corrupt aristocrat. In the French decadent worldview any modern man is a decadent by virtue of being what he is in space and time, and since he reacts in relation to the great city, he is also a cosmopolitan. The decadent is not exclusively a latterday dandy, a refined pervert, a polished wastrel. Decadence refers to more than wine and women. The cosmopolitan's responses to Babylon vary according to his social milieu, his background, and his pocketbook, though this is not always apparent in the exaggerated fiction of Mendès, Lorrain, or Péladan.

In a more realistic vein the Goncourt brothers depict the fatal attractions of the city. Their heroes, too, are decadents struggling for fortune and love in the bazaar of modern Babylon. Their metaphysical antipathy for the city, like that of Balzac, Flaubert, and writers of comparable stature, is not so evident or didactic as with the minor writers of the decadence proper. But it is nonetheless evident. In *Charles Demailly,* where the tensions of the city finally destroy the hero's sanity, the physician obviously speaks for the Goncourts. He gives the following diagnosis of the megalopolis:[10]

Tout se précipite à la centralisation, à la formation de grandes et de petites capitales. La vie moderne va du plein air de la vie agricole à la vie concentrée, à la vie assise, à la vie au gaz du charbon de terre, à la vie des lampes, à la vie nourrie par une alimentation falsifiée, sophistiquée, trompeuse, à tous les renversements des conditions normales de l'être physique.

His Rousseauistic idea characterizes the decadent vision of Babylon. By a strange paradox the decadents, though drawn to artificiality, believe in the simplicity of living. They are convinced that the life they lead and love is yet fatal and will destroy them, as Demailly's physician explains. The sheer tempo of Babylon exhausts its creatures. Hence the Goncourts observe that Paris has a clean sweep almost every year, with fortunes given to the new, destruction to the old, while another crop will follow the next year.[11]

Greed and lust are the traits of Babylon, as Louÿs observes, and these vices leave their tortured imprint upon the cosmopolitan's taut face. In *Germinie Lacerteux,* for instance, the Goncourts portray the effect of the city upon a man. They describe Jupillon as incarnating upon his face the greedy scepticism characteristic of the Parisian; his face is drawn in a mocking smile.[12] Such implicit observations about the cosmopolitan are sharper than the explicit diatribes voiced when the author's mask of impersonality falls away. Rather than decrying Babylon, decadent writers like the Goncourts simply depict Parisians as lunatics, misers, wastrels, perverts, *hystériques,* idiots, psychotics, egomaniacs—human wrecks of the most pitiable kind. Such a portrait of Paris is more devastating in effect than any philosophical denunciation: it shows the great city, concretely, as Babylon.

Perhaps more than any other writer in the French decadence Zola is obsessed with the megalopolis. Indeed his abstraction, Paris as the great city, brings out and magnifies his characters, who often seem real only as they move against the backdrop of Babylon. *Les Rougon-Macquart,* to be sure, is the portrait of a family, but of that family within a particular megalopolitan context. Zola's creatures are unimaginable without Paris.

The Rougon-Macquart swarm into Babylon from their little provincial town, Plassans. Lured by visions of success, they rapidly spread like poison through the arteries of the city. In varying settings they reveal their hereditary ills, the result of *la tare initiale*. Tante Dide is the mother of all illness. The members of the family achieve different stations as cosmopolitans, but they remain a diseased and doomed unit. Paris acts on them like a hothouse on the growth of malignant plants. Such an image recurs throughout Zola, in fact, notably in the love scenes of *La Curée*. It is significant that novels taking place outside Babylon, like *Le Rêve* and *La Faute de l'Abbé Mouret,* are attenuated, more poetic and authentically hopeful, than the passionate and violent struggles occurring in the city. Paris magnifies the very worst in the Rougon-Macquart.

In *La Curée,* for instance, Aristide Saccard arrives from Plassans, in the healthy South, determined to gain wealth by any means. His attitude is typical. Zola describes the peasant upon his eagerly anticipated arrival:[13]

Le soir même de son arrivée, pendant qu'Angèle défaisait les malles, il éprouva l'âpre besoin de courir Paris, de battre de ses gros souliers de provincial ce pavé brûlant d'où il comptait faire jaillir des millions.

After his wife dies he unscrupulously marries Renée Saccard, who is pregnant by a married man, in an effort to get her family fortune. The callous bargain is concluded with his receiving the money for giving his name, such as it is, to Renée's illegitimate child. The novel portrays scenes of fantastic decadence—all documented, Zola believes, by the period itself of the Second Empire. Liaisons are too numerous to mention.

The height of decadence is the incest between Renée Saccard and her wastrel stepson, Maxime. Bored with familiar vices, she leads him on in the hope of "un nouveau frisson." Finally he seduces her at her half-repressed invitation. Such a plot might evoke the best tragic efforts of a Sophocles or a Racine. But this is Paris, Babylon, in the utter corruption of the Second Empire. What happens, then? When Aristide finally learns of his son's flagrant adultery with his wife, he does not throw a tirade or lash out in anger. He does not even mind too much and certainly not for long.

He is too concerned with the more serious business of making money. He even advises his son, like a good father, to forget Renée, and concern himself with the serious and pressing business of life: a good marriage and financial speculations. Such fatherly counsel and indeed such a reaction are unthinkable outside the context of a decadent Paris. But in this modern Babylon the novel rings true to life. Aristide, Maxime, and Renée, acting in a gothic nightmare, are psychologically true.

Son Excellence Eugène Rougon is Zola's portrayal of a modern Macbeth, a cosmopolitan athirst with an unquenchable ambition. Paris appears like a jungle where, as in Darwin, only the strongest and cleverest will survive. Rougon is determined to be among them. He is an egomaniac who almost mystically tries to absorb Paris into himself. His ambition knows no bounds.

Zola's great epics of men and movements give a vast panorama of corruption. Indeed the vista, Paris, is the real hero, and men and women act more in relationship to it than to themselves. The megalopolis is, so to speak, the first cause. *L'Assommoir* is notable for the amorality of its men and women— brutish, vicious, drunken. Gervaise Macquart, typically, runs away from Plassans to the city with the conviction that a better life awaits her. Her aspirations are soon dashed. Her destruction takes place in the biologically living city, with its moving masses, twisting streets, personified stores. Gervaise, in spite of her pathetic appeal, is always of secondary interest. The city itself captivates the reader.

It is symbolic that Zola turns to the great department store, Au Bon Marché, to inspire his portrait of the fictional store, Au Bonheur des Dames, in the novel of that name. It is his epic poem to modern activity in commercial Babylon. Though he claims to be singing a hymn to work, happiness, and success, his personification of the store is horrifying, and he has to remind himself in his *ébauche* to the novel to be optimistic. Zola's optimism, as usual, is forced. The picture of the store and of Paris as Babylon is brutal. The callous Octave Mouret, who has made a previous appearance in

Pot-Bouille, speculates on the artificiality and whimsy of Parisian women. For them the department store is not only a commercial house but also, and more importantly, a temple to modern life. Zola is explicit. He describes it as such, with worshipers filing in and out amid the personified offerings of silks, satins, tapestries. The symbolism is transparent:[14]

Là apparaît le côté *poëme* du livre: une vaste entreprise sur la femme, il faut que la femme soit reine dans le magasin, qu'elle s'y sente comme dans un temple élevé à sa gloire, pour sa jouissance et son triomphe.

Zola's ambivalence in depicting the store is evident. While trying to suggest its real beauty, he rather testifies to its horrors. The colossal department store ruthlessly destroys the surrounding shopkeepers, just as Paris drains the provinces. The high priest, Mouret, is vain, smug, greedy, licentious. He is the priest of Baal, not Jehovah. And what purpose does the modern temple fill in the new Babylon? The image of the temple, let it be remembered, is Zola's own idea. The store is a temple to anti-nature. It appeals to modern woman's cult of artificiality. It serves humanity by satisfying greed and the Babylonian frenzy for movement. The joy of work, which Zola claims for the store, is only the happiness of obtaining money by any possible means. Man's goal is to enjoy his vices, wines, women, with the offerings garnered in the new temple.

In *Le Ventre de Paris* Zola is even more intimately concerned with the organic city. The viscera are not man's most beautiful organs, but they are certainly among the most vital. Moreover, Les Halles answers man's most modern aspirations: the satisfaction of his avaricious appetite inculcated by Babylon. It is as important a symbol in the decadent worldview as the mediaeval cathedral in the Catholic scheme of things in the Middle Ages. Man cultivates his monstrous gut, in short, and the tone of the novel is a lugubrious Rabelaisianism. Zola baldly states his purpose:[15]

L'idée générale est le ventre de Paris, les Halles où la nourriture afflue, pour rayonner sur les quartiers divers;—le ventre de l'humanité, et par extension la bourgeoisie digérant, ruminant, cuvant en paix ses joies et ses honnêtetés moyennes. . . .

The words seem like a parody to the modern reader. Zola does not perceive the utter incongruity of his stated aim with the bourgeois horrors actually depicted. This glaring lack of self-knowledge, of perceiving self in perspective, reflects the decadent's essential ambiguity in his idea of the city and his ambivalence in response to it. The writer is a cosmopolitan in Babylonian captivity no less than his fictional heroes.

Concern with the city is omnipresent. In *Germinal* Paris is the backdrop for striking laborers fighting against capitalism—the joy of cosmopolitan labor and the death struggle for money and power. *La Terre,* according to Zola himself, is meant to contrast with the decadent commercialism of Babylon. Hence it is best understood as the other side of the coin. The heroine of the novel is the earth itself as the sustainer of life. Unlike the cosmopolitans the characters are filled with a smell of and an abiding love for the earth. It is a mystical love, a natural affection. They are the philosophical antitheses to the artificialities of the city. The novel is a far cry from *La Débâcle,* a portrait of Paris during the fall of the Second Empire. It is a personal story contrasted with the swirling masses of *La Débâcle,* a typical Zola novel. *La Terre* is a poetic idyll.

L'Argent is an important document on Babylon. It shows the effect of money on the cosmopolitans. Zola claims to be impartial in this novel; hence his comment is all the more interesting:[16]

Montrer que l'argent est devenu pour beaucoup la dignité de la vie: il rend libre, est l'hygiène, la propreté, la santé, presque l'intelligence. Il n'y a que l'amour et l'argent.

Zola might have added, as Balzac does, that money is ever the stronger motivation. Once again Zola reminds himself to be fair and optimistic in his notes. Surely these are the marks of a man who has grave reservations about the validity of his beliefs. Money does improve the social lot of mankind, to be sure, but it does not ennoble men's souls. *L'Argent,* like most of his novels, is another testimony to the power of greed and viciousness in an insane drive for power. Zola stresses the theme to the point of monotony.

Paris, though outside the *Rougon-Macquart* series, still attests to Zola's preoccupation with the city and city-living. He maintains that "Paris est donc une adaptation saisissante des événements de l'époque,"[17] and documents his novel with the Panama fiasco, anarchistic riots, and scandals of the epoch. Pierre Froment, a young priest who loses his faith after his mother dies, is almost a fictional pretext. His story is a secondary theme. The real topic, as elsewhere, is life in Babylon. Hence Victor-Meunier puts his finger on Zola's ultimate concern by writing vividly in *Le Rappel* of 21 March 1898:[18]

. . . Paris qui s'épanouit, dans le ruissellement de l'or, dans le resplendissement des chairs nues, et Paris qui, dans l'ombre, écrase entre ses dents longues des imprécations de haine; le Paris qui jouit, côtoyant le Paris qui râle; Paris-noblesse, Paris-finance, Paris-politique, Paris-débauche, Paris-crime; tout fumant ensemble dans le même chaudron monstrueux. . . .

Not only does the critic seize the author's fundamental idea and concern, but he also senses Zola's ambivalent attitude towards the city. Victor-Meunier's series of antitheses, the white and the black Paris, evidence the polarities of Zola's typically decadent vision of the megalopolis. Essentially, however, the dark side is much stronger than the light. That is the decadent message. Zola gives a vividly putrefying portrait of modern Babylon in *Paris*. While he may admire the grandeur of the megalopolis and its possibilities, he abhors its basic artificiality. Zola's condemnation is explicit. The cosmopolitan is not only anti-natural, and hence reprehensible, but repulsive. In his *ébauche* to *Nana*, for instance, Zola describes Parisian life in these unforgettable words:[19]

C'est toute une société se ruant sur le cul, une meute derrière une chienne qui n'est pas en chaleur et qui se moque des chiens qui la suivent.

A stronger image is hardly possible.

Les Rougon-Macquart has two great themes: the city and
the city-dweller (the cosmopolitan) reacting to stress. In this
case Babylon intensifies the hereditary ills and weaknesses
deriving from Tante Dide. Zola's study is of psychological
and physiological degeneration, and despite its appended
optimism the series is profoundly pessimistic. Paris is destructive and modern man is anti-natural; he will be destroyed
for his transgressions against nature. This is his constant
theme. The follies of the example, the peculiar foibles of
the Rougon-Macquart families, provide another theme. The
motifs are of course inextricably related. But by separating
them, somewhat artificially, the importance of Paris as Babylon, and of *all* cosmopolitans reacting to the city, becomes
much clearer.

Zola may not have realized what an abject picture of Paris
he has really drawn. In his notes, as previously stated, he is
constantly reminding himself to be "optimistic," to show the
"real joys of life and work." His efforts seem unconvincing.
The weakest link in the *Rougon-Macquart* series is his final
novel. *Le Docteur Pascal,* as a dénouement, is neither logically nor artistically satisfying. Dr. Pascal is made into something of a superman so that Zola could verify, he thought,
his scientific theories on progress. Pascal's medical discoveries
and miraculous cures seem, artistically, like a *deus ex ma-
china.* They are totally unconvincing and obviously forced.
Thematically they are incongruent with the tragic vision of
Babylon given in his long epic of despair and degeneracy.
Le Docteur Pascal is jarring. The reader has been prepared
for nineteen novels to expect a *Götterdämmerung* the like of
which literature has seen neither before nor after. Instead of
that he receives a pious sermon on the necessity for hygiene.
There is no greater anti-climax in the whole of literature.

Such is the idea of the city in decadent literature. Years
later Spengler is to formulate definitions of decadent concepts
which have long been current. He speaks with the experience
of his French predecessors: the concept of decadence is in
the air. For instance, he contrasts the cosmopolitan with the
provincial much as Péladan, to name one of a number of
writers, always thinks of them:[20]

The peasant is the eternal man, independent of every Culture that ensconces itself in the cities. He precedes it, he outlives it, a dumb creature propagating himself from generation to generation, limited to soil-bound callings and aptitudes, a mystical soul, a dry, shrewd understanding that sticks to practical matters, the origin and the ever-flowing source of the blood that makes world-history in the cities.

The description applies to any number of decadent heroes. Let the reader recall the peasants of *La Terre* and contrast them with the uprooted laborers of *Le Ventre de Paris* or the sophisticates of *Son Excellence Eugène Rougon*. Zola's lesson is plain, and it is typical. The peasant is healthy because he participates in nature, the cosmopolitan corrupt because he is anti-natural. This is, rephrased, what Spengler writes, schematizing the various portraits of the decadent writers into a composite whole. And when he places his cosmopolitans in the great city, Spengler understands the megalopolis like Mendès, Péladan, Lorrain. His condemnation is pointed:[21]

The Megalopolis is "free" intellect. It is in resistance to the "feudal" powers of blood and tradition that the burgherdom of bourgeoisie, the intellectual class, begins to be conscious of its own separate existence.
Intelligence is the replacement of unconscious living by exercise in thought, masterly, but bloodless and jejune. The intelligent visage is similar in all races—what is recessive in them is, precisely, race. The weaker the feeling for the necessity and self-evidence of Being, the more the habit of "elucidation" grows, the more the fear in the waking-consciousness comes to be stilled by causal methods. Hence the assimilation of knowledge with demonstrability, and the substitution of scientific theory, the causal myth for the religious.

This is the long sermon which Péladan, for instance, preaches in other words to the same effect throughout the *Décadence latine*. Modern man as a cosmopolitan, he warns, is doomed because he has succumbed to the great harlot, Babylon. She has seduced him from nature, from the ways of righteousness. Thus man has passed from his holy communion with nature to the cult of artificiality, of anti-nature, in idolatrous harlotry. And life without nature, he warns, is ultimately sterility—death without resurrection. These images are his own. Péladan is nothing if not a religious mystic.

Thus the decadent vision of the city is starkly moral, not hedonistic: it is even Calvinistic. To this extent the decadent writer, often without knowing it, is like an Old Testament prophet crying out to the cosmopolitan sinners from his wilderness. Who would ever have dreamed, for instance, of Alphonse Daudet in this guise? He is whimsical, amusing, yes, but also the political satirist of *Numa Roumestan* and the acid commentator of the Duke de Morny in *Le Nabab*. In his way too Daudet, the most unlikely of "decadent" writers, makes his comment. He adds his voice to the resounding chorus of fatalists comprising the decadence proper as they exclaim, over and over, in poem, story, and book: Alas, alas, that great city Babylon, that mighty city! for in one hour is thy judgment come!

FIVE

THE DECADENT: A CEREBRAL HERO

THE WORLD is too heavy for the decadent. It does not meet his expectations, it disgusts him, it overwhelms him. Nature has a negative not positive value, and reality never meets his wish. Thus the decadent rejects actuality, he retreats into himself, and he creates a more satisfactory world of his own. Hence he becomes a cerebral hero, the ideal man of inaction. For what is the purpose of engaging on idealistic quests in a most imperfect world? To do so is not only useless but even naïve. Crushed by spleen, the decadent leads a cerebral existence, spelling out his days as so many disappointments.

The decadent is cerebral because activity is infantile. In *The Decadent: Being the Gospel of Inaction,* an American classic which typifies French decadent values, this is, succinctly, the thesis. The lines are drawn. Ralph Adams Cram, the author, sets his scene in Boston (which may be any megalopolis), a city which he abhors so much that he actually prays that rats will one day crawl through its ruins. Malcolm McCann, a Faustian man of action, a kind of pre-decadent, visits his former friend, Aurelian Blake. The latter now devotes his days to opium and burgundy. A philosophical dialogue ensues in which each tries to convince the other that he is right. McCann represents energy, machinery, reform, and as a socialist he incarnates the materialism of the masses. Blake discounts his argument. He detests the republic and longs for the monarchy; he stresses the importance of individualism and *l'art pour l'art*. Fighting for social reform, Blake answers, is only replacing a sordid gang of capitalists by a corrupt mob of emancipated slaves. Life, with all the ugly tensions of city-living, would be just as stagnate in the new order.

The cogency of his argument shatters McCann. He begins to reflect. What, he asks, is possible? There is nothing, Blake replies, for life is futile. The free man in a dying society is the decadent—a libertine who does nothing because in the long run nothing can change the relentless concatenation of events spelling inevitable doom. The decadent, in short, can *do* something only for himself. He can make Aurelian Blake's choice. He can become a cerebral hero, apart from the world, devoting himself to art and philosophy, and assuaging his spleen with drugs and liquor. For he is a civilized man, marked by a declining *élan vital*, as Brooks Adams writes, and he should use the last sparks of his energy on himself. The cerebral hero suffers from a psychic fatigue beyond soma and human understanding. He is a microcosm of the macrocosm, a man who mirrors the world with his dissipations and his fatal disenchantment. He is superannuated, older than mere years, and he rejects reality, life, action. These traits characterize the cerebral hero of the French decadence.

One fact is cardinal: Reality and ideality are antipodes. In his failure to resolve these polarities, the decadent hero falls victim to abulia, like Des Esseintes in Huysmans' *A Rebours*. He becomes cerebral. Des Esseintes wants to go to London, but he listlessly falls back into his chair. He reflects on what he will undoubtedly see in London. The cerebration overwhelms him. He no longer has the strength to make the trip. He has used up his energy in thinking about London. Thought (ideality), he knows, is infinitely more satisfactory than the actual visit (reality). This incident exemplifies admirably the unresolvable polarities of decadent thought. The dream is more perfect than life. The final scene, as he prepares to leave his pleasure-house at Fontenay, is instructive in this connection:[1]

Des Esseintes tomba, accablé, sur une chaise.—Dans deux jours je serai à Paris; allons, fit-il, tout est bien fini; comme un raz de marée, les vagues de la médiocrité humaine montent jusqu'au ciel et elles vont engloutir le refuge dont j'ouvre, malgré moi, les digues.

Between reality and the dream there is a ceaseless conflict which saps the decadent's energy. Tension, however, is not expressed in action. Abulia is the result. It is an extreme indolence, or lethargy, in which cerebration prevents the hero from acting.

This concern with cerebration recurs throughout Huysmans' fiction. In *Là-Bas* he discusses it as a form of pygmalionism, in which the dream replaces reality. Mme Chantelouve suffers acutely from this vice. This *femme fatale* tells Durtal, the decadent hero:[2]

—Je dis que je n'ai qu'à les désirer, qu'à vous désirer tous, maintenant, avant de m'endormir...
—Et?
—Et vous seriez inférieur à ma chimère, au Durtal que j'adore et dont les caresses rendent mes nuits folles.

Her words almost parallel those of Léonora in Péladan's *Le Vice suprême,* whose cardinal sin is, significantly, a similar kind of pygmalionism. Other decadents voice the same thought in other words. The point is that life is a poor second to fantasy. The Baudelaire of her dreams, as Mme Chantelouve explains, is a perfect lover beside whom reality pales. Actuality could never compete successfully with a phantom. The elusive has too much charm, and most of that charm resides precisely in its unsubstantiality. Thus her vice is a cerebral sexualism, an obsession with her erotic dreams. She entices men while rarely gratifying them, for the dreams themselves assume the proportion of reality—but of an insatiable, and therefore satisfactory, reality. *Lassata, sed non satiata*, in the recurrent decadent phrase, depicting the *femme fatale*, refers to the body, not the decadent soul. Thus Mme Chantelouve, typically, is a succubus, a sexual will-of-the-wisp flitting through an elaborate tissue of dreams. And why? Reality has lost its savor and the dream-world alone can tempt the decadent. He knows reality; he does not know the dream. Perhaps even the dream will not, or cannot, maintain his interest forever.

The Hamlet figures of the French decadence increasingly inhabit a static world of abulia as the *fin-de-siècle* draws nigh. To be sure, the decadent as a cerebral hero, like any hero-type, has his antecedents. Though romantic heroes are generally dynamic, certain exceptions tend to foreshadow the inactive decadent. Adolphe is a classic example, and at least in theory the dandy frowns upon action. Participation in life is too much for the former, too vulgar for the latter—*in theory*, let it be added at once, for later French dandies, particularly, are men of action, although they thereby deviate from the archetypal ideal.

As the romantic hero passes into a new hero-type, one which is best called "decadent," cerebral figures begin to appear with alarming frequency. In Baudelaire's *La Fanfarlo* Samuel Cramer presages the new man as he tries to lash himself into movement every morning. Action, the young dandy says, is scarcely worth the effort. Baudelaire depicts him:[3]

C'est à la fois un grand fainéant, un ambitieux triste, et un illustre malheureux; car il n'a guère eu dans sa vie que des moitiés d'idées. Le soleil de la paresse, qui resplendit sans cesse au dedans de lui, lui vaporise et lui mange cette moitié de génie dont le ciel l'a doué.

His efforts are fruitless and abortive. Likewise Frédéric Moreau, of Flaubert's *L'Education sentimentale*, suffers from a well-documented case of abulia, which is only partly due to his unrequited love for Mme Arnoux. Inactivity is his nature. He merely focuses it, in a way, upon her as an object.

Life simply enervates him like a strong perfume, and his weakness for Mme Arnoux then lapses into "un mode nouveau d'exister." He is too weak to act. His life would have been the same without Mme Arnoux or without any woman. He is a cerebral hero by nature. Any reasons, if such they are, are actually rationalizations of the fact.

There is a philosophical cause for the inactivity of both Cramer and Moreau, however, as indeed for all decadent heroes. Their expectations in life have been dashed to pieces by actual events. Disappointment has crushed their will. They have in a sense lost hope, and with it their *élan vital*, and they now lack the energy to participate in life. They have given up the struggle, and they look for solace in their dream-world of fantastic chimaeras. They are imprisoned in their abulia, in their dream-life, to the exclusion of action and actuality. Their pale inactivity, at length, becomes so painful that it even begins to lose its seductiveness. This is the painful point of no return. Thus Rimbaud cries out desperately in *Une Saison en enfer:*[4]

"Où va-t-on? au combat? Je suis faible! les autres avancent.
Les outils, les armes... le temps!...
Feu! feu sur moi! Là! ou je me rends.—Lâches!—Je me tue!
Je me jette aux pieds des chevaux.
Ah!...
—Je m'y habituerai...
Ce serait la vie française, le sentier de l'honneur."

In this bitterly ironic passage abulia reaches its apogee. The cerebral hero loathes himself for his lethargy, his weakness. Abulia becomes a destructive inactivity in its final form— the deathwish. The cerebral hero's will is so crushed that he often welcomes annihilation as his release from an insupportable reality.

By definition the cerebral hero is introspective. He turns within. He is dreamily languid, reclines on cushions, reads symbolist poetry. He may listen to the delicate strains of subdued music. His abulia has aesthetic overtones, certainly:[5]

La décadence, c'est Sardanapale allumant le brasier au milieu de ses femmes, c'est Sénèque s'ouvrant les veines en déclamant des vers, c'est Pétrone masquant de fleurs son agonie. C'est encore . . . les marquises marchant à la guillotine avec un sourire et le souci de ne pas déranger leur coiffure. C'est l'art de mourir en beauté.

The cerebral hero is usually an artist of a special sort. He merely contemplates art passively; he is not a creator. And it is a corrupt and intellectualized art, the super-refinement of an aging civilization, which he admires. The cerebral decadent is sensitive to the voluptuous nuances of bloodless literature and painting. To a certain extent, then, he resembles the Eastern mystic as, divorced from reality, he contemplates his own navel.

Abulia provides the psychological setting for a Des Esseintes, for a Duke Jean de Fréneuse (Lorrain's *Monsieur de Phocas*), and for numerous other cerebral decadents. In *Pelléastres* Lorrain peoples an entire society with languishing decadents who, symbolically, have taken their name from Debussy's *Pelléas*. They have a great affinity for his subdued tonalities, and they tend to be all that the term *pelléastre* might suggest. In the same volume Lorrain execrates the malignancy of decadent cerebralism by terming it "le poison de la littérature." He should know. He discusses the influence of art on society, marks the impact of Huysmans' *Là-Bas,* for instance, and how the young decadents of the age imitate Durtal, and how young girls paint themselves like *femmes fatales.* It is amusing but also foreboding. His *pelléastres* are twilight creatures, listless, amoral, and sensual, of a moribund world. Their horizons are limited by fat cherubs posing erotically around a silken bed in a pink boudoir.

Catulle Mendès similarly evokes a cerebral world. As a psychological motif cerebralism colors the heroes and heroines of his interminable novels and stories. Lise de Belvèlize, Mme de Ruremonde, Valentin himself, whatever the name may be, the same type recurs throughout *Monstres Parisiens, Arc-en-ciel et Sourcil rouge, Le Confessionnal, Les Romans d'innocence,* and *Rue des Filles-Dieu, 56.* The provocative

titles speak for themselves. They suggest an over-intellec-
tualized vice in which original sin, guilt, barbarity, real passion have lost all meaning. Decadence is the epoch of cerebralism, and even its sinners are often too tired and blasé to
react to stimulation. Their sins are frequently peccadilloes
of the imagination. Spleen is the greatest single theme from
Baudelaire through the French decadence. It is the scarlet
thread which ends, if not culminates, in poetry like Maeterlinck's *Serres chaudes*, with poems entitled "Lassitude," "Ennui," and "Ronde d'ennui."

Any decadent is by definition a kind of cerebral hero. But
some decadents are much more completely dominated by
abulia than others. With them inactivity becomes a cult,
and they seem stasis incarnated. Among them are, for example, the men and women of Pierre Louÿs. In *La Femme et
le pantin* Don Mateo Diaz, as the puppet, is typical. Démétrios is a classic instance in *Aphrodite*. A great sculptor, he
is a listless genius; the queen's lover, he is given to introspection and indolence. Indeed he is fatally attracted to
Chrysis, the courtesan, because of his abulia. By eluding him
she momentarily whets his jaded appetite and dormant energies. He perpetrates the three enormous crimes which she
demands of him in return for herself. But afterwards, even
before possessing her, he loses interest in Chrysis. He is again
victimized by abulia. He simply no longer cares. He possesses
her in a dream, as he explains, and that vision replaces reality.
In fact, it heightens reality to such a pitch that repetition
seems sacrilegious, superfluous. In comparison with such an
experience reality itself is vulgar. Consequently Démétrios
disregards Chrysis. After she is executed, he turns to art for
consolation. His energy sapped, he turns from the world and
his cerebralism reappears with all its impotency.

Marcel Schwob's heroes are invariably cerebral. The writer
of *Le Livre de Monelle* is much preoccupied, in his cerebral
existence, with the streetwalkers whom he chances across.
They symbolize vitality, energy, for him. His lassitude re-
quires their presence. They seem to lend him their own life
for a time, and the weak decadent draws energy from the

strong female. Yet nothing suffices for long. Always obsessed with "le monde intérieur," Schwob's hero reflects upon the *mal du siècle*—spleen, abulia:[6]

La maladie du siècle commença. On voulut être aimé pour soi-même. Le cocuage devint triste. La vie aussi: c'était un tissu d'aspirations excessives que chaque mouvement déchirait. Les uns se jetèrent dans des mysticismes singuliers, chrétiens, extravagants, ou immondes; les autres, poussés du démon de la perversité, se scarifièrent le coeur, déjà si malade, comme on taquine une dent gâtée.

The succinct analysis is deadly accurate. After hoping for too much, the hero becomes disenchanted, his will is crushed, and abulia is the result. Then he cannot act, i.e., participate in life. He no longer even wishes to. The fear of defeat evidenced by the late-romantic hero (the anti-hero) disappears when the sophisticated decadent enters the literary scene. But the powerful sense of defeat remains, and he wryly accepts the utter futility of life and action. As the dandy knows instinctively, sophistication is a mighty defense against disappointment, frustration, involvement. By turning away from the world and to himself the decadent, for all his sophistication, comes to suffer the illness of abulia. The word is well-chosen. Abulia is quite incapacitating.

Barrès formulates a famous "culte du moi" in his philosophy of cerebralism. In his important trilogy the decadent shows himself hypersensitive to egoistic nuances. In *Sous l'oeil des barbares* Philippe is helplessly immobile before the *barbares,* or bourgeois. He turns from the world to himself in a desperate attempt to free latent energies. In *Un Homme libre* he consciously develops his ego through "moral mechanics," and he strives to overcome his abulia. He never succeeds. In the final volume of the trilogy, *Le Jardin de Bérénice,* he is continually self-preoccupied. Despite his good intentions he cannot muster enough energy to woo the elusive but willing Bérénice, and he sadly watches her succumb to another man. She marries him. Philippe, in actuality, never achieves his professed goal of freedom towards which he so earnestly strives—i.e., the release of his energy. He is paralyzed. Unlike Hamlet he does not even enjoy momentary outbursts of action.

Remy de Gourmont portrays many cerebral heroes. Among them Mr. James Sandy Rose, of *Une Nuit au Luxembourg,* is a famous example. An introverted writer, he wanders aimlessly about Paris, jotting down his impressions of a world in which he cannot really participate. Gourmont's cerebralism is reflected in *Lettres d'un satyre* and *Lettres à l'amazone* in particular. In the latter work a weak hero writes effusively to a masterful woman. Cerebration makes Gourmont's fiction static, so that the hero ever shows a peculiar lack of kinesis.

In *Les Chevaux de Diomède* Gourmont's hero is cerebral in the extreme. He is dissatisfied with life in general and with his rather extensive harem in particular. He is the disenchanted victim of moral indolence—a solidification of his passions, so to speak, through constant disappointment and betrayal. He is in love with an ideal which constantly eludes him. He suffers an agonizing frustration as a result. Pascase, a friend of Diomède, reflects this essential cerebalism when he says:[7]

J'ai réfléchi. Je crois que je l'aime parce que je ne la connais pas. L'ayant vue, elle me déplaira peut-être. Alors je serai tranquille et guéri. Si au contraire, ce qui est possible, elle me séduit, je ne serai pas plus malheureux qu'avant.

The decadent again refers to the polarities of actuality and of ideality. Woman is seductive, he argues, only when she is unknown, mysterious, not possessed, for then she is an ideal for man. Possession means actuality, and in turn it entails disappointment. The destruction of the will is inevitable when one is disenchanted. The dream must never be realized, or it forever loses its ephemeral appeal.

Diomède likewise philosophizes over cerebralism throughout the novel. He analyzes it in himself, in his friends, in the social structure. He even formulates a hypothetical man of the future, while pointing a finger of scorn at modern society for a social context making cerebralism inevitable.

This hypothetical man antedates and resembles Huxley's tragic man of *Brave New World*. He is a human robot running on social propaganda rather than oil, the helpless creature of mass media through constant bombardment of the newspaper, radio, television, and an unthinking, well-conditioned consumer who is titillated by advertisement and then satisfied momentarily before the endless procedure is again repeated. It is a terrifying portrait:[8]

A des hommes parqués par la science et par le socialisme dans des besognes et des plaisirs prévus et ordonnés une fois pour toutes, quelques idéogrammes suffiront pour dire toute la pensée humaine, qui sera brève; les besoins physiques, les désirs sexuels, bon, mauvais, pluie, soleil, froid, chaud.

The logical conclusion of cerebration in society is a totally cerebral society. Such a man will be an object which experiences sensations without being truly alive. He lacks vitality, which alone can produce meaningful choice. He is no longer attuned to the cosmic beat of nature that is the harmony of animals, children, primitive peoples. The civilized man, by living in modern society, is necessarily afflicted with abulia because that society subtracts from the sum of his natural inclinations. Inactivity is the price which one pays for civilization. It is the natural consequence of the unnatural life.

At the end of the novel Diomède, as a cerebral hero, wallows in self-depreciation. He despises himself for being weak, but he is powerless to change. He simply does not have the strength of will. Yet he intends to adopt the lamb of his best friend, the painter Cyran, in order to attune himself with nature. Diomède knows that he is ill, and he wants to be well again. This, he thinks, may be his prescription for a cure. His act is symbolical, as he explains:[9]

Je vais adopter Agneau. Selon le voeu de Cyran, j'en ferai un bélier qui perpétuera sa race, sans perpétuer la pensée qui corrompt les raccs et brise l'harmonie de l'unité. Agneau est un être dont les actes seront toujours purs, puisque leur rythme ne pourra être troublé par aucun scrupule. Le mal, c'est la pensée déformatrice avec toutes ses tentations, ses labyrinthes d'où nul n'est ressorti, sinon estropié par les luttes, enfiévré par les angoisses intellectuelles. Sois maudite, Pensée, créatrice de tout, mais créatrice meurtrière, mère maladroite qui n'as jamais mis au monde que des êtres dont les épaules sont l'escabeau du hasard et les yeux, la risée de la vie.

The apostrophe to Thought is indicative of the cerebral hero's intellectual assessment of his predicament. He is fatally attracted to intellect, which will destroy him by drying up the springs of vitality. Diomède is thinking aloud. He is truly a decadent, i.e., a civilized man, a sophisticate, because he feels a discordant relation with nature. He has lost the rhythm of the animal, the throbbing beat of life. He hates himself for being intelligent, i.e., civilized, sophisticated, self-consciously aware of himself even as he is thinking, a homo-duplex, because that destroys his will-power and ability to act. The die is cast. His self-loathing becomes so strong that it is an active wish for self-destruction. His abulia results, as with so many others, in an active deathwish. Cyrène might speak for all cerebral heroes when he sadly observes in a moment of decadent truth:[10]

Ma vie se trouble et mon coeur se durcit. D'heure en heure, je désire moins de choses et les désirs que je réalise me donnent des joies chaque fois diminuées. J'avais tant espéré vous voir épouser Néo et vivre avec elle et moi, et nous, une large vie de philosophe ironiste. Vous deux, moi et Cyran, c'était un monde en quatre personnes; du haut de notre planète nous aurions jugé les hommes avec un dédain aimable et presque divin. Cyran tout rêve, moi tout coeur, Néo tout esprit, vous toute âme et lien des autres âmes . . . Cela aurait duré peu d'années, oui, je sais: Cyran s'est vieilli, sont sort me guette . . . Mais nous aurions vécu en vous au delà de la tombe . . . Absurde, n'est-ce pas? Tout est absurde, hormis les sensations. Je crois que les hommes reviendront des animaux.

Once again the hero draws the lines between expectation and fulfilment, hope and disappointment, the ideal and the real. And again he bears witness to the crushing effect of actuality —a sinking into despondency, spleen. This is the essence of decadent psychology: The cerebral hero abhors himself because he is a Hamlet figure, a man of pale thought and not of action, while he realizes, like Hamlet, the necessity for action. In his abulia he formulates a creed of sensationalism. Life is nothing, he maintains, but a series of sense-impressions which he, like a good Epicurean, should enjoy to the fullest without bothering himself over other problems. All else is illusory. But intellectualizing over life, he finds, is no substitute for living. All the nuances of his sensualism, at length, are a pale shadow of the fundamental, animal life which he thirsts for. The cerebral hero, then, is profoundly unhappy with himself. But he cannot change what he is. His anguish lies in being condemned ever to watch himself like Tantalus —the spectator of a spectator at the banquet of life—while suffering the gnawing pangs of a hunger which will never be satisfied.

The cerebral hero appears again and again in Gourmont's fiction. In *Sixtine,* "un roman de la vie cérébrale" as it is frankly subtitled, the hero, Hubert d'Entragues, for example, is so given to introspection that he actually wonders:[11]

Y a-t-il un monde de vie extérieure à moi-même? C'est possible, mais je ne le connais pas. Le monde, c'est moi, il me doit l'existence, je l'ai créé avec mes sens, il est mon esclave et nul sur lui n'a de pouvoir. Si nous étions bien assurés de ceci, qu'il n'est rien en dehors de nous, comme la guérison de nos vanités serait prompte, comme promptement nos plaisirs en seraient purgés.

Entragues lives solely with his sense-impressions, which are totally divorced from reality. Gourmont describes him: "Le monde idéal, tel qu'il le détenait, suffisait à son activité mentale et trop inerte pour la lutte."[12] He lacks the energy to fight the game of life or, for that matter, even to continue to live. He inhabits an unreal city of phantoms, not of the living men and women of a vital Paris:[13]

Paris, ce n'était pour lui, ni la rue, ni le boulevard, ni le théâtre; Paris, pour Entragues, était confiné dans les bornes assez étroites du "cabinet d'étude" peuplé des bons fantômes de son imagination.

The cerebral hero is isolated as well as impotent. Indeed his impotence largely causes his isolation.

The plot of this novel turns upon the hero's cerebralism, his tragic flaw. Entragues is in love with Mme Sixtine Magne, a widow, whom he unsuccessfully tries to seduce, though she seems sufficiently willing. He is simply not forceful enough to carry through the seduction. This motif is amusing. From the first page to the dénouement the reader wonders: Will he, will he not? But Entragues' agony is real. He does not. He is a dreamer who cannot bring himself to act in a real life situation, though he always intends to. He lacks the necessary energy and drive. Sometimes he seems to love an ideal, not a real woman, and this fact accounts, at least partly, for his strange irresolution. Sixtine does not flee from him too fast. A perceptive woman, she senses this and says as much:[14]

Vous aimez une créature de rêve que vous avez incarnée sous les apparences qui sont les miennes; vous ne m'aimez pas telle que je suis, mais telle que vous m'avez faite. Vous n'aimez pas une femme, mais une héroïne de roman, et tout n'est pour vous que roman.

She analyzes the cause of his cerebralism, the opposition between ideality and reality. An ideal is such, she implies, because it is unattainable. He does not really want to possess her. A romantic type might pursue an ideal woman across a continent, but the decadent is too sophisticated. He knows that realization means disappointment while at least disenchantment alone, totally divorced from reality, can maintain a certain aura of charm. It is no wonder, then, that Entragues cannot act. He sadly watches Sixtine elope with her forceful Russian suitor, Moscowitch, who, like an animal, takes matters in hand and crushes her will. The old relation between man and woman is reasserted. The will to power, the will to love, two natural instincts, are all important. But a cerebral decadent like Entragues takes a sad pleasure in his unhappiness. He is, ironically, quite glad that he has been disappointed again. He would not have had a different outcome for the world.

Entragues knows he suffers from cerebralism. He mumbles repeatedly, obsessively:[15]

J'ai de particulières facultés de vision et maintes fois je vous appelai près de moi par des magies. L'objet auquel je pense très fortement s'incorpore devant mes yeux en une forme visible, et à mes sens tactiles en une palpable matérialité, quelquefois. J'ai senti des présences de personnes certainement bien loin de moi, selon le commun jugement, et cela ne m'étonne point, car la sensation régulière n'est qu'une hallucination vraie. Vraie ou fausse, pour moi, cela est bien indifférent, je ne m'en inquiète guère.

He testifies to the fatal attraction of the dream. His words recall Mme Chantelouve's pygmalionism and evidence his belief in the strong power of the imagination. His dreams, enigmatically, suffice while at the same time, from another point of view, they are insufficient:[16]

Nous sommes dans les imaginaires, c'est-à-dire dans la réalité transcendante ou surnaturelle, pourquoi donc, alors, ne pas mettre les deux pieds sur le même plan? Ai-je besoin, pour rêver à des amours, d'avoir serré contre ma chair de la chair aimée? Naïveté. Est-ce que Guido a touché à sa madone? Est-elle une femme avec qui il ait dormi dans un lit, ou seulement joué sur un canapé? Pourtant il y a une vraie joie d'amour à revêtir son illusoire charnalité pour aimer, en sa personne, l'intangible créature de ses songes.

His fantasies are all the more seductive because they are unrealizable. Actuality is drab. The cerebral hero's idea of nature is again ambiguous, his attitude towards it ambivalent. In a philosophical dialogue one of Entragues' friends exclaims:[17]

La nature! mais c'est l'artiste qui le crée, la nature, et l'art n'est que la faculté d'objectiver en un simulacre la représentation individuelle du monde.

It is a complete philosophy of sensualism, sense-perception, and reaction, like that of Hume. Entragues replies, formulating the decadent doctrine of reality:[17]

On se raconte soi-même, on ne peut même raconter que cela: l'oeuvre d'un artiste, c'est la lente et quotidienne réaction de l'intelligence et de la volonté sur tel amas de cellules individuelles.

His words echo Schopenhauer's dictum "the world is my idea," and they reflect Kant's influence with his conviction that the thing-in-itself is absolutely unknowable. Hence all knowledge is extremely relative. It is only an impression of the thing-in-itself seen through imperfect eyes. The cerebral hero inhabits this tenuous world of reflection and curious insubstantiality. His life is somnolent. It is small wonder that, with such a worldview, he is afflicted with abulia: life, being unknowable, is too essentially unreal to justify action.

The symbolist poets are greatly concerned with the dream and unreality. Their verse is purposefully suggestive, in fact, because they frankly admit that they cannot perceive reality. They can only suggest certain attributes of the thing-in-itself, not recreate it. The corollary of this proposition is that the hero of a shadowy world will act accordingly—that is, he will not act at all. He will think, he will reflect, but he will not act.

Symbolist "reality" is vague, indefinite, blurred over. Verlaine expresses a kind of symbolist ontology as well as an aesthetic credo in the following verses:[18]

De la musique avant toute chose,
Et pour cela préfère l'Impair
Plus vague et plus soluble dans l'air,
San rien en lui qui pèse ou qui pose.

Il faut aussi que tu n'ailles point
Choisir tes mots sans quelque méprise;
Rien de plus cher que la chanson grise
Où l'indécis au Précis se joint.

C'est des beaux yeux derrière des voiles,
C'est le grand jour tremblant de midi,
C'est, par un ciel d'automne attiédi,
Le bleu fouillis des claires étoiles ...

and further:

> Car nous voulons la Nuance encor,
> Pas la Couleur, rien que la nuance!
> Oh! la nuance seule fiance
> Le rêve au rêve et la flûte au cor!

Verlaine's atmosphere is that of the *hantise de l'idéal*. The *ideal*, imperfectly perceived, is *being* in the symbolist ontology. Reality lies behind the trembling veil which, though diaphanous, cannot be rent. The symbolist poet, his fictional hero, wavers because he responds to the veil, not to the actuality behind it. If the symbolist poet only did not know, was not conscious of the fact, that he was reacting at second remove, he could then act freely. But the cerebral decadent does know that he reacts to impression, suggestion, an inaccurate and imperfect perception, not to actuality. And this knowledge tends to paralyze him. It makes of him a poet of abulia.

More than any other symbolist poet Stéphane Mallarmé is obsessed with *l'idéal* and afflicted with sterility and abulia. In his poems he depicts himself as a cerebral hero whom reality disgusts and ideality eludes. He constantly suffers from a defeatism reflected in his sterility and nihilism. He is an aged Faust in whom the will has been crushed and whose sad knowledge is no longer equal to the world. This hero cannot lash himself into action; he is too weak to raise the whip. In "Brise marine," for instance, Mallarmé contrasts ideality and reality, he speaks of his ennui, and he bears witness to the crushing sense of sterility which always prevents him from writing as he wishes:[19]

> La chair est triste, hélas! et j'ai lu tous les livres.
> Fuir! là-bas fuir! Je sens que des oiseaux sont ivres
> D'être parmi l'écume inconnue et les cieux!
> Rien, ni les vieux jardins reflétés par les yeux
> Ne retiendra ce coeur qui dans la mer se trempe
> O nuits! ni la clarté déserte de ma lampe
> Sur le vide papier que la blancheur défend
> Et ni la jeune femme allaitant son enfant.

Je partirai! Steamer balançant ta mâture,
Lève l'ancre pour une exotique nature!

Un Ennui, désolé par les cruels espoirs,
Croit encore à l'adieu suprême des mouchoirs!
Et, peut-être, les mâts, invitant les orages
Sont-ils de ceux qu'un vent penche sur les naufrages
Perdus, sans mâts, sans mâts, ni fertiles îlots...
Mais, ô mon coeur, entends le chant des matelots!

In his poetic creativity, or rather the moments in which he
tries to overcome his sterility, Mallarmé confronts the haunt-
ing whiteness of the unwritten page. Its pallor fascinates him
as a kind of unblemished ideality, but the inspiration at the
tip of his pen lingers, halts, does not blacken the page with
words: reality would then spoil ideality. The cerebral hero
is statically present with himself, torn between the familiar
polarities, an agonized victim of abulia.

In "L'Azur" Mallarmé uses other symbols, but the fundamental theme is the same. Life is empty, static, motionless,
and the cerebral hero is enticed by visions dancing ever so
slightly upon the horizons:[20]

—Le Ciel est mort.—Vers toi, j'accours! donne, ô matière,
L'oubli de l'Idéal cruel et du Péché
A ce martyr qui vient partager la litière
Où le bétail heureux des hommes est couché.

Car j'y veux, puisque enfin ma cervelle, vidée,
Comme le pot de fard gisant au pied d'un mur,
N'a plus l'art d'attifer la sanglotante idée,
Lugubrement bâiller vers un trépas obscur.

En vain! l'Azur triomphe, et je l'entends qui chante
Dans les cloches. Mon âme, il se fait voix pour plus
Nous faire peur avec sa victoire méchante,
Et du métal vivant sort en bleus angélus!

Il roule par la brume, ancien et traverse
Ta native agonie ainsi qu'un glaive sûr;
Où fuir dans la révolte inutile et perverse?
Je suis hanté. L'Azur! l'Azur! l'Azur! l'Azur!

The vision which he will never capture tantalizes him. He is too weak, now, to pursue a quest across lost horizons. Life has weighed too heavily upon him. In a famous sonnet Mallarmé says that, at length, the poet will realize that his final poetic function is to write no more:[21]

> Le vierge, le vivace et le bel aujourd'hui
> Va-t-il nous déchirer avec un coup d'aile ivre
> Ce lac dur oublié que hante sous le givre
> Le transparent glacier des vols qui n'ont pas fui!
>
> Un cygne d'autrefois se souvient que c'est lui
> Magnifique mais qui sans espoir se délivre
> Pour n'avoir pas chanté la région où vivre
> Quand du stérile hiver a resplendi l'ennui.
>
> Tout son col secouera cette blanche agonie
> Par l'espace infligée à l'oiseau qui le nie,
> Mais non l'horreur du sol où le plumage est pris.
>
> Fantôme qu'à ce lieu son pur éclat assigne,
> Il s'immobilise au songe froid de mépris
> Que vêt parmi l'exil inutile le Cygne.

The cerebral hero has become so sterile that he will not even record his own decline and fall—the last function of the decadent man. The symbolist poet stops just short, just as sterility sets in like rigor mortis. The symbols of sterility are numerous: the frozen lake that has captured the swan, the glittering hoarfrost and the transparent ice, the pale agony and the cold dream. The images of purity and pallor, in different guises, appear over and over. There is no action in the poem. The inert poet is emprisoned by his cerebralism in a nonmoving world. The scene leaves the impression of an engraving, glittering with white, sharp lines, as a clean portrayal of a static and sterile poet who will write no more. The decadent dirge has ended with the faintest whimper.

A history of the cerebral hero is the entire record of the protagonist in decadent literature. Abulia, as Adolphe evidences, has its aetiology in romanticism. But as the nineteenth century gains velocity and passes on, abulia becomes more symptomatic. Each decadent hero in almost his every act could exemplify the cerebral protagonist. Certain ones, of course, are more noteworthy than others, and the wellsprings of abulia are seen more clearly in some than others. To enumerate them is superfluous. What is important is the role of cerebralism in decadent psychology: the fact that the hero, unable to resolve the polarities of ideality and actuality, his energies sapped by modern life, drops the sword of action and does not cut the Gordian knot of inactivity, as he is increasingly caught, like Mallarmé's swan, in abulia and sterility. The decadent is cerebral as his response—even the failure to respond—to the tragedy of his aging, dying civilization. In him the poet comes to a dead-end. The old poetic themes of life, vigor, activity vanish, as in Mallarmé, while a new theme emerges: Will the poet write? and finally, Can he write? Sterility is the subject of the decadent's final poems, and the poet, moreover, decides that he cannot and will not write. There is no dirge after the twilight of the gods.

SIX

THE DECADENT: AN AESTHETE

PERHAPS the aesthete is the decadent in his most characteristic role in the French decadence. Indeed, the aesthetic idea of life is essentially decadent. Art is the highest value posited and often excludes other values. This fact sets the decadent apart from his immediate predecessor, the romantic hero. As a hero the romantic takes himself quite seriously, and his lack of humor is with his lack of perspective a most cardinal trait. The romantic hero is grandiose as a rebel, poet-prophet, seeker, but he is never an aesthete. Only as a dandy, a special case of the romantic hero, does he pass into the decadent hero, for here too there is much emphasis on aesthetics.[1] The romantic hero is essentially a man of nature whereas the decadent aesthete is, of course, the prototype of the anti-natural. The romantic is non-aesthetic, the decadent aesthetic, and in the paraphrase never shall the twain meet.

Gautier is the harbinger of *l'art pour l'art*. He states the new doctrine succinctly in "L'Art" and several other poems. He elaborates upon his theory in the famous preface to *Mademoiselle de Maupin,* which as a document in the French decadence may well be second only to his preface to Baudelaire's *Fleurs du mal* in its resounding impact. In the preface

Gautier stresses the luxury of art, its basic impracticality and non-utilitarian nature, and attacks the vulgarities of the newspaper world. Baudelaire's Samuel Cramer, from *La Fanfarlo*, lives an aesthetic life according to the principles enunciated in Gautier. He exemplifies the French dandy who responds aesthetically to life. Cramer's worldview is more "aesthetic" and typically French than might be realized. Certainly the French dandy is more of a true aesthete than his English counterpart. There is a basic difference, as Prevost, among other commentators, points out:[2]

Le dandysme français ne fut pas la simple copie du dandysme anglais. Les modes et les goûts venus d'Angleterre n'en constituaient que l'aspect le plus superficiel. Le caractère particulier du dandysme français se fait sentir dans l'impatience témoignée par Roger de Beauvoir à l'égard de Beau Brummell, aussi bien que dans son enthousiasme pour le "dandysme" de Lord Byron, qui ne fut guère un *dandy*. Puis, effet du tempérament, le dandy anglais se distinguait par la froideur et la réserve, le dandy français par une gaîté franche et animée. Enfin, *dandyism* ne voulait guère dire autre chose que le fait de se présenter toujours en une tenue soignée où tout est propre et à sa place. En France, le dandysme c'était en partie cela, mais c'était surtout l'art de vivre. . . .

It is at this point that the dandy merges with the aesthete, for both are artistically oriented towards a decadent ideal in life: Existence, as they perceive it, has value only as a super-refined sense of art makes it so. They respond to the subtle and the delicate, not to the bombastics of romanticism.

The archetypal aesthete of the French decadence is Des Esseintes of Huysmans' *A Rebours*. He is the typical decadent for whom life without art is pointless. He identifies art with life, in fact, or even makes it larger than life. Art is deified. Effeminate and abnormal, Des Esseintes tires of the city, Paris, and retires to his country manor, Fontenay, in an infamous pursuit of pleasure. This does not mean that he is given to crasser pleasures, like sexual excesses, but rather that, like his master Epicurus, he lends himself to a philosophical sensualism. He savors fine wines and liqueurs, atomizes perfume pictures in the air, smells exotic plants and flowers, contemplates the harmonies of all his senses. He is "partly the father, partly the off-spring, of the perverse art he adores,"[3] as all critics have recognized. Finally, when his supersensitivity causes his nervous system to collapse, he must either die or go mad, or return to nature and normalcy. Art exacts a fearful toil of the decadent aesthete.

Des Esseintes' choice is basically that of all decadents. His actions are those of all aesthetes when confronted with their terrible world of horror and ugliness, for they conceive modern society in this guise. The legend of the Fall of Imperial Rome lies beneath the surface, and the aesthete turns to art, among other reasons, with an ultimate social cataclysm in mind. Thus Gautier writes about the decadent and his station in the modern world in his famous preface to Baudelaire's *Les Fleurs du mal*:[4]

Ne semble-t-il pas au lecteur, comme à moi, que la langue de la dernière décadence latine—suprême soupir d'une personne robuste déjà transformée et préparée pour la vie spirituelle—est singulièrement propre à exprimer la passion telle que l'a comprise et sentie le monde poétique moderne? La mysticité est l'autre pôle de cet aimant dont Catulle et sa bande, poètes brutaux et purement épidermiques, n'ont connu que le pôle sensualité.

Decadent aesthetics, then, is natural for the poet in a moribund society: He attempts to transfigure language, and indeed life, during the great moment of cataclysm, when all the ugliness and wretchedness of man come to the fore in a final catastrophe. Ancient Rome always preoccupies the decadent, and he draws his obvious parallels with the Second Empire and with Western civilization. For the decadent aesthete, consequently, art *is* life. In fact, Désiré Nisard criticizes modern writers in his *Etudes sur les poëtes latins de la décadence* largely because they make art their *raison d'être* rather than subsuming it, as classical writers do, as only one aspect of the many factors comprising man's totality. Under the guise of assessing the Romans he really lambastes nineteenth century French authors. In "Lucain, ou la Décadence," especially, he delineates the parallels between Roman antiquity and modern France. His focus of scorn is the "aesthete," the "decadent," who lives for art and, in so doing, corrupts it.

The proper relationship of art to life, in the theory of *l'art pour l'art*, should be stressed. The concept has been imperfectly understood for much too long. When practiced for its own sake, art is not necessarily divorced from life, as myopic critics still maintain in curious arguments. Indeed, art is its own morality in life:[5]

C'est que l'art, qui est en dernière analyse la représentation de la vie, et plus spécialement l'Art pour l'Art, n'est pas moral toujours ni pour tous. Il requiert chez ceux auxquels il s'adresse certaines conditions de moralité, certaines facultés d'interprétation qui ne se trouvent pas toujours réunies à un degré suffisant pour que ses leçons portent tout le fruit dont elles sont susceptibles. C'est là son infériorité sur la morale proprement dite, au point de vue moral. Il ne serait pas juste, et il serait inutile de la lui reprocher.

The aesthetes of *l'art pour l'art* are firmly grounded in a social context. Indeed, they turn to art because they abhor their wretched society. It is *ugly* in the full meaning of the word. Sin, vice, perversion are traits they can tolerate, even admire for their artificiality, but not vulgarity and ugliness. The aesthete, like any other hero-type, acts in response to his society. In this case it is an ugly, decadent society. He withdraws from it in disgust, but the very withdrawal, let it be stressed, is assuredly a form of response.

Numerous works illustrate this fundamental point about *l'art pour l'art*. The most transparently clear is Cram's *The Decadent: Being the Gospel of Inaction*, an American classic in the French tradition. Like the work of Oscar Wilde, it is more French than the French itself. The socialist hero of the short novel, Malcolm McCann, becomes an aesthete through the arguments of his decadent friend, Aurelian Blake. McCann is a philistine who naïvely believes that social reform is possible and necessary in a crumbling world. He is certain that he can set society aright again. Blake, addicted to opium, tobacco, and liquor in that order, is too sophisticated to heed such idealistic nonsense. It is delusion, he says. The book is a philosophical dialogue in which each develops an opposing position. Finally Blake convinces McCann that he too should become a decadent, an aesthete:[6]

I believe only in art as the object of production,—art which shall glorify that which we eat, that wherewith we clothe ourselves, those things whereby we are sheltered; art which shall be this and more,—the ultimate expression of all that is spiritual, religious, and divine in the soul of man. I hate material prosperity, I refuse to justify machinery, I cannot pardon public opinion. I desire only absolute individualism and the triumph of idealism.

The idealism to which Blake refers is the possibility of the good life through art. This is art for art's sake. Significantly he does not suggest a total withdrawal from life, for that is manifestly impossible. The decadent aesthete is simply one who transvalues his life through surcharging nature with art.

Hence the decadent aesthete, like Baudelaire, Flaubert, Gourmont, the Goncourts, Barrès, indeed all the decadent writers, despises the bourgeoisie and its values. The *bon bourgeois,* as the sobriquet goes, is assuredly against art. He is too enamored of his machinery and his creature comforts. In this sense, enigmatically, the aesthete, the very epitome of the sophisticated, civilized, and anti-natural, still yearns for nature, while the philistine turns away from it. The aesthete is a kind of megalopolitan primitive whose space and time exoticism often attest to his real desire for a simpler life. At the same time he is the slave of convenience, luxury, sensuality. The difficulty may be resolved. From the philosophical standpoint the aesthete's ideal parallels that of Epicurus. Pleasure is certainly the aim of a civilized man, but true pleasure lies in his sensitive and artistic ordering of life. It is a beautiful simplicity, not a sensual excess. But just as Epicurus' adherents often violate his precepts, decadent aesthetes frequently deviate from the ideal they project. Des Esseintes is again instructive. He travels to Fontenay, Huysmans writes, like a monk to his cloister. His life, while sensually oriented, is far from riotous. But he gets out of hand. He degenerates, like perhaps all aesthetes, into a sensualism that is a corruption of the ideal of artistic living. But such is not the professed aim of *l'art pour l'art,* just as hedonism is by no means the goal of the real Epicurean. The aesthetes merely attest once more to the difference between intention and deed, between ideality and reality.

L'art pour l'art is an aristocratic notion. Asthetic living, it maintains, is possible only for an intellectual élite. Decadent predilections for the *ancien régime* and for conservatism are natural corollaries of their anti-bourgeois bias. One who hates the mediocre must thereby love the exceptional; he turns from the bourgeois to the aristocratic. The aesthete has good reasons for despising democracy:[7]

The attitude of the so-called Decadent was then something else and something more than merely an attempt at "astonishing the bourgeois." It was an unequivocal way of affirming his esthetic individualism, denied to him either of science or of Democracy. It was a way of affirming his right to create an aristoratic art, the delectation of a minority, even when the majority did not approve of its existence.

L'art pour l'art has as a fundamental tenet that art is quite useless, i.e., non-functional. It serves no utilitarian or social purpose. Thus art can hardly find approval with a bourgeoisie concerned with practical affairs like making money. The aesthete, on the other hand, searches for finer things. He is an aristocrat of the senses when not by birth or pocketbook. Des Esseintes, the archetypal aesthete, typically rejects the "modern world," i.e., the commonplace bourgeois society, in order to turn to other lands and times. His space exoticism is evident, for example, in his love for England and Holland, and his time exoticism in his admiration for Latin writers:[8]

Enfin, depuis son départ de Paris, il s'éloignait, de plus en plus, de la réalité et surtout du monde contemporain qu'il tenait en une croissante horreur; cette haine avait forcément agi sur ses goûts littéraires et artistiques, et il se détournait le plus possible des tableaux et des livres dont les sujets délimités se reléguaient dans la vie moderne.

His retreat from the contemporary scene is evident. Escape lies through antiquity or the Middle Ages, through the convolutions of decadent art and literature, just as through drugs and drink—through anything, in fact, antipodal to modern bourgeois values. In his adamant insistence on his own individuality and his determined opposition to the bourgeois, the decadent aesthete recalls the modern beatnik with his attack upon the "square."

Contemporary life, the aesthete believes, is not only ugly but vulgar. He wants none of it. Yet he is a part of his society, and however he may try he cannot escape his social context. He must react in response to it, whether favorably or not. Thus decadence, which cuts across the artificial boundaries of the various schools in a common concern, is peculiarly ambiguous and certainly ambivalent. The aesthete wants to escape an age which he feels is "decadent," yet cannot, and perhaps would not, and certainly recognizes that he is himself decadent. He adhors the city, as has been seen, but cannot live without its luxuries. He yearns for the simpler life but would not be strong enough to survive in it, as he realizes. *L'art pour l'art* is all he has, consequently, and there are times when even art does not suffice.

Contrary to what many critics seem to feel, the aesthete is neither hypocritical nor superficial. At least the "aesthetic pose" characterizes only some decadents, by no means all of them, and disguises an element of depth. It is a persona which masks the deep anguish which the aesthete truly feels: his frustration with modern life and his despair in failing to come to grips with it. Hence he turns to art as his succor. In so doing he distorts and often inverts deliberately the bourgeois values of his society. This fact, however, does not mean that he is "superficial" or simply cantankerous. The aesthete believes in his ideals. They are those of *l'art pour l'art*. He might well argue, with justification, that the bourgeoisie has inverted his ideals, deliberately, for money, power, things.

The aesthete turns to art in various ways. His painful confrontation with the world does not always elicit an identical response. He ranges through the gamut of experience and

aesthetic possibility. Yet in *l'art pour l'art* the aesthete tends
to fall into one of two categories. He tends to respond like a
parnassian or a symbolist, since the so-called schools of parnassianism and symbolism, in contradistinction to realism and
naturalism, are most intimately concerned with ideas of art.
The aesthete of these movements is generally the poet himself, the decadent *Moi*, as he speaks, often in the first person,
through his poems. Here he is explicit. The aesthetic hero
is generally more implicit in the decadence proper, and for
a good reason. Parnassianism and symbolism have poetry
almost as an exclusive province. In fiction, however, the
aesthete must frequently combine with other roles as a
cerebral hero, a cosmopolitan, or, say, a pervert.

As a parnassian the aesthete's ideal is to sculpt a lasting
beauty in a perfect immobility of form: He captures time as
process in one beautiful and meaningful moment. He hones
his verses to a fine point, for absolute perfection is his goal.
Never has form been a more obsessive concern than in parnassianism. In *Emaux et camées* Gautier is the harbinger of
the movement, and perhaps the first great modern poet of
the sculpted form. He practices his professed ideal. In
"L'art" he formulates the idea of *l'art pour l'art*:[9]

> Oui, l'oeuvre sort plus belle
> D'une forme au travail
>   Rebelle,
> Vers, marbre, onyx, émail.
>
> Point de contraintes fausses!
> Mais que pour marcher droit
>   Tu chausses,
> Muse, un cothurne étroit....
>
> Peintre, fuis l'aquarelle
> Et fixe la couleur
>   Trop frêle
> Au four de l'émailleur....
>
> Tout passe.—L'art robuste
> Seul a l'éternité,
>   Le buste
> Survit à la cité.

Et la médaille austère
Que trouve un laboureur
        Sous terre
Révèle un empereur.

Les dieux eux-mêmes meurent,
Mais les vers souverains
        Demeurent
Plus forts que les airains.

Sculpte, lime, ciselle;
Que ton rêve flottant
        Se scelle
Dans le bloc résistant!

It is evident from these lines that the aesthete makes an important assumption: There is an eternal value in art, residing in the perfection of its form, which transcends the transient ages. It is this perfection of form which he seeks as his immortality. It is his way of coping with an ephemeral and obscenely vulgar society. He chisels perfect beauty like a statue. His verse is hard, clean, firm. It is small wonder that Des Esseintes, in *A Rebours*, adores Gautier's work, and that Oscar Wilde's Dorian Gray, at the end of the century, turns back to *Emaux et camées*.

The same idea recurs throughout Leconte de Lisle's poetry. The aesthete rejects the delusions of life while he finds his solace in art. Leconte de Lisle's world is, he feels, an accurate portrait of dying animals, guttural primitives, great battles and bloody struggles, all scenes of unceasing strife, and all forms of historic and modern ugliness. In "Aux Modernes" he drops his pose of impersonality, and he speaks directly to his times:[10]

Vous vivez lâchement, sans rêve, sans dessein,
Plus vieux, plus décrépits que la terre inféconde,
Châtrés dès le berceau par le siècle assassin
De toute passion vigoureuse et profonde.

Votre cervelle est vide autant que votre sein,
Et vous avex souillé ce misérable monde
D'un sang si corrompu, d'un souffle si malsain,
Que la mort germe seule en cette boue immonde.

Hommes, tueurs de Dieux, les temps ne sont pas loin
Où, sur un grand tas d'or vautrés dans quelque coin,
Ayant rongé le sol nourricier jusqu'aux roches,

Ne sachant faire rien ni des jours ni des nuits,
Noyés dans le néant des suprêmes ennuis,
Vous mourrez bêtement en emplissant vos poches.

The powerful image of modern man as a coward, stuffing his pockets with money, too weak to survive in the jungle of nature, testifies to Leconte de Lisle's scorn for and disgust with society. This is his constant theme, expressed in a wide variety of images and across many dead civilizations. Man's absolute hope from the pains of life is death, he argues, but his contingent release may come through art—if he is wise enough to heed. Hence Leconte de Lisle is an aesthete, who writes starkly in "Vénus de Milo":[11]

Marbre sacré, vêtu de force et de génie,
Déesse irrésistible au port victorieux,
Pure comme un éclair et comme une harmonie,
O Vénus, ô beauté, blanche mère des Dieux! ...

Si mon berceau, flottant sur la Thétis antique,
Ne fut point caressé de son tiède cristal;
Si je n'ai point prié sous le fronton attique,
Beauté victorieuse, à ton autel natal;

Allume dans mon sein la sublime étincelle,
N'enferme point ma gloire au tombeau soucieux;
Et fais que ma pensée en rhythmes d'or ruisselle,
Comme un divin métal au moule harmonieux.

The parnassian line of development from Gautier to Leconte de Lisle and his followers is evidently direct, even imagistically so. Art alone is the aesthete's consolation for a most imperfect world.

Heredia's *Les Trophées* epitomizes the hard form of which Gautier and Leconte de Lisle write. Heredia molds his verses in tightly knit Italian sonnets. Though he has fallen somewhat into disrepute, none can deny him the perfection of form which he seeks above all else. His theme is always

the permanence of beauty as opposed to the transiency of
the world. In sonnets like "Un Peintre," "Michel-Ange,"
and "Sur un marbre brisé" he lauds the indestructibility of
art, as in these lines upon the broken statue:[12]

> La mousse fut pieuse en fermant ses yeux mornes;
> Car, dans ce bois inculte, il chercherait en vain
> La Vierge qui versait le lait pur et le vin
> Sur la terre au beau nom dont il marqua les bornes.
>
> Aujourd'hui le houblon, le lierre et les viornes
> Qui s'enroulent autour de ce débris divin,
> Ignorant s'il fut Pan, Faune, Hermès ou Silvain,
> A son front mutilé tordent leurs vertes cornes.
>
> Vois. L'oblique rayon, le caressant encor,
> Dans sa face camuse a mis deux orbes d'or;
> La ligne folle y rit comme une lèvre rouge;
>
> Et, prestige mobile, un murmure du vent,
> Les feuilles, l'ombre errante et le soleil qui bouge,
> De ce marbre en ruine ont fait un Dieu vivant.

Again the world appears transient, ugly, and parnassian art
alone ennobles it. It is the omnipresent theme of the
aesthete.

Both the parnassian and symbolist aesthete live for art.
But the parnassian sculpts in clean lines and clear imagery
whereas the symbolist evokes, suggests, in vague, musical
language. The symbolist aesthete knows that he cannot capture reality, or even know it in its frightful totality, and
hence his art is differently oriented. Perhaps, then, the
poem, i.e., the poet's transfiguration of imperfect nature into
lasting beauty, is as much the reader's response to a *suggestion of beauty* as the poem itself. Symbolism permeates
the whole of life; it is not merely an elaborate literary device. It transfigures the vulgarity of the world with new
aesthetic meanings and values.

Baudelaire presages the symbolist aesthete and his worldview in his famous sonnet "Les Correspondances," where he
writes:[13]

La Nature est un temple où de vivants piliers
Laissent parfois sortir de confuses paroles;
L'homme y passe à travers des forêts de symboles
Qui l'observent avec des regards familiers.

Comme de longs échos qui de loin se confondent
Dans une ténébreuse et profonde unité,
Vaste comme la nuit et comme la clarté,
Les parfums, les couleurs et les sons se répondent.

Il est des parfums frais comme des chairs d'enfants,
Doux comme les hautbois, verts comme les prairies,
—Et d'autres, corrompus, riches et triomphants,

Ayant l'expansion des choses infinies
Comme l'ambre, le musc, le benjoin et l'encens,
Qui chantent les transports de l'esprit et des sens.

Surely symbolist eyes, when they behold nature, transform it into a thing of exciting beauty. This is the recurrent theme of *Les Fleurs du mal;* nature is beautiful only when transfigured by art. In symbolism proper the theme becomes obsessive.

In the famous "Art poétique" Verlaine formulates the symbolist ideal of writing poetry:[14]

De la musique avant toute chose
Et pour cela préfère l'Impair
Plus vague et plus soluble dans l'air,
Sans rien en lui qui pèse ou qui pose.

Il faut aussi que tu n'ailles point
Choisir tes mots sans quelque méprise:
Rien de plus cher que la chanson grise
Où l'Indécis au Précis se joint.

C'est des beaux yeux derrière des voiles,
C'est le grand jour tremblant de midi,
C'est, par un ciel d'automne attiédi,
Le bleu fouillis des claires étoiles.

The symbolist aesthete is of course a man who writes poetry, but he is also a hero who sees nature poetically. There is a vast difference. The classical lines of parnassianism with its emphasis on clarity, restraint, and sculptured form vanish in the symbolist mists: Beauty is to be suggested, not described, for it can be only apprehended, not known. So it is with nature.

At this point the symbolist aesthete tends to merge roles with the metaphysical decadent. There is no cause for concern. The lines dividing the subtypes of the decadent hero are frequently blurred. Hence the symbolist is a kind of metaphysician who assuages his painful knowledge of life with the balm of beauty, *l'art pour l'art,* which he refines more and more. Thus Wallace Fowlie observes rightly:[15]

The decadent poets, for example, reflected an age-old conflict between man's reason and his heart. They believed in the rights of the inner life, of a sensitivity which would cultivate the subconscious and the intuitive aspects of a poet's life. A deeper belief in idealism presided over the aspirations of the symbolists. Their mediaeval settings, their attraction to Wagner, to Lohengrin's swan and Parsifal's grail, all denote a nostalgia for the past, for a sense of purity and a striving for the absolute.

As a symbolist the aesthetic hero worships abstract forms of beauty that transfigure the things themselves. His nature is one comprised of almost Platonic forms, but through symbolist eyes they appear blurred. The human intellect is not acute enough to perceive them clearly. Beauty is sensed. Such an ideal transfigures the most abject reality into a permanent vision of the beautiful. This is the function of the poet. Rimbaud testifies to this in "Ma Bohème":[16]

> Je m'en allais, les poings dans mes poches crevées.
> Mon paletot aussi devenait idéal.
> J'allais sous le ciel, Muse, et j'étais ton féal:
> Oh là là, que d'amours splendides j'ai rêvées!
>
> Mon unique culotte avait un large trou.
> Petit-Poucet rêveur, j'égrenais dans ma course
> Des rimes. Mon auberge était à la Grande-Ourse.
> Mes étoiles au ciel avait un doux frou-frou.

Et je les écoutais, assis au bord des routes,
Ces bons soirs de septembre où je sentais des gouttes
De rosée à mon front, comme un vin de vigueur;

Où, rimant au milieu des ombres fantastiques,
Comme des lyres, je tirais les élastiques
De mon souliers blessés, un pied contre mon coeur!

This is truly a metamorphosis of the homely into the sublime.

The symbolist aesthete strains to express sensations of beauty. He constantly experiments with the new and the involuted in a desperate effort to avoid the hackneyed. Any experience once felt tends to become vulgar, i.e., diurnal, and is therefore excluded from the symbolist ideal. The new aesthetics demands constant striving from the symbolist poet. André Barre describes the aesthete's plight in this regard:[17]

Il fallait du nouveau à tout prix dans le fond comme dans la forme: "L'un des éléments de l'Art, affirme péremptoirement Remy de Gourmont, est le Nouveau, élément si essentiel qu'il institue presque à lui seul l'art tout entier et si essentiel que sans lui, comme un vertébré sans vertèbres, l'Art s'écroule et se liquéfie dans une gélatine de méduse que le jusant délaissa sur le sable."

Thus Rimbaud, for example, cannot confine himself to merely repeating Baudelaire's idea in "Les Correspondances." He must pen a manifesto that is at once different in content and more striking in form. His poem must supersede the older, now worn experience. Hence Rimbaud feels compelled to exaggerate Baudelaire's thesis and to twist his imagery in his own sonnet on the aesthete and symbolism, the famous "Voyelles":[18]

A noir, E blanc, I rouge, U vert, O bleu, voyelles,
Je dirai quelque jour vos naissances latentes.
A, noir corset velu des mouches éclatantes
Qui bombinent autour des puanteurs cruelles,

Golfes d'ombre; E, candeurs des vapeurs et des tentes,
Lances des glaciers fiers, rois blancs, frissons d'ombelles;
I, pourpres, sang craché, rire des lèvres belles
Dans la colère ou les ivresses pénitentes;

> U, cycles, vibrements divins des mers virides,
> Paix des pâtis semés d'animaux, paix des rides
> Que l'alchimie imprime aux grands fronts studieux;
>
> O, suprême clairon plein de strideurs étranges,
> Silences traversés des Mondes et des Anges:
> —O l'Oméga, rayon violet de Ses Yeux!

In "Voyelles" the poet is still the aesthete who perceives beauty in various guises. But he is also something of a seer, as the aesthete passes into the metaphysical decadent. The juxtapositions of sense-impressions, *les correspondances* of Baudelaire, are not only aesthetic perceptions but also mystical or at least philosophical knowledge—a kind of systematic insanity for a purpose. Rimbaud develops the theme in his doctrine of the *dérèglement de tous les sens*. He professes such aesthetic experience as his ideal:[19]

> Je dis qu'il faut être *voyant*, se faire VOYANT. Le poète se fait *voyant* par un long, immense et raisonné *dérèglement* de *tous les sens*. Toutes les formes d'amour, de souffrance, de folie; il cherche lui-même, il épuise en lui, tous les poisons, pour n'en garder que les quintessences.

At this point the symbolist aesthete ceases to practice *l'art pour l'art,* in the narrowest sense, and broadens out the doctrine to include the greatest metaphysical pretentions. The demarcation is, however, quite tenuous.

More than any other poet Stéphane Mallarmé is the prototype of the symbolist. In "L'Après-midi d'un faune" he draws, for instance, upon familiar themes and poetic situations in symbolism proper. Erotic love, the high aspiration of symbolist poetry, a search for reality poetically conceived—such are his themes. The situation, or setting for the poem, could hardly be more "symbolic," with the faun, the nymphs, the psychological monologue, the dream, with Eros flitting about in the air. The poem is indeed misty, as any good symbolist poem should admittedly be. The faun, or symbolist aesthete, asks himself a familiar question:[20]

> Aimai-je un rêve?
> Mon doute, amas de nuit ancienne, s'achève
> En maint rameau subtil, qui, demeuré les vrais
> Bois même, prouve, hélas! que bien seul je m'offrais
> Pour triomphe la faute idéale de roses.
> Réfléchissons. . .

Again the symbolist aesthete transmutes the raw material of nature into a kind of ideality, just as the mediaeval alchemist, in an actual image recurring through symbolism, turns his metal into gold. The aesthete not only writes poems but lives artistically. This is the fullest meaning of the poetic experience. Thus the poet asks himself whether he loved a "dream." The resolution to this symbolist question lies in living for art's sake. Nature becomes art if it is beautiful. It cannot remain simply a disconnected, ugly, commonplace series of things.

The relationship of the symbolist aesthete to the decadent archetype must never be forgotten. The aesthete is the decadent in one of his several roles. Symbolism, in fact, is meaningless outside a decadent context, at least the symbolism visualized in the late nineteenth century. For here the symbol does not refer to a thing in a simple one to one equation; a symbol rather opens the door to an entire experience. *L'art pour l'art* becomes supra-natural art, and the symbol is the *durée profonde* of Bergson. Consequently even the great apologist for symbolism, Michaud, takes care to place the movement in the broader framework of the decadence:[21]

Décadence et symbolisme sont, non pas deux écoles, comme on tend généralement à le faire croire, mais deux phases successives d'un même mouvement, deux étapes de la révolution poétique . . . La Décadence . . . nous apparaît comme le moment du lyrisme, l'épanchement d'une sensibilité inquiète, à l'état de crise, le Symbolisme étant le mouvement intellectuel, la phase de réflexion sur ce lyrisme. . . .

Michaud's interpretation is a bit vague. But interpreted within *l'art pour l'art*, it may well read, correctly, that *decadence* shows the aesthete enjoying his senses directly, immediately, sometimes hedonistically, whereas *symbolism,* still a part of decadent concern, tends to portray him reflecting upon his sense-pleasures. The aesthete has a carnal side, as the public insists on understanding decadence, and an intellectual (or symbolist) side. Verlaine himself recognizes as much: [22]

J'en révoque, bien entendu, toute imputation injurieuse et toute idée de déchéance. Ce mot suppose au contraire des pensées raffinées d'extrême civilisation, une haute culture littéraire, une âme capable d'intensives voluptés. Il est fait d'un mélange d'esprit charnel et de chair triste et de toutes les splendeurs violentes du bas-empire; il respire le fard des courtisanes, les jeux du cirque, le souffle des belluaires, le bondissement des fauves, l'écroulement dans les flammes des races épuisées par la force de sentir, au bruit envahisseur des trompettes ennemies.

The symbolist aesthete, as a hero, recalls the supreme arbiter of good manners, Petronius, ever sensitive to pleasure but also philosophical in his pleasures, and always aware that nature is too complex to grasp: He has epicurean not parnassian calm. There are no sharp corners to art, no clean-cut lines of demarcation. Art, as he sees it, lies like a diaphanous mist over nature, thereby enhancing the glimpsed beauties that are so soon to be enshrouded again.

Decadent, symbolist, parnassian, all three types of the aesthete are sensualists. Their sensualism, or their acute sensitivity to sense-impressions, to rephrase the word, relates them closely to the decadence proper. The aesthete of this body of decadent literature, the core, is a sensualist who often borders on perversion. In fact he is sometimes an overt pervert. He is obsessed with the delicate and subtle sensation, for the unimagined and the unexperienced, and his philosophy of art is colored by his quest of sensation in his peculiar view of man and nature. In *Les Chevaux de Diomède* Gourmont speaks for an entire generation: [23]

Tel qu'il est devenu, l'homme est un être contraire à la nature: là est sa beauté. Mais il n'est pas mauvais que la nature parfois le rappelle à son origine, l'incline vers ses mamelles dures et ses hanches de pierre, afin qu'il sache que la joie est d'être un homme et non d'être un animal.

Art being antithetical to nature, the aesthete is naturally drawn to the abnormal in *l'art pour l'art,* whether it is an accentuation of the normal or an outright perversion. The line separating the two is often quite tenuous. But the aesthete sensualist should not be regarded, necessarily, as a pervert. Des Esseintes has homosexual interests, but it is erroneous to consider him a homosexual. The aesthete tries all experiences. He simply possesses the faculty, or virtue as he looks upon it, of intense living through hypersensitivity.

Baudelaire is among the first writers of the century to experience the acme of hypersensitivity. His sense of smell, for instance, is developed almost to the point of perversion. The case is instructive. In "Parfum exotique," "La Chevelure," and "Le Flacon" he records his ecstasy before certain scents. He is overpowered. In "Le Parfum" he describes his reaction:[24]

> Lecteur, as-tu quelquefois respiré
> Avec ivresse et lente gourmandise
> Ce grain d'encens qui remplit une église
> Ou d'un sachet le musc invétéré?
>
> Charme profond, magique, dont nous grise
> Dans le présent le passé restauré!
> Ainsi l'amant sur un corps adoré
> Du souvenir cueille la fleur exquise.
>
> De ses cheveux élastiques et lourds,
> Vivant sachet, encensoir de l'alcôve,
> Une senteur montait, sauvage et fauve,
>
> Et des habits, mousseline ou velours,
> Tout imprégnés de sa jeunesse pure,
> Se dégageait un parfum de fourrure.

Such an obsession with smell, and there are more striking examples, can hardly be called normal. In the entire section of poems comprising "Le Vin" in *Les Fleurs du mal* Baudelaire attests to the sense attraction of drink, elsewhere to

drugs. In "Les Bijoux," among other poems, there is a kind
of voyeurism. It is a perversion of sight. Sensuality is rampant
throughout. It is only a step, moreover, from Baudelairean
sensualism to the perversion of Des Esseintes and the "monstres parisiens" of the decadence proper. There is a direct
lineage to effete megalopolitans like Georges Vasseur, the
jaded dandy like Durtal, the neurotic *femme fatale* like Mme
Chantelouve, or the horror chambers of Mirbeau's *Le Jardin
des supplices.* But there are attenuated sensations as well.
Pierre Louÿs, for example, symbolizes the aesthete's eternal
search for the unfamiliar titillation in *Une Nouvelle Sensation.* A resuscitated Callisto argues with a nineteenth century
decadent, the writer himself, that there is no new voluptuousness under the sun. They debate the matter, and the aesthete
almost capitulates. He absent-mindedly lights a cigarette
while Callisto, a new gaze in her eyes, looks at him curiously.
A moment later she is reclining on the sofa, ecstatically savor-
ing the (to her) new sensation of the cigarette! In *Une Nuit
au Luxembourg* Gourmont portrays the aesthete's sensualist
role when "Lui" tells Sandy Rose: "Oui, je veux que tu sois
un nouvel Epicure et que tu redises aux hommes d'aujour-
d'hui ce que mon ami enseignait jadis aux Athéniens."[25]
The aesthete sensualist makes a philosophy of voluptuousness
as the dandy does of his dress.

In his philosophy, as well as in external traits, the aesthete
sensualist merges almost imperceptibly into the metaphysical
decadent. Many decadent writers are aware of this combina-
tion of roles. Lorrain makes the point, implicitly, in *Monsieur de Phocas:*[26]

*L'homme moderne ne croit plus, et voilà pourquoi il n'a plus
de regard.* Les yeux modernes? Il n'y a plus d'âme en eux; ils ne
regardent plus le ciel. Même les plus purs n'ont que des pré-
occupations immédiates: basses convoitises, intérêts mesquins,
cupidité, vanité, préjugés, lâches appétits et sourde envie: voilà l'abominable grouillement qu'on trouve aujourd'hui dans
les yeux.

Monsieur de Phocas, like a good aesthete, attacks the philis-
tinism of the *bon bourgeois.* Sensuality is a valid expression

of *l'art pour l'art,* he maintains later, since it opens un-
dreamed vistas to the jaded decadent. It is a narcotic. Monsieur de Phocas' obsession with jewels, eyes, the unseeing orbs
of the statue, is metaphysical as well as aesthetic. The vacant
eyes of the sightless statue are those of modern man, he
claims: unperceptive, undiscriminating, nerveless, *sensation-
less,* dead. The aesthete, on the other hand, can make them
glisten like emeralds in their empty sockets; he can transfigure nature with an eerie light. The sensualist lives for
beauty by keying his nerves to the finest pitch of the five
senses. Life is then a moving canvas, an incessant symphony,
an endless poem. The aesthete writes sensualism as the first
article of his metaphysical creed. He lives up to it religiously.

The sensualist, like his brother aesthetes, the parnassian
and the symbolist, responds in a particular way to his own
ideas of art and nature inherent in the all-embracing doctrine
of *l'art pour l'art.* Art is good, nature bad, or, rephrased, art
makes nature tolerable. It is the old theme. The familiar
catchwords, which become hackneyed by the *fin-de-siècle,*
ring true for the sensualist at this time. With his fibers and
in his viscera he makes aesthetics into metaphysics, and he
can say, like Kant, that the world is only his idea of it. In
Sixtine Entragues and his friend debate this very point over
and over. Entragues speaks for all decadents when he says:[27]

On se raconte soi-même, on ne peut même raconter que cela:
l'oeuvre d'un artiste, c'est la lente et quotidienne réaction de
l'intelligence et de la volonté sur tel amas de cellules individuelles.

The sensualist is indeed a perambulating organism of millions of cells, each delicately attuned to nature artistically
perceived through hypersensitive antennae. Life is literally
his feast. He gorges himself upon sight, sound, smell, as well
as upon liquor, drugs, women, perversions. He does not conceive of nature in the clean contours and the sharp outlines
of the parnassian, and he does not concern himself with the
subtle distinctions and the uncertainties of the symbolist. But

the sensualist, too, lives for art in his own way. His gourmandism and licentiousness, no less than his calmer sensations, are his defense, as an aesthete, against the vulgar encroachments of an ugly and dehumanizing world.

SEVEN

THE DECADENT: A PERVERT

THE pervert is the best-known type of the decadent hero. The very word "decadent" suggests, unfortunately, a rich wastrel moving through the licentious circles of a very opulent and very wicked Paris. The picture is of course distorted. The metaphysical, aesthetic, and cerebral heroes are more basic to the decadent worldview, and the "pervert," to use the loose synonym for "decadent," is the least interesting and essential of the various hero-types. Yet the pervert is a fact that cannot be glossed over. He does appear in decadent literature, and so he must be accounted for.

Perversion is simply a departure from normalcy, an exaggeration of one or more of the so-called normal responses to stimuli. This medical definition is surely not exciting, but it serves at the outset to show how rapidly the "luster" associated with perversion disappears in the cold light of a denotative definition. Any decadent hero fits this portrait by definition, for his very concept of art as anti-nature and of himself as the artificial man causes him to violate normalcy either instinctively or deliberately. But while, strictly speaking, every decadent is "abnormal," the term "pervert" has come to refer to a *sexually* abnormal type. Decadent literature has always been identified with sexual licentiousness, erroneously of course, and educed comparisons with post-Augustan banquets of ease or late-Alexandrian orgies of food and sex. Readers of this current in decadent literature have drawn an obvious conclusion. They have generalized its hero into a satyr, its heroine into a nymphomaniac (or *hystérique,* as she is almost always called), or worse. Such a falsification of decadent literature is preposterous, but it is also understandable. Certain streams of decadent fiction, in particular, overflow with perverts.

Yet one point must be clarified. The word "pathology," applied to decadent literature, is meaningless. The decadent is not pathological in a literary sense, despite psychoanalytical miaulings to the contrary. Unlike his literary predecessor, the romantic hero, the typical decadent pervert, if there is such a thing, *tends* to maintain some kind of intellectual control over his emotions and indeed over his very perversions. He is infrequently insane. Sometimes the excess of his perversions causes even the decadent pervert to feel guilty, but often he feels no qualms of conscience for the most outrageous crimes against God and man. He tends to be a latter-day Sade, wallowing in sensuality for the sheer joy it affords. But licentiousness, while frankly appreciated, does not usually deprive him of his reason. Most decadent perverts are coolly, consciously, and systematically perverse. They are not insane in the sense that romantic heroes often are.[1] The pervert is simply a decadent whose suppurating emotional refinement is attuned to sexuality. He often searches for the delicate sexual sensation as the aesthete looks for the new and involuted in art, and both heroes do so for the same reason: a new titillation. Sexuality is the pervert's *raison d'être* as intellect is the cerebral hero's or art the aesthete's. One might even call the decadent pervert, with much reason, an aesthete of his senses. At any rate, the pervert's quest of sexual pleasure runs throughout the literature as a guiding motif from the brightest to the dimmest stars of the writing constellations.

Great poets of the stature of Baudelaire, Verlaine, Rim-

baud, and Mallarmé are obsessed with perversion. Verlaine
and Rimbaud are bisexual; certainly they have homosexual
tendencies. Baudelaire, at one time, is almost ready to use
the title *Les Lesbiennes* for *Les Fleurs du mal*. In countless
poems Verlaine turns to the theme of lesbianism, as in "Sur
le balcon," "Pensionnaires," "Per amica silentia," "Prin-
temps," "Eté," "Sapho," and the section "Filles" from *Paral-
lèlement*. Nor does the list stop there. By a frequency count
homosexuality is by far his greatest theme. Rimbaud alludes
to his homoerotic relationship with Verlaine in several cryp-
tic passages. Mallarmé pens a suprisingly erotic poem of
lesbianism in "Une Négresse" with one of the most startling
metaphors in literature. Baudelaire often turns to the subject, sometimes with a frank eroticism, at other times with
a kind of mysticism. In "Lesbos" he sings frankly:[2]

> Lesbos, terre des nuits chaudes et langoureuses,
> Qui font qu'à leurs miroirs, stérile volupté!
> Les filles aux yeux creux, de leur corps amoureuses,
> Caressant les fruits mûrs de leur nubilité;
> Lesbos, terre des nuits chaudes et langoureuses. . . .

The poem is a virtual hymn to lesbianism. Baudelaire glori-
fies female homosexuality, while stressing the theme of "sterility," much as Gide is later to do, in the twentieth century,
in *Corydon*. Homosexuality is not only tolerated, in short,
but even recommended. This should not be surprising, however, for a dandy who tries hashish and deliberately cultivates
the more exotic vices of the day. Hence in "Femmes dam-
nées" he couples the lovers, Delphine and Hippolyte, with
intensely erotic quatrains:[3]

> Etendue à ses pieds, calme et pleine de joie,
> Delphine la couvait avec des yeux ardents,
> Comme un animal fort qui surveille une proie,
> Après l'avoir d'abord marquée avec les dents.

> Beauté forte à genoux devant la beauté frêle,
> Superbe, elle humait voluptueusement
> Le vin de son triomphe, et s'allongeait vers elle,
> Comme pour recueillir un doux remercîment.

> Elle cherchait dans l'oeil de sa pâle victime
> Le cantique muet que chante le plaisir,
> Et cette gratitude infinie et sublime
> Qui sort de la paupière ainsi qu'un long soupir.

Baudelaire also makes numerous allusions to lesbianism in other poems. The theme is to recur throughout the decadence. Lesbianism is a fetish. It is the entire theme of Louÿs' *Les Chansons de Bilitis,* and appears as well with Chrysis in *Aphrodite* and with Mirabelle and Princess Aline in *Les Aventures du Roi Pausole.* At least the motif receives the attention of great poets like Baudelaire and Verlaine, or the whimsical attention of fine poets in prose like Louÿs. Perversion, here at least, is embodied in beautiful workmanship. This will not always be true in the decadence.

The darker side of homosexuality appears like an ugly shadow, a gothic horror, in the interminable novels and stories of the *bas-décadents.* In *Les Hors nature,* for instance, Rachilde weaves a frightful story of perversion between two German noblemen, in fact between two brothers. Jacques Reutler de Fertzen, a Hercules, has a homosexual attachment for his brother, the effeminate Paul-Eric. Both decadents, of course, enjoy numerous orgies in Paris before they return to their German manor, to the thundering strains of a night storm. The plot becomes more absurd as it progresses. By the end of the novel Reutler has promised to marry Marie, a pyromaniacal streetwalker, if she will only consent to seduce Paul-Eric in an attempt to cure him. She hesitates. The effeminate young man disgusts her, and besides she loves Reutler. But Paul-Eric, hearing of the vow, makes his more masculine brother renounce his intention to marry her. He is jealous. Then Marie, eavesdropping, runs out and sets fire to the great manor. Succumbing at last to the temptation he has so valiantly fought for so long, Reutler makes love to his brother before strangling him in shame (to protect the family name), while the dark house bursts into the fiery holocaust of an operatic finale. The novel is so preposterous that it is actually funny, but the *bas-décadents* remain ponderously solemn while portraying their chamber of horrors.

The nightmares can become even more lurid. In *Méphis-tophéla*, for example, Mendès relates the nefarious life of the arch-lesbian Baroness Sophor d'Hermelinge, née Luberti, who, as a child, has a homosexual attachment for her good friend, Emmeline. Her ambition, when she grows up, is to seduce Emmeline. Indeed, Sophor even marries her brother, and suffers rape from him on the nuptial night, when she conceives Carola, in order to be close to Emmeline. When the brother learns, however, that his wife has designs upon his own sister, he looks somewhat askance upon this state of affairs and rather indecorously chases Sophor away. But the Baroness retires to Paris, where she becomes a notorious pervert. She is part of a large circle infesting the *haut monde*. There are actually love rites between mothers, daughters, and perverted friends. And to make bad matters worse, Sophor falls in love with her own daughter, Carola, who is precocious at age sixteen and already frequents the worst les-bian circles of Paris. Alas, jealousy ruins their relationship. Both mother and daughter have fallen in love with a cheap bi-sexual prostitute, Magalo, who prefers the younger and prettier Carola. In despair Sophor increases her dope intake and becomes an addict. By the final page she has completely collapsed. The decadent tragedy is complete!

Such plots are commonplace in the decadence proper. The worst that might be said of them, artistically, is that they soon cease to be funny and become tedious. Suffice it to say, thematically, that the decadent writers are obsessed with homosexuality, and that while the great poets in the era dignify a delicate theme in fine verse, the *bas-décadents* merely poke about in the sewers and cesspools. They feel they are depicting modern society as it is, whereas in truth their lurid imagination is alternately surprising, humorous, or boring. But their literature nonetheless remains a social document and their preoccupation with the problems of homosexuality very real.

This preoccupation is understandable when it is fitted into the decadent worldview. Then the problem is not basically that of one lecher's desire for another but that of man and

woman. The natural relationship of man and woman, the
decadent writers repeat again and again, has been disrupted
by the artificialities and tensions of megalopolitan society.
Rampant homosexuality is the social consequence. Modern
man has become feminine and modern woman masculine.
They have reversed the roles which nature, in her biological
wisdom, intends for them to fill. They are androgynes, perverts. Androgynism is the broader topic which subsumes
homosexuality.

The decadent male is weak and the decadent woman
strong. This is a fundamental article of the decadent worldview. It is not logically consistent throughout the literature,
but the attitude, or pose as it sometimes is, is characteristic:
man is androgynous. Now, the androgyne has different traits
according to the particular writer. In Péladan the androgyne
is[4]

... cet être qui n'existe plus physiquement chez l'homme dans
nos races. Il désigne un idéal classique analogue au page, au
très jeune chevalier, et un type moral où l'amante se double
de l'ami, et la maîtresse du compagnon, c'est le type créé pour
représenter les Saint Georges.

The variations of type are endless. But Péladan liberally
peoples his *roman fleuve, La Décadence latine,* with such
androgynous men and women, usually women, among whom
the most famous is the sadistic prostitute Claire, La Nine,
reigning amidst unbridled feasts of sensuality as queen over
the fifteen notorious decadents of an atheistic social club.
And during these Alexandrian orgies the perverted heroes
and heroines engage in deep philosophical conversation. In
its most sensual moments the decadence proper has philosophical pretensions.

French decadence numbers in its vivid pages countless
men and women of dubious sex. In *Princesses d'ivoire et
d'ivresse* Lorrain creates a race of pinkcheeked men:[5]

Il est même des princes dans le nombre, mais si délicats, si
chimériques, si androgynes dans leur adolescence de jeunes

dieux qu'ils en sont presque des princesses, princes de nacre et
de caresse. . . .

A certain aerial prose keeps the book from becoming completely tasteless. The physical androgynism of a Lorrain
becomes a psychic androgynism in other decadent writers.
Remy de Gourmont is a notable example. In *Lettres à l'amazone* he observes: "Mais il y a des volontés mâles en des corps
féminins"[6] and portrays himself, in the fictional correspondence, as a feminine young man writing to a tough-spirited,
utterly masculinized modern woman. His *Lettres d'un
satyre* is even more explicit. It is the connected story of
Antiphilos, the satyr or man of nature, as he lives first in
Greece and Italy, and then becomes a decadent in modern
times. The *Lettres* allegorizes the changing fashions of love
and the roles played by man and woman. Antiphilos is
quite disturbed, as his conversations with Diogène testify,
by the prevalence of androgynes in modern women.

The most famous androgyne of decadence proper, in one
of its most lurid seedpots, is Rachilde's Monsieur Vénus in
the well-known novel of the name. The plot is fantastic.
Raoule de Vénérande is a typical, rich Parisienne, a liberated
modern woman with more money than good sense, utterly
immoral, with a drawer full of gigolos in a room overflowing
with lovers. One day she stops by her fleuriste's room to buy
artificial flowers, but discovers brother Jacques working at
his sister Marie Silvert's table. She is immediately smitten by
his smooth cherub skin, his full lips, his coquettish eyes, and
his deliciously modest air. She establishes him as a gigolo and
abandons her stable of lovers. He is the perfect androgyne
of her dreams. Into his luxurious apartment of hanging mirrors (all decadent boudoirs have an ample supply) Raoule
comes to visit him, dressed like a man, and belabors his
slight body with rough, demanding caresses. She finally marries him to spite the rich society to which she belongs and
which has come to bore her. It affords a new sensation.

In the meantime, Raoule's maiden aunt, suspecting that
her niece may not be altogether what she should be, bribes

Marie to tell her the truth. She does, gladly. Then the aunt retires to a convent, broken-hearted, while Marie opens a thriving house of prostitution which especially caters to androgynes and other perverts. Matters become even more complex. Baron de Raittolbe, at first grief-stricken to see his beloved Raoule marry Jacques, finally succumbs to his coquettish charms. This is a strange turn of affairs. One must admit it is somewhat rare for a rejected suitor to fall in love with his own successful rival. At any rate, he resists Jacques with increasing difficulty, mostly out of deference for Raoule's feelings, but Jacques, carried away with Raoule's insistence upon his femininity, tries to seduce the baron. Raoule is outraged. She orders Raittolbe to kill Jacques in a duel which the latter believes is mock. The experience is shattering for Raoule and her baron. After his death they both worship, literally worship, at a great life-size statue of him as Eros, with a fine wax as substitute for the cherub skin they loved to touch.

The novel ends with Raoule distraught. She sadly recollects her first meeting when she had returned to the Baron to tell him in open-mouthed astonishment, licking her lips:[7]

Il existe, mon ami, et ce n'est même pas un hermaphrodite, pas même un impuissant, c'est un beau mâle de vingt et un ans, dont l'âme aux instincts féminins s'est trompée d'enveloppe.

It is difficult to speculate whether Raoule or Raittolbe weeps more for him in this highly erotic novel. But certainly *Monsieur Vénus* explores the depths of erotic degradation. It is almost the nauseating apogee of an incredible literature.

But while decadence does not ever again, perhaps, reach these heights of the imagination, the androgyne appears throughout the literary epoch. In *Isis* Villiers de l'Isle-Adam creates a memorable transvestite, Marquise Tullia Fabriana, who wanders about as a man in the company of her effeminate guide and lover, Comte de Strally-d'Anthas. Even Nana, in Zola's novel of the courtesan, seeks for a new sensation when, tired of her lovers' masculine kisses, she fondles, like a man, the effeminate and helpless adolescent who has trailed her to her summer house. One of the most famous of all androgynes is Des Esseintes of Huysmans' *A Rebours*. Androgynism is a salient aspect of his curious and complex character. At Fontenay he daydreams of the masculine acrobat from America, Miss Urania, his former mistress. They had been admirable lovers, he reflects. They perfectly complemented each other with their sexual polarities. Her masculinity had merged with his femininity until it seemed they had completely changed sex. It had even startled him at first.[8]

Cet échange de sexe entre Miss Urania et lui, l'avait exalté; nous sommes voués l'un à l'autre, assurait-il; à cette subite admiration de la force brutale jusqu'alors exécrée, se joignit enfin l'exorbitant attrait de la boue, de la basse prostitution heureuse de payer cher les tendresses malotrues d'un souteneur.

Like a good pervert, however, Des Esseintes had come to enjoy his androgynism. Soon even that was to tire him. He would have to seek rarer perversions.

There is no need to multiply examples. These heroes and heroines evidence the point amply, and the student of the French decadence knows very well that androgynes abound throughout. The "sexless" man or woman, i.e., the hero with reversed sex, is in the order of the day. Androgynism, which is closely related to homosexuality while still preserving a special character, even spills over into the border areas of decadence, into symbolism, realism, naturalism. The message is uniform even in other guises through the various schools: the man is always weak, the woman ever strong and destructive. Modern man is truly a pervert because he has violated nature and nature's aims.

Even more horrors confront the decadent pervert. Incest is naturally a favorite theme, but it is not that of romanticism or gothicism. Its tone is more erotic. Many perverts commit incest along with the more homely vice of homosexuality. This is true, for example, of the fraternal incest in *Les Hors nature* and the filial incest in *Méphistophéla*. Incest is also a theme in Barbey's *Les Diaboliques*, Louÿs's *Contes*, and countless other works.

Since incest is the supreme violation of man's social and

moral law, it affords the pervert the rarest of rare sensations. This quest for the new titillation is actually why Renée Saccard, in Zola's *La Curée,* turns almost unconsciously to incest with her stepson, Maxime. She is bored by the Parisian *haut monde,* and her numerous liaisons no longer distract her. She wants a new thrill. Thus she forces Maxime into such a situation that he must seduce her. Her jaded appetite quickly becomes insatiable. They begin to meet constantly in her hot-house, where, true to decadent form, she plays the man and he the woman in the familiar decadent reversal of the sexes:[9]

Renée était l'homme, la volonté passionnée et agissante. Maxime subissait. Cet être neutre, blond et joli, frappé dès l'enfance dans sa virilité, devenait aux bras curieux de la jeune femme, une grande fille, avec ses membres épilés, ses maigreurs gracieuses d'éphèbe romain. Il semblait né et grandi pour une perversion de la volupté. Renée jouissait de ses dominations, elle pliait sous sa passion cette créature où le sexe hésitait toujours.

Their many encounters in the hot, oppressive nights are embarrassingly frank. But Zola, as a naturalist and a great talent, is much more restrained with the sexual motif than the *bas-décadents.*

In *Le Chercheur de Tares* Catulle Mendès recounts another gothic tale of incest. It is the story of Arsène Gravache, who, in his search for truth, turns to ugliness and self-destruction. Thanatos is an omnipresent motif. He is a nervous child with moments of seizure, the illegitimate son of a profligate mother and libertine father. A thorough masochist, Arsène falls in love with a young girl named Myrrhine (the symbolism of the name is evident), daughter of a rich slave trader who drunkenly boasts that she was sired on an Algerian prostitute and that he wants to have sexual relations with her. She commits suicide in despair and shame when she hears his besotted raving. Arsène strangles himself with a scarf after he has been commited, insane, to an asylum. The novel is typical of the *bas-décadents.*

Even when incest is not the principal theme, it is a

secondary motif. In Lorrain's *Monsieur de Phocas* the hero, Duke Jean de Fréneuse, is a neurotic who moves through a world of lesbianism, incest, drug addiction, sado-masochism. Maud White, a beautiful English actress, carries on an open affair with her brother. In the Wagnerian *Le Crépuscule des dieux,* by Elémir Bourges, there is, among all conceivable crimes and fornications, a subtale of incest between Hans Ulric, an illegitimate son of Charles d'Este, and his sister, Christiane. He finally kills himself from guilt, and she retires to a convent to atone for her sins. Incest is a secondary theme so frequently encountered in decadent literature that examples abound.

Probably the most absurd novel of incest is Mendès *Zo'har.* Its one redeeming grace is that the horrors are so numerous, preposterous, and stark that the novel is actually funny. At any rate, Léopold de Roquebrussane, the effeminate hero, is the child of an old tyrant who has raped a woman, Léopold's mother, then dastardly refused to marry her, but has adopted the child after her death solely in order to corrupt him. He proceeds to sire another infant, Stéphana, on another woman, and rears her apart in a convent. When Stéphana finally meets her half-brother, they fall madly in love with each other. But she gloats in her incestuous passion while he flees from it. By a complicated series of events he comes to believe that Stéphana is not his sister, after all, and they happily elope to the mountains of Norway. While there, alas, he learns the truth and almost goes insane from guilt. Stéphana admits that she has suspected as much all along and enjoys their relationship immensely. Their incest, she argues, makes their sensuality more savory. Why should he not be reasonable and admit as much? But Léopold, unheeding her cold logic, leaps from a high cataract and kills himself on the sharp rocks below. After he is safely buried, his sister-mistress-wife, Stéphana, her life having lost its savor, enters his tomb. She sadly lies down to die beside his rotting corpse. The dénouement is so fantastic that the story reads like a parody of the decadent novel. But the epilogue tempers the hilarious satire, as one may read it, with a note of disgust:

Years later their skeletons are discovered along with that of an unborn, half-developed foetus inside Stéphana's.

After homosexuality and incest a more homely vice like nymphomania must seem restrained. But the decadent writers surcharge hypersexuality with a medley of other perversions and thus achieve the desired effect. Poor Germinie Lacerteux, in the Goncourts' novel, is not only an *hystérique* but a masochistic, half-mad streetwalker. Zola's Nana dies with a horrible, disfiguring case of smallpox after an innocuous life of using up one man after the other. In Huysmans' *Là-Bas* Mme Chantelouve mixes nymphomania with sacrilege. She is a priestess in a love cult, she cultivates pygmalionism, she is the lover of a defrocked priest, and she participates in the multiple love rites of the black mass. In addition she loves to profane the consecrated wafer sexually. Altogether she may be regarded as a somewhat spiteful woman. In Rachilde's *L'Animale* little Laure Lordès, as a child, indiscriminately seduces the neighborhood children, causes one suicide, and attempts to make love to the village priest in, of all places, the confessional. And she almost succeeds. This situation somewhat discomfits her parents, who rather unceremoniously chase her away from home. Their lack of understanding, the modern psychologist might add, makes matters worse. She flees to Paris and entertains a succession of lovers with frantic sexuality. She even becomes obsessed with Lion, a handsome tom-cat of dubious parentage. Nymphomania, one might say, finally shatters her nervous system. When Laure plans to run away to Algeria with her newest paramour, Lion, rabid and perhaps a bit jealous, attacks her just as her current lover knocks on the door. She goes screaming to the roof only to hurtle to her death to the street below. She makes a wet imprint upon the pavement. As usual, one horror is piled upon another.

Mendès pens a classic tale of bourgeois horror in *La Première maîtresse,* which is likely the funniest of all the decadent novels. It is the story of seventeen-year-old Evelin Gerbier who, "les cheveux coupés comme ceux d'une femme garçonnière," falls in love with a thirty-two-year-old nymphomaniac of courtly manners, Mme Honorine d'Arlement. She is a sweet lady with many virtues and only a single failing: she has killed a husband and an entire series of lovers through her sexual excesses. A model bourgeoise in all respects save one, Honorine is insatiable. The novel is fantastic. Honorine and Evelin have sexual relations after their very first meeting, after tea of course, and thereafter always have an assignation after tea, cakes, and genteel conversation in her room at precisely eleven o'clock. Only the fact that he is happily afflicted with satyriasis saves him from expiring because of her nymphomania, but Mendès notes that even he is taxed to the limit. Unable to satiate each other, they start walking the streets at night in search of new partners for their multiple amours. Mendès analyzes their motives with all the psychological deftness, i.e., pretension, of the *bas-décadents*:[10]

Des damnés, élus pourtant, pour qui l'on aurait inventé un supplice fait d'une intensité formidable de délices, voilà ce qu'ils devaient être; et leur enchantement se multipliait de leurs angoisses, comme leurs angoisses s'exaspéraient de leur enchantement. A ce degré de sensation, la qualité de la sensation disparaît, s'évanouit, n'est plus. On ignore si l'on souffre, ou si l'on est heureux. Ce qu'on sait, c'est que toutes les vigueurs de la vie, tendues, jusqu'à l'impossibilité de l'être davantage, vibrent comme des cordages qui vont rompre. Et l'on crie! et l'on meurt!

Each novel has its outstanding scene, which is almost a perfect parody, except for the writer's ponderous solemnity, of the decadent novel. In *La Première maîtresse* it occurs when Honorine strangles her sister, Antoinette, who has just had relations with Evelin, because she refuses to commit the sororal incest which he wishes to see as a voyeur. Alas, sentenced to twenty years in prison, but released in only eight for good behavior, she is discharged to find Evelin happily married, a successful writer of bourgeois novels, and a fine *père de famille*. But love has its way: he returns to her nymphomaniacal embrace, by an eagerly accepted invitation, after, of all things, a friendly cup of tea.

Another amusing tale of horror is Mendès' *La Femme-*

Enfant. It is the story of a middle-aged artist, Faustin Laveleyne, who loves a woman old enough to be his mother (incest revisited) but is suddenly captivated by the "femme-enfant," the nymphette heroine, Liliane Forli, who seems to have been a model for Lolita. She is supposedly an insatiable girl of seventeen who has been everyone's mistress. She becomes an ideal woman for Faustin. He adores her, idolizes her, but nevertheless makes love to her and mistreats her. Liliane has momentary fits of insanity, but she soon regains control. Later Mme Laveleyne discovers that the poor child is only ten—though somewhat advanced for her age—an amoral sprite of a girl whose passions have made her the willing accomplice of man's lust.

Decadence ceases to have its amusing side and becomes disgusting with such novels as Mirbeau's *Le Jardin des supplices.* Not even Sade at his worst in *La Philosophie dans le boudoir* or *Les Cent vingt jours de Sodome* can surpass the nauseating horrors or perversions of the Chinese torture gardens. The sadistic English nymphomaniac, Clara, is so despicably evil and perverted that hypersexuality is one of her minor vices. She gives herself to every conceivable profligacy with man, woman, and animal, whetting her sensuality with indescribable scenes of filth, blasphemy, murder, mayhem, and cruelty.

In Lorrain's *Le Vice errant* all the women of the accursed House of Noronsoff have been nymphomaniacs for centuries, a curious and unflattering record. It is futile to enumerate their amours, for they defy mathematics. Nor is it necessary. Sexuality becomes tedious after a time. The point is that Lorrain explicitly attributes their profligacy as the reason for the fall of the House, of France, and thereby of Europe and the whole of Western civilization. It is perhaps a good bit to claim, even for nymphomania, but Lorrain intones like a prophet against the licentious decadents of his day. The nymphomaniac, he says, is more than merely sexually destructive: she disrupts the family, infects the social organism, sacrifices the nation and humanity for her fleeting pleasures. Lorrain's thesis is explicitly or implicitly that of most decadent novels.

Violence is a common trait among these decadent perverts. It colors homosexuality and androgynism, incest and nymphomania. The pervert can be understood, then, through his common denominator, violence. It is a violence of a peculiar sort: the pervert is a sado-masochist whose inversion, hypersexuality, and other vices are expressed on a pleasure-pain spectrum. This is what most notably sets the decadent apart from earlier types of the pervert in literary history. There are many. After all, these vices, while abominable, are not unknown, from the revolting homosexuality of Petronius' *Satyricon* and the bestiality of Apuleius' *Golden Ass* to more contemporary expressions of similar themes. Their heroes are not sado-masochists. Sado-masochism as a guiding motif enters literature obsessively with Sade, and it is developed to its highest point in the decadence proper.

Thus the decadent pervert is by definition a sado-masochist. The reader has only to turn, for verification, to the heroes already discussed for their other inversions. Sado-masochism is always covert, and frequently overt, in their character.

Maurice Barrès, who is ironically regarded as a revitalizing force in French letters, is obsessed with sado-masochism. In *Le Jardin de Bérénice* Philippe feels a strange pleasure as he watches his beloved Bérénice languish and slowly die against an oppressive background of swamp-fever. In *Les Déracinés* the beautiful Armenian heroine, Astiné, is brutally murdered by two sex perverts. Sado-masochism colors the theme of incest in "Un Amateur d'âmes" in *De la Volupté, du sang et de la mort*. In "Le Fantôme," from *Le Pèlerin du silence* Gourmont joins the sado-masochistic camp by having his narrator flagellate Hyacinthe, his beloved, before making love to her, of all unlikely places, in the darkened church. The blasphemy titillates them as much as the sado-masochism.

Rachilde's women, as *Monsieur Vénus* surely proves, are so lurid that a generalization is in order. In the preface to *La Sanglante ironie* Camille Lemonnier observes, as no critic has ever denied:[11]

Ces étranges jeunes filles (et c'est par là qu'elles s'attestent bien modernes) répudient toute analogie avec leurs soeurs antérieures, les amères possédées des âges de la Damnation, les cruelles amazones des batailles de la chair s'amputant le coeur et le donnant à manger aux pourceaux des grandes luxures. Névrosées, les sens précocement excités par des ferments d'hérédité, malades d'un excès de songerie qui les livre déjà savantes et dévirginisées à l'homme, elles assument une façon de perversité ingénue. . . .

The words accurately describe Rachilde's psychology of the modern woman. Her heroines are sado-masochists who, like Raoule de Vénérande, always control, corrupt, and destroy their pliable men. Whereas sado-masochistic elements are present in both men and women, the man generally tends to be masochistic and the woman sadistic. This is the point. It is a reversal of the sexes, as the decadent writers look upon their natural function, and both sexes welcome it as a perversion. They typify civilized perversion at its decadent worst. The barbarians, for all their faults, are not perverts. They are instruments of nature.

Lorrain invariably portrays a sado-masochist as a hero, whatever particular form of perversion he might assume. Thus in *Buveurs d'âmes* he typically describes his hero as an androgynous male:[12]

Une étude très curieuse et très creusée d'un caractère d'homme amoureux de la souffrance, en proie à la plus inquiétante des sensualités, la sensualité de la douleur.

And as if this were not enough, he presents an archetypal portrait of the sado-masochist in *Monsieur de Phocas:* It is Duke Jean de Fréneuse who, struggling with his perverse phantoms, finally kills the sadistic Englishman, Claudius Ethal, his evil genius, and who mumbles feverishly over and over to himself:[13]

La palpitation de la vie m'a toujours rempli d'une étrange rage de destruction, et voilà deux fois que je me surprends des idées de meurtre dans l'amour.

The literary expression of the theme is not of a high quality, to be sure, as it is in Baudelaire with "Héautontimorou-ménos" and certain other poems. But from great writer to

bas-décadent sado-masochism is the great motif which subsumes, like articles of a creed, the various perversions like
homosexuality, bestiality, incest, nymphomania.

Among the *bas-décadents* Péladan may always be counted
upon for baldly overt presentation of a decadent theme if
for no more. In *Istar* the heroine, Mme Istar Capimont, a
beautiful Jewess, married and with a young daughter, falls
in love with Nergal, the callous novelist who writes thinly
disguised novels about the perverts whom he encounters on
his many peregrinations. The perverts do not like his novels,
it might be added. After he and Istar have a platonic relationship which the city misunderstands, Mme Capimont is
ostracized and persecuted. She dies of an hallucination in-
duced by a rejected suitor. In revenge M. Capimont poisons
a hoyden, la Malabierne, with poison dipped on his piercing
fingernail. He scratches her arm like a hypodermic needle,
injecting the fatal poison into her bloodstream. It is an effective and ingenious device. Péladan's sadistic psychology demands an even more horrible death for Leclerc, Istar's
assassin. He is driven into a gibbering maniac when Nergal
wraps himself in a shroud, in a fog-covered graveyard, disguised as a resuscitated Istar come back from death to exact
a frightful vengeance.

Absurd as these plots make sado-masochism seem, the
decadent writers take themselves quite seriously, and they
firmly believe that sado-masochism is modern man's dominant
trait. They are explicit. In *Gog,* for instance, Catulle Mendès,
a wretched but sincere writer, describes a sado-masochistic
family which obviously represents all the great houses of
Europe. In depicting their sado-masochistic venom as it
spreads throughout the veins of the family, Mendès constantly
underscores his didactic message. He says with pontifical
bluntness:[14]

En un mot, c'est de sa fenêtre qu'il considère ce soleil couchant,
l'antique splendeur monarchique; mais il croit que, de partout
on le verrait descendre de même. Puis voici dans la nuit où les
étoiles, comme des lys d'or, s'éteignirent, des mânes de rois, et
des spectres de sceptres. . . .

It is a melancholy thesis which the *bas-décadents* with a customary lack of finesse belabor endlessly. It is unfortunate, perhaps, that they cannot cloak their good intentions within the framework of well-written and psychologically valid novels. But their obsession with social philosophy interferes with the limited abilities which they do possess.

Sado-masochism recurs throughout Bourges' *Le Crépuscule des dieux*, which is so Wagnerian in its Götterdämmerung that the author actually plagiarizes title and themes. Only the names have been changed, and they do not protect the innocent. Everyone is a sadist and/or masochist amid thundering crescendos of brass: Giulia Belcredi, who pits son against father, sleeps with both, and tries to get Otto to poison his father, Charles d'Este; Hans Ulric and Christiane, who torture themselves, ludicrously of course, with the ecstasy of incestuous love; the blustering and tyrannical Charles d'Este himself, cruel to his children, a Kronos figure, fawning before his mistresses. Bourges is not recounting their story simply for the shock effect, as many critics erroneously interpret decadent literature. He is exemplifying a Grand Thesis by their wretched lives: "On passera du crépuscule d'une famille, ou d'une caste, au crépuscule de l'humanité,"[15] as André Lebois justly observes.

Sado-masochism, the search for the new, the involuted, and the perverse, ends by replacing the doctrine of love that characterizes earlier stages of development in the West—love of oneself, his family, his nation, even humanity. This is the decadent theme bandied about, over and over, in works of varying quality. Whether right or wrong, the decadent writers believe that this fundamental change has been effected in the psyche of modern man, i.e., the "decadent," and has made him something less than a man. This is the new psychology which governs modern man: No longer love, but a perversion and travesty of love, sado-masochism with all its concomitant perversions, is the decadent's *raison d'être,* his principle of being, and will lead him not to happiness, as he fondly believes, but rather to catastrophe and to destruction.

EIGHT

METAMORPHOSES OF THE VAMPIRE: MODERN WOMAN AND THE *FEMME FATALE*

THUS far our study has primarily concerned the decadent hero, and the heroine has appeared in relationship to him. The decadent heroine is a striking figure that justifies a chapter of her own.

In "Les Métamorphoses du Vampire," from *Les Fleurs du mal*, Charles Baudelaire casts modern man and woman in a graphic scene that is to obsess writers of the French decadence. Modern man is shown as a weak decadent consumed by modern woman, who is a vampire or a *femme fatale*. Their love is a passionate deathstruggle in which the active female, like a spider, destroys the passive male. It is an ironical poem. In it man searches for beauty but finds ugliness, and he looks for love in woman's arms only to confront destruction. The beautiful *mannequin* of his dreams, his ideal woman, is actually a vampire who drains him of his energy, i.e., his life. This terrifying image of the vampire recurs throughout decadent literature.

This literary image also reflects the social ethos of decadence. There is a striking parallel between the woman of

141

fiction and of reality. The *femme fatale* emerges in the baroque tragicomedy of the Second Empire and the *fin-de-siècle* and moves through opulent salons and boudoirs, racetracks, and private clubs. Perhaps women even more than dandies characterize this effete society—tantalizing women like Lola Montez or the Russian prostitute La Païva (Thérèse Lachmann). In *Gaslight and Shadow* Roger L. Williams delineates the world of reality, the artificial society of intrigue, corruption, strained gaiety, that is to be reflected in the world of fiction:[1]

Hortense Schneider did not limit her attentions to crowned heads. For a time she was mistress to the Duc de Gramont-Caderousse, who was the unofficial leader of the *Cocodès.* The latter, a slang expression roughly equivalent to *swells,* included nearly one hundred fast-living gentlemen, mostly of aristocratic origin but with a sprinkling of officers of the guard. Their activities encompassed gambling, racing, dueling, and making love. Rich young men of the bourgeoisie were usually able to crash this élite, but Russian aristocrats, known in particular for their immoderation, were always welcome.

"The Ogresses" were the female counterpart of the *Cocodès:* nearly one hundred women of obscure origin who lived in a dazzling state of unrelieved luxury and who favored members of the Jockey-Club in particular. The prestige of these courtesans was so great that it was common, during the Second Empire, not only for the *demi-monde* to meet the *haut monde* socially, but for the latter to emulate the former.

The citation sets the tone of the woman in decadent literature. It also depicts the historical cadre of the French decadence. The luxury and licentiousness are fairly astonishing. It is small wonder, then, that the bewitching *femme fatale* is a literary heroine, and even ideal, of the decadent society.[2] The Second Empire, in fact and in fiction, is an artificial world devoid of natural values.

The *natural woman*—wife, mother, earth-woman—disappears and the *modern woman* appears in her stead. As Brooks Adams points out she emerges with the economic man and the artificial society.[3] Thus the new woman, rouged and flirtatious, appears like a provocative beauty from Offenbach. The sounds of the can-can echo in the background. Her appearance and the role she plays are major themes in French decadent literature. At first she appears as the object of man's vanity—a delicate and expensive bauble—but in time she becomes, biologically, a functionless sex. This is not to say that she has no sex, by any means. The decadent writers feel, some explicitly, others implicitly, that she is no longer the woman nature means for her to be. The modern woman, or *femme fatale*, incarnates destruction rather than creation. She has lost her capacity to love, and with it her role as wife and mother. She is now a mistress, beautiful but profoundly unnatural. The new heroine has a malevolent influence on men, who may in fact be degenerate themselves but who become even worse because of her. This is woman as the French decadent writers perceive her.

Woman is manifestly a problem. Whereas the romantic heroine is subdued and invariably passive, the decadent *femme fatale* is active and violent. Hugo's Dona Sol, in *Hernani*, is an impossible heroine for the decadents. They conceive of no such women, for their heroines are pale and rouged, with green eyes, or tall, lithe, strong, fatally seductive. Whatever their physical traits, they are always sadomasochists. Thus Péladan typifies an entire generation of literary heroines by observing about one of his women characters:[4]

Les natures violentes comme celles de Francesca ne sont sensibles qu'à deux sortes d'êtres; les dominateurs dont elles se font les esclaves, souvent rébellionnées, et les faibles dont elles se déclarent les tutrices et les fées.

The description is recurrent. With such writing in mind James M. Smith comments upon the emergence of the new heroine:[5]

With the Decadence the "fatal woman" comes into her own, a reflection of the greater emphasis upon masochism in the latter period. The fatal woman, who suffers from ennui, is possessed of irresistible charm, often centered in her green eyes; her body is an end in itself to the unfortunate male, whom she usually kills. Her lover is generally a youth, passive, obscure, and inferior.

There are infinite variations to this theme. Writers conceive of woman's role vis-à-vis different kinds of men in various ways. The many such comments, by actual frequency count, only contribute to the total impression. Mendès, for instance, discusses the modern woman as she reacts to the physician:[6]

D'ailleurs, la femme moderne a un dominateur: le médecin. Et il ne pourrait pas en être autrement. Du temps qu'elle avait une âme, ou croyait en avoir une,—ce qui est absolument la même chose,—la femme dépendait du prêtre; à présent qu'elle est seulement un corps, un corps tressaillant de nerfs ou s'imagine n'être que cela,—ce qui revient tout à fait au même,—elle se soumet au médecin.

Other writers depict the modern woman kaleidoscopically in her relationships with all kinds of men and in her several roles. But irrespective of details the constant theme is sadomasochism. This is the dominant trait of the modern woman, and it differentiates her sharply from her passive and subdued predecessor, the romantic heroine.

Modern woman is malevolent and has a malignant effect upon men. Although this is baldly the decadent thesis, there are nonetheless different categories of the modern woman. They are not all "evil" in the same way. The most salient strain, noted by Praz and other commentators, is the *femme fatale*, or the fatal woman. She recalls a flashing-eyed Theda Bara with red lips and white skin, leading men on to their doom. Yet there are more domestic types who are nonetheless "fatal," i.e., malevolent, and more attenuated, though no less devastating passions motivate them. The effect, however, is the same: the man always withers and dies. Neurotic women often destroy themselves with their catabolic energy while they are devouring their unfortunate lovers. The deviates, as we have already seen, are a particular class. Many decadent heroines, too, are "bad" rather than fatal

by modern understanding, for a romantic titanism characterizes the fatal women in the grand style. Certain categories
of the modern woman, as might be expected, tend to merge.

Just as romanticism passes imperceptibly into decadence,
so vestiges of the romantic heroine are still evident in many
decadent "fatal women." Perhaps the more "romantic" are
less sharply characterized, "paler" so to speak, whereas the
moré "decadent" heroines have greater psychological depth.
This is a matter of interpretation. But it is certain that, on
an activity-passivity pole, the "romantic decadents," like
Salammbô and Sara, have much less energy than the "decadents proper," like Clara and Léonora d'Este, who often
possess demonic energy. There are of course notable exceptions, notably from le bas-romantisme like Dumas père's
work, e.g., La Tour de Nesle. Yet there is a clear trend
based on activity and energy: the more "decadent" the heroine, the more active she generally is and the greater energy
potential she certainly possesses.

Salammbô, in Flaubert's novel of the same name, is a transitional figure who is at once a romantic heroine and a decadent femme fatale. "Il s'exhale du fond de mon être comme
de chaudes bouffées plus lourdes que les vapeurs d'un vol-
can,"[7] she describes herself like a female René. Her romantic
grandiloquence, however, is tinged with decadent sensibility.
She is a fatally seductive temptress. Yet there is a distinction.
Mathô is destroyed because of her, to be sure, but she does
not really manipulate him or lure him to his doom. Her
sensibility is decadent while, psychologically, she remains
a romantic figure. Her behavior in the pompous dénouement
illustrates this duality.

Sara, in Villiers de l'Isle-Adam's Axël, is also a curious
mixture of romantic and decadent. Like Salammbô she has
a morbid, decadent sensibility. Yet she exclaims in the grand
style of romanticism: "Là-bas, tout nous appelle, Axël, mon
unique maître, mon amour . . . de grandes causes à défendre,
tous les rêves à réaliser."[8] No femme fatale calls her lover
her unique maître or amour. Besides, her naïve idealism is
foreign to decadent sophistication. Sara is a specter of death

who begins in a decadent framework but then progresses along old romantic lines. The tone or sensibility of the closet drama, rather than its psychology, is decadent.

Transitional figures like Sara and Salammbô are to be expected. Of course romanticism does not suddenly end with the failure of Hugo's *Les Burgraves* or decadence begin, say, with Baudelairean sensibility in 1857. The matter is complex. Romanticism and decadence usually merge with graying tonalities in the fifties and sixties. Many of the women whom Praz enumerates as fatal women in *The Romantic Agony*, somewhat erroneously, are best understood in this light. Rosalba (Barbey, "A un Dîner d'athées," *Les Diaboliques*), Cléopâtre (Gautier, *Une Nuit de Cléopâtre*), Marguérite (Dumas père, *La Tour de Nesle*), Nyssia (Gautier, *Le Roi Candaule*), the Vénus d'Ille (Mérimée), Clarimonde (Gautier, *La Morte amoureuse*), Marie (Flaubert, *Novembre*), or the Queen of Sheba (Flaubert, *La Tentation de Saint Antoine*)—all these heroines contain romantic as well as decadent elements, and probably more of the former than of the latter. As fatal women they are the psychological if not always chronological predecessors of the decadent *femme fatale* of literary decadence proper. There is an essential difference between them and the mainstream of decadent heroines.

This difference becomes glaringly apparent with Clara in Mirbeau's *Le Jardin des supplices*. Some mention of her has already been made. As a *femme fatale* she is a sadistic Englishwoman who, with her many other amours, has an affair with the unnamed narrator of the novel. Her adventures as a sado-masochistic nymphomaniac defy description, for the Chinese torture gardens harbor incredible crimes of violence and sexual passion. Clara is an archetypal whore. In the frontispiece a Darwinian scientist announces the theme which Clara develops in the course of the novel: "Le meurtre est la base même de nos institutions sociales, par conséquent la nécessité la plus impérieuse de la vie civilisée."[9] Murder, he concludes, is indispensable to modern life, and the novel certainly shows it indispensable to contempo-

rary sexuality. Love and destruction are inextricably inter-
twined. Thus the narrator's question is rhetorical as he asks
his paramour:[10]

—Chère Clara, objectai-je, est-il donc naturel que vous recher-
chiez la volupté dans la pourriture et que vous meniez le trou-
peau de vos désirs s'exalter aux horribles spectacles de douleur
et de mort?
—Non! fit Clara vivement . . . puisque l'Amour et la Mort, c'est
la même chose! et puisque la pourriture, c'est l'éternelle résur-
rection de la Vie.

This metaphysical thread is cut time and time again by vivid
scenes of sexual orgy multiplied to sharp pitches of horror.
Lesbians embrace in a death-struggle, men and women cop-
ulate like animals, human beings in cages are fed raw meat—
tainted at that—while spectators torture them with sticks
and stones. These are the more mentionable details. The
novel throughout preaches a decadent message which the
hero at last enunciates after viewing the torture gardens:[11]

Ce que j'ai vu aujourd'hui, ce que j'ai entendu, existe et crie
et hurle au delà de ce jardin, qui n'est plus pour moi qu'un
symbole, sur toute la terre. . . . J'ai beau chercher une halte dans
le crime, un repos dans la mort, je ne les trouve nulle part.

The contrast between Clara and the narrator is striking. She
acts while he watches; she is force while he is intellect. She
is not a magnet, like Salammbô, to which men are drawn
and thereby destroyed. She is an active force of malevolence.
She is herself destructive energy, and she actively directs it
against all men.

Léonora d'Este is another decadent heroine in Péladan's
Le Vice suprême. This "monstre métaphysique," as the
author calls her, is "une vivante allégorie de la décadence
latine."[12] She is a perambulating symbol. Her decadent sensibility is such that[13]

De l'artiste, elle n'avait que la perception du laid. Comme certaines lentilles, ses yeux décomposaient en grotesque ce qu'elle
regardait. Elle voyait les gens comme Granville les a dessinés,

dans leurs similitudes avec les bêtes. Tout lui arrivait à l'état caricatural; ridicule était le prisme dont elle teignait les choses. A l'église, le bedeau lui masquait Dieu.

Léonora soon reveals herself as a latter-day Circe, a witch, a *femme fatale*. Péladan generalizes about the modern woman by noting about her:[14]

Passive, absolue, injuste, la femme n'admire la grandeur que par espoir d'en obtenir le sacrifice. Elle aime les chastes pour les corrompre; les forts pour les asservir; les indépendants pour les avilir.

In short, she has within her a *principle* of demonic energy that compels her to be destructive. Her fatal beauty entices men to their doom. Léonora attempts to seduce even Mérodack, the mystic, and later Père Alta, the priest—unsuccessfully in both cases. But she enjoys much success as a fatal woman in ruining human lives. After failing to seduce Père Alta, for instance, she falsely accuses him of having tried to make love to her. Her stratagem is clever. In the dénouement he is still in serious trouble with the Church. In turn Mérodack infuriates her when he tells her bitterly:[15]

J'ai deviné l'énigme et le sphinx féminin m'a léché les pieds; mais ce spectacle: la femme dominant l'homme, m'a toujours indigné comme un antiphysisme. Esclave à plaindre ou tyran à mépriser, la femme vibre à tout, ne raisonne à rien, inconsciente dans la sublimité et dans la boue; elle reste éternellement réfractaire à l'idée, et c'est l'idée qui meut les mondes.

His words are incisive. Léonora knows fully well, like Clara, that she is a sado-masochistic demon venting her fatal energy against the passive male.

Pierre Louÿs portrays many fatal women. The general decadence of his work, first, is reflected by his philosophical preface to *Aphrodite,* in which he equates licentiousness with civilization, and in such scenes as the following orgy, where the slave Aphrodisia entertains with sickening solicitude:[16]

Aphrodisia, encore esclave, triomphait dans un cercle d'hommes et fêtait sa dernière nuit de servitude par une débauche dé-

sordonnée. Pour obéir à la tradition de toutes les orgies alexan-
drines, elle s'était livrée, tout d'abord, à trois amants à la fois;
mais sa tâche ne se bornait pas là, et jusqu'à la fin de la nuit,
selon la loi des esclaves qui devenaient courtisanes, elle devait
prouver par un zèle incessant que sa nouvelle dignité n'était
point usurpée.

Another character in the novel, Chrysis, a beautiful courtesan, tempts Démétrios, the great sculptor of the sacred statue
Aphrodite, and Queen Bérénice's lover. On a cruel whim
Chrysis, who sells herself indiscriminately, refuses to give
herself to Démétrios until he perpetrates three sacrilegious
crimes. As a fatal woman she ensnares him with her strength
and by his weakness. His life is thereafter ruined, as the
novel foreshadows, but at her death-scene he manages to
tell Chrysis:[17]

L'Esclavage! voilà le vrai nom de la passion. Vous n'avez toutes
qu'un seul rêve, qu'une seule idée au cerveau: faire que votre
faiblesse rompe la force de l'homme et que votre futilité gouverne son intelligence! Ce que vous aimez, dès que les seins vous
poussent, ce n'est pas aimer ni être aimée, c'est lier un homme
à vos chevilles, l'abaisser, lui ployer la tête et mettre vos sandales
dessus. Alors vous pouvez, selon votre ambition, nous arracher
l'épée, le ciseau ou le compas, briser tout ce qui vous dépasse,
émasculer tout ce qui vous fait peur, prendre Héraclès par les
naseaux et lui faire filer la laine! Mais quand vous n'avez pu
fléchir ni son front ni son caractère, vous adorez le poing qui
vous bat, le genou qui vous terrasse, la bouche même qui vous in-
sulte! L'homme qui a refusé de baiser vos pieds nus, s'il vous
viole, comble vos désirs. Celui qui n'a pas pleuré quand vous
quittiez sa maison peut vous y traîner par les cheveux: votre
amour renaîtra de vos larmes, car une seule chose vous console
de ne pas imposer l'esclavage, femmes amoureuses! c'est de le
subir.

Once again sado-masochism is the principal theme. The decadent heroine, Louÿs infers, is fatal as she overwhelms the
weak male. Cruel self-sufficient pride is her spirit. Unchang-
ing and indomitable, Chrysis ascends the city tower, nude,
with the stolen necklace of Aphrodite about her, supremely

proud in her sacrilege, while the crowds below stand aghast and gape.

Conchita, or Concepcion Garcia, is the fatal woman and Don Mateo Diaz, a middle-aged Spanish nobleman, the puppet in Louÿs's *La Femme et le pantin*. The plot, based upon Casanova's adventure with La Charpillon, is baldly simple. For two years Conchita wheedles Don Diaz out of his money by promising herself but eluding him at the final moment. She is a curious woman, living dutifully with her mother, while exciting his jealousy by sleeping with other men. She even seduces a boy in front of him. As a fatal woman she absorbs his entire interest in life, then systematically ruins him. She respects him only momentarily when he becomes inflamed enough to beat her:[18]

Pour que tu me battes, Mateo. Quand je sens ta force, je t'aime, je t'aime; tu ne peux pas savoir comme je suis heureuse de pleurer à cause de toi. Viens, maintenant. Guéris-moi bien vite.

But Diaz's masochism soon gets the better of him. He relishes suffering at the beautiful hands of this cruel woman. At the end of the novel, Don Diaz still grovels at her feet even as André Sévenol plans to take Conchita away to Paris. Activity (the woman) destroys passivity (the decadent male) and respects only dynamic force, e.g., Sévenol. It is the familiar decadent theme.

As a fatal woman Stéphana, from Mendès' *Zo'har*, has already been scrutinized. She is the incestuous *femme fatale* who destroys her brother. Mendès' description of her adamantine energy in comparison with his pliability, however, may be interesting:[19]

Et, de tout son jeune corps, où une vitalité incoercible devait battre les veines et courir sous la peau comme un pigment de feu, s'exhalait une chaleur d'épanouissement.

Wild-eyed, taut-nerved, she resembles a panther more than a woman. Stéphana can even tell her brother after he learns of their incestuous marriage:[20]

T'aurais-je voulu avec la même ferveur, s'il m'avait été permis de te vouloir? Ne dois-je pas, peut-être, l'excès délicieux de mon désir à ma colère contre tes remords? Toi-même,—descends au fond de ta pensée, interroge l'inavoué de ton être,— toi-même, tu m'aurais moins aimée si ton amour ne t'avait pas semblé un crime.

To the end she is demonic energy and activity, he utter passivity, and she is strength while he is weakness.

The fatal woman is often a bitch, for lack of a better word, like Marthe in the Goncourts' *Charles Demailly*. Marthe is a beautiful woman, a demanding actress who wages conjugal war upon her husband, Charles Demailly. In the vicious megalopolis and the newspaper world, where each man is every other's enemy, Marthe as a modern woman is the apogee of artificiality. Her energy waxes while Charles's wanes, and she finally drives him insane by betraying him with certain letters to his "friends." He is destroyed. His illusions shattered, his belief in life vanished, Charles is overwhelmed by the stronger woman. In long passages on the modern woman[21] the Goncourts attest to the destructive power of the fatally attractive modern woman. This misogynism, if such a philosophical belief may be so called, reflects similiar passages in their *Journal*. Even Demailly, stronger and less "decadent" than the heroes of the decadence proper, falls victim to the familiar sado-masochistic impulse. The modern woman is seemingly irresistible.

In *Le Livre de Monelle* Marcel Schwob further attests to the activity of the woman and the fundamental passivity of the male. For instance, Monelle, as an acutely alive prostitute, contrasts sharply with the lethargic narrator. This unnamed writer is so indolent, in fact, that he relies upon streetwalkers for his energy. He must come into contact with life in the raw, he feels, merely to keep going. Thus he comes to idolize the prostitute. Monelle says about this common decadent failing:[22]

Aucune d'elles, vois-tu, ne peut rester avec vous. Elles seraient trop tristes et elles ont honte de rester. Vous ne les connaissez

que pendant qu'elles sont compatissantes. Il ne faut pas penser
à autre chose. Il ne faut pas penser à ce qu'elles ont pu faire
dans les ténèbres. Nelly dans l'horrible maison, Sonia ivre sur
le banc du boulevard, Anne rapportant le verre vide chez le
marchand de vin d'une ruelle obscure étaient peut-être cruelles
et obscènes. Ce sont des créatures de chair.

Indeed they are carnal women. That is precisely why the
narrator, as a decadent, must be close to them. They warm
him, give him life, like the young women who console King
David in his old age. The hero is impassive in his cerebral
existence, the victim of his inertia. The women act while the
decadent observes. The women live while the decadent
languishes.

The cold heroine of Gourmont's *Les Chevaux de Diomède*,
Néobelle, contrasts sharply with the cerebral Diomède. She
has complete control over her actions and emotions. On the
other hand, he has no strength of character, no will-power,
no drive. She tells him matter-of-factly after having spent
the night with him:[23]

Je vous ai déjà dit que je ne me sentais pas sensuelle. Je ne suis
donc ni surprise, ni humiliée, ni effrayée, et je ne trouve pas
que j'ai payé trop cher une notion, comme vous dites, si pré-
cieuse et qui me sera très utile pour me diriger dans la vie. Je
sais ce que je puis donner à un homme et je sais ce qu'un homme
peut me donner. Je puis lui donner tout; il ne peut rien me
donner que le plaisir de le voir heureux. Ainsi, sûre de moi-
même, je dominerai facilement les passions excitées par ma
beauté inutile.

She is coldly self-sufficient. She uses her beauty simply as
a snare for the weak and the unwary, as she does with Lord
Grouchy. She emprisons him with sex, then marries him. In
Gourmont, too, men are weak, women strong.

Hyacinthe Chantelouve is a *femme fatale* with demonic
energy in Huysmans' *Là-Bas*. A familiar figure, she is already
known as a pervert. Her opinion of herself is interesting,
however, as when she frankly describes herself as a modern
succubus:[24]

Il n'est pas facile à expliquer; je vais essayer néanmoins; dans la province de Luxure, on relève, si je ne me trompe pas, le péché ordinaire, le péché contre nature, la bestialité, ajoutons-y, n'est-ce pas, la démonialité et le sacrilège. Eh bien, il y a en sus de tout cela, ce que j'appellerai le Pygmalionisme, qui tient, tout à la fois, de l'onanisme cérébral et de l'inceste.

Durtal is crushed by her disarming candor. He soon succumbs to her fatal attraction, and she leads him on a trail of witchcraft, sexual orgy, and black masses in the back-alleys of modern Paris. At length she almost robs him of his manhood and his soul, as old Carhaix the bellringer suspects. Her weapons are mighty. With cold self-sufficiency, modern woman's cardinal trait, she explains her pygmalionism:[25]

—Enfin, tenez, je vous possède quand et comment il me plaît . . .
—Vous dites?
—Je dis que je n'ai qu'à les désirer, qu'à vous désirer tous, maintenant, avant de m'endormir . . .
—Et?
—Et vous seriez inférieur à ma chimère, au Durtal que j'adore et dont les caresses rendent mes nuits folles!

Mme Chantelouve is at least consistent. She consumes men one after the other in her role as a modern vampire.

The list of *femmes fatales* may be endlessly extended. There is no need, however, to pile up examples. Lorrain's *Le Vice errant,* an important novel already cited, admirably summarizes the type of *femme fatale* and the diabolical role that she plays in the French decadence proper. The novel is about the fall of the House of Noronsoff, which has been enchanted for centuries by a gipsy's curse. All women loved or married by the Noronsoffs will be faithless, cruel, destructive, i.e., *femmes fatales.* This is not merely a domestic situation. Lorrain carefully shows the relationship of the family to the entire society: the family is the microcosm, the social structure the macrocosm. When the family falls the society which it represents must surely disintegrate, and the family will indeed collapse when the wife, mother, earth-woman, is supplanted by the vampire, bitch, *femme fatale.* It is a simple matter of cause and effect. The fall of the Noronsoffs is also the symbolical collapse of European civilization:[26]

Il invectivait sa mère et le pope et Gourkau et nous tous; il appelait la ruine et l'incendie sur cette ville qui l'avait bafoué, l'incendie et la ruine avec le feu du ciel et celui des Barbares sur cette vieille Europe qui l'avait corrompu; et cette agonie furieuse avait quelque chose de grandiose. Halluciné, tordu de spasmes et d'épouvante, il appelait les Asiatiques et leur future invasion, leur trombe vengeresse sur la décomposition du vieux monde. Il mourait de Nice, de Florence et de Londres; c'étaient Paris, Vienne et Saint-Pétersbourg qui l'avaient gangrené et pourri; ses instincts barbares enfin réveillés conviaient les Barbares au châtiment. Il réclamait les Huns d'Attila et les Tartares de Genghis-Khan, toutes les hordes des races jaunes pour tuer, piller, voler, massacrer les Niçois, les médecins et Gourkau lui-même et sa mère. "Oui, qu'ils viennent. Viendront-ils enfin? Qu'ils brûlent tout ici, qu'ils pillent cette villa, qu'ils vident mes écrins, qu'ils écrasent mes perles, qu'ils crucifient Gourkau, qu'ils torturent Filsen, qu'ils empalent Ytroff et qu'ils violent ma mère!" Et dans un hoquet suprême il crachait enfin la vieille âme de Byzance trop longtemps attardée en lui.

The thoughts of the decadent are startling, the images shocking. It is an omnipresent theme. It summarizes the main idea of decadence and stresses the role of the *femme fatale,* the presiding witch of ruin and degradation. Prince Noronsoff gives vent to his self-disgust and to his loathing for his class and society. His deep grief arises principally because of his disenchantment with women. The woman he knows is the *femme fatale.* His misogynism is much deeper than a mere bias, an intellectual pose. As with all decadents it has roots extending deeply into his soul and with social ramifications: the man who rejects woman renounces life, for woman is the matrix of the life-process. It is in this sense that decadent misogynism must be understood.

The message is plain. The decadent society, the putrefying megalopolis, is rotten because of its *tare initiale*—the decay of modern woman. With wife and mother gone the family inevitably disintegrates, like the House of Noronsoff, and with the family the entire society. Retribution, the decadent believes, will inevitably come. He recalls the German barbarians overrunning a moribund Roman Empire. His eyes narrow at the thought of the cataclysm to come. He sees again the barbaric hordes, of the East this time, marching against the citadel of civilization. They are crude, ruthless, cruel, yet healthy, because they are still men of *nature* and their women are *natural,* i.e., wives and mothers, and their actions are the expression of the natural animal in them. With a conscious deathwish Noronsoff welcomes the destruction of his world and of himself. He abhors his society because it does not deserve to live. He hates himself. Europe is, like Byzantium, personified by an archetypal *femme fatale*—a seductive queen of vice and luxury, a beautiful prostitute, a Theodora, who this time will not save the citadel of culture, but will rather betray it to the barbarians awaiting at the gates, through her uncontrollable sado-masochistic impulses.

The modern woman is not necessarily a separate category from the *femme fatale.* Indeed the terms seem confusing. Perhaps it is wise, in this confusion, to examine the connotations.

In the decadence proper, where woman is invariably seen as fatal, i.e., destructive to men, certain categories tend to merge. But just as the romantic heroine passes, sometimes imperceptibly, into the decadent heroine, so the "fatal woman" frequently has other characteristics. She is not always the same. The archetypal *femme fatale* is always self-possessed; she would otherwise be a contradiction in terms. Yet there are other decadent heroines, no less fatal, who do not possess her astonishing *sang-froid.* These women are still oriented towards sado-masochism, and unlike the romantic heroine of sweetness and subdued light, they also have a great reservoir of energy. Their activity, however, is often abortive because their energy remains untapped or becomes warped. In this role the modern woman becomes a neurotic who cannot control herself. The development is natural. Few social commentators could describe modern society since Napoleon without almost equating the modern woman with neurosis.

Some of Gourmont's heroines evidence this trait. Like Sixtine, they move away from the type of *femme fatale* and into this direction. In this "roman de la vie cérébrale," Hubert d'Entragues, the hero, is in love with Mme Sixtine Magne, widow and modern woman, whom, as we have already seen, he tries unsuccessfully to seduce. Entragues has already been discussed as a prototype of the cerebral hero. Now attention must be focused upon Sixtine. For not only is he a lethargic dreamer suffering from abulia, but she too, unlike the demonic *femme fatale,* chatters about philosophy and art. She recalls the type of the modern neurotic—well-dressed, frequenting salons and art museums, and, accompanied by her French poodle, seeing her psychiatrist. The comparison is just. Sixtine is certainly neurotic. She falls prey to her violent Russian suitor, Moscowitch, who takes her by force and crushes her will. She suffers from what might be termed, rather crudely but accurately, the rape complex. The civilized woman, the neurotic, welcomes assault from the barbarian. Sixtine feels this instinctively. In her farewell letter to Entragues she even states that she feels she still loves him, yet is irresistibly drawn to the Russian's brute strength. This is what Entragues, like any decadent, does not have, and the lack alienates him from the modern woman who, in her sado-masochism, wants to be forced, even raped. Passivity fails to respond to passivity, while it does respond to activity. The neurotic woman demands action: it is sensed as a kind of return to nature and natural function that cuts her neurosis like a sword through the Gordian knot of lethargy, moral indolence, sado-masochism. For the decadent, however, this kind of modern woman is still fatal. Yet, unlike her sister-heroine, the *femme fatale,* she is victim as well as executioner. She, too, suffers. She, too, can be destroyed. At all events sado-masochism remains her dominant trait.

In Zola's modern epic the women of the Rougon-Macquart family are noteworthy examples of modern woman on the contemporary scene. Zola's great theme is decadence, conceived in terms of pathological degeneration, and he pursues the initial *tare* through several generations of women to develop this idea. He expounds on the role of woman in the family and her relationship through the family to society.[27]

Physiologiquement les Rougon-Macquart sont la lente succession des accidents nerveux et sanguins qui se déclarent dans une race, à la suite d'une première lésion organique, et qui déterminent selon les milieux, chez chacun des individus de cette race. . . . Historiquement, ils partent du peuple, ils s'irradient dans toute la société contemporaine, ils montent à toutes les situations, par cette impulsion essentiellement moderne que reçoivent les basses classes en marche à travers le corps social, et ils racontent ainsi le Second Empire, à l'aide de leurs drames individuels, du guetapens du coup d'Etat à la trahison de Sedan.

Zola's condemnation of woman is startling, even brutal. He maintains that woman is of prime importance in forming and transmitting the traits bedeviling this particular family, the Rougon-Macquart. He early describes the fatal influence of the mother, Félicité, on her husband Pierre's sons by stating that "la race devait s'épurer par les femmes."[28] Then he records the decline and fall. The decadence of modern woman, symbolized in this family, Zola explicitly says, is mirrored in the social decline of contemporary France. Félicité, as an example of the pathologically degenerate wife and mother, the modern woman gone bad, is wholly responsible for the French defeat at Sedan.

In *Le Docteur Pascal,* the conclusion of the series, it is true that Zola preaches man's regeneration through rationalism, hygiene, social reform. But this optimistic message seems somewhat forced, as though Zola feels compelled to testify to a ninteenth-century idea of unilinear progress in which he does not really believe. Certainly his work does not support the hopeful note voiced in *Le Docteur Pascal.* The overall impression of the entire series is profoundly pessimistic. While decadence and pessimism are by no means identical, the idea of decadence certainly emerges, clearly, from a philosophy of pessimism. The two ideas are inseparably related. Zola portrays degeneration far too often and vividly to counterbalance his essential message of doom, despair, destruction, by forcing an artifical and optimistic dénouement. This pessimist is telling himself to be hopeful. The conclusion is contrived. This interpretation is of course debatable like all critical exegeses. Yet decadence is admittedly present in *Les Rougon-Macquart* and it must be accounted for. In this sense the Zola of mechanistic degeneration and cosmic pessimism is a much larger figure than Zola as a social reformer, advising universal sanitation.

Germinie Lacerteux, in the Goncourts' novel of that name, is a modern woman from the lower classes. A simpleminded country girl, Germinie comes to Paris to work as a servant. The megalopolis destroys her natural instincts. She succumbs to the penurious solitude forced upon her by the money-loving city. She grasps desperately for love. She smothers Jupillon with affection and would have destroyed him except for his protective cynicism. She, too, becomes sado-masochistic. Her love is lust, as this scene with Gautruche amply shows:[29]

Et c'étaient entres ces deux êtres, des amours terribles, acharnées et funèbres, des ardeurs et des assouvissements sauvages, des voluptés furieuses, des caresses qui avaient les brutalités et les colères du vin, des baisers qui semblaient chercher le sang sous la peau comme la langue d'une bête féroce, des anéantissements qui les engloutissaient et ne leur laissaient que le cadavre de leur corps.

It is an ugly picture. Germinie, unsatisfied at first, then insatiable, becomes a nymphomaniac. She begins to walk the streets:[30]

Elle ramassa les amours qui s'usent en une nuit, ce qui passe, ce qu'on rencontre, ce que le hasard des pavés fait trouver à la femme qui vague. Elle n'avait plus besoin de se donner le temps du désir: son caprice était furieux et soudain, allumé sur l'instant. La dernière pudeur et le dernier sens humain de la débauche, la préférence, le choix, et jusqu'à ce qui reste aux prostituées pour conscience et pour personnalité, le dégoût, le dégoût même,—elle l'avait perdu!

Her annihilation is soon complete. The megalopolis destroys the capacity for love which she at first showed for her illegitimate daughter. Even maternal love disappears. Then, twisted by the cruel city, Germinie ends her days as a neurotic prostitute tortured by nymphomania. A pauper's grave awaits her after years of poverty and disease.

In Mirbeau's *Le Journal d'une femme de chambre* Célestine is servant to a decadent bourgeoisie. Attacking Bourget for idealizing the monied class, Mirbeau portrays it as an artificial society of sexual perversion, hypocrisy, and degeneration. Célestine neurotically responds to her brutish employers. She is fatally attracted to the barbaric Joseph, who brutally rapes and kills a child, little Claire. As a modern woman Célestine feels a sado-masochistic attraction to him but no love for him. She tries to master Joseph, or failing she will be dominated by him. By the end of the novel she is his neurotic slave. In her sado-masochistic submission she is no longer concerned about his depravity or her own.

Rachilde has already been discussed. With her women decadence is in full bloom. In *La Sanglante ironie,* as throughout her numerous novels, she dissects the soul of the modern woman and concludes: "Névrosées . . . elle assument une perversité ingénue."[31] She lays her finger upon the modern woman's sore: her soul is corrupt as indeed it must be in its total isolation from nature. When the modern woman is not a flamboyant *femme fatale* who exults in love (and there are many such women in Rachilde), she is a neurotic victimized by her sado-masochism. Again she must dominate or be dominated, for love as the fundamental partnership of man and woman is not within her province.

Laure Lordès is the *hystérique* of Rachilde's *L'Animale.* Her nymphomaniacal seductions of Lucien Séchard, Henri Alban, and Auguste, and her attempt to seduce Père Armand de Bréville have been discussed. Her bestial attraction to her *gros matou,* Lion, has been noted as an example of the deca-

dent pervert. But her neurosis is stronger than one might
think even from these facts. Laure, interestingly enough,
feels that she is normal and natural (and here she may well
reflect Rachilde's thinking), as she justifies herself with
Henri Alban, her lover and a young law student:[32]

—L'hystérie, répéta Laure, c'est une maladie à la mode dont
tu m'as parlé, mais je ne me sens pas malade, mon pauvre Henri,
et ce sont peut-être les hommes de cette époque, les hommes
comme toi, qui sont malades! Ne crois-tu pas qu'il y ait eu
jadis . . . oh! il y a des siècles, une population ne faisant que
s'aimer sur un tapis d'herbe bien verte et avec beaucoup de
soleil autour. . . .

The neurotic always tries to justify herself. But instead of
a natural woman, loving in the sun, she is a sordid nymphomaniac trying, as a child, to seduce her village priest in
the confessional for the perverse pleasure of sacrilege. Laure's
ideas are modern madness. When her last decadent lover
calls her sane, healthy, good, his words only show how topsy-
turvy contemporary values have become:[33]

La vraie femme, selon la nature, c'est toi, sans les préjugés, sans
les détours de nos sociétés modernes, sans la stupide crainte de
paraître autre chose que la belle créature que tu es!

The words are an ironical culmination in the twisted story.
Laure is no creature of love. She is a sado-masochist who
titillates and tortures her many lovers in a neurotic attempt
to dominate and destroy them.

Even Mme Istar Capimont, of Péladan's *Istar,* already
mentioned, is a sado-masochist. Though reserved, she knows
she is seductively beautiful. She is chaste, indeed, but with
a lecherous chastity. She is a masochistic woman who yet
takes a psychic delight in making her husband suffer the
pangs of jealousy, as he believes she is betraying him with
Nergal, the scornful novelist. Everyone in the novel tortures
either himself and/or the others. Even the platonic relationship between Istar and Nergal is a refusal to culminate their
desires for the pleasure of self-abnegation. In a letter opened
after her death Istar requests Nergal to spend a night alone
with her corpse. She wants to torture him, and he relishes

the excruciating experience. He fondles and caresses her cold body, lies upon her breast, breathes through her mouth, and struggles against himself in his almost uncontrollable lust: he almost has relations with her. He finally gains control, or loses it, depending upon one's viewpoint, not because he respects her but because the denial of his desire affords him more masochistic satisfaction than self-indulgence would afford. Sado-masochism could hardly be more complete.

In Péladan's *Curieuse!* Paule Riazan, a familiar androgyne, is a modern woman intrigued by the evils of the megalopolis. She has a fatal attraction for the young "Chatterton," Jean Davèzc. She wants to destroy him. She is in turn fascinated by Nébo Mérodack because she cannot destroy him. Like Virgil with Dante, he escorts her through the inferno of Paris in quest of cerebral sins: she will scrutinize the perverts, like a voyeur, and thereby have her pleasure while remaining a virgin. She is callous about it all. Hence she moves like a wraith through the labyrinths and finds a city populated by *maquereaux* like Alphonse and streetwalkers like La Porporata. She discovers the truth of the comment: "Une chose inédite, inavouée . . . c'est de considérer Paris comme le grand mauvais lieu de l'Occident, le vilain quartier de toute l'Europe."[34] This is the Paris that Paule Riazan encounters. She is not disappointed in her quest of evil and violence. The novel is a study of the development of her neurotic self-consciousness. Just as Paule becomes aware of her own sado-masochism, she discovers a society of sadists and masochists, as she says, in which love, the primordial bond of man and woman, has been forever snapped.

Mme Honorine d'Arlement of Mendès' *La Première maîtresse,* already mentioned as a nymphomaniac, is also a sadomasochist. She drains her lovers like a vampire. She weakens them, as Mendès takes care to point out:[35]

Mais il y a des hommes que la femme saisit, torture, ne lâche pas, en qui elle pénètre, s'installe, demeure. Inférieurs? sans doute, faibles, incertains, trop dociles, mais si malheureux! la femme les tient. La femme les charme, les allanguit, les édulcore; elle fait d'eux quelque chose qui ressemble à la femme.

Her sado-masochism makes her feed like an animal upon her prey. She does not resist her psychological compulsions. Her fatal attraction overcomes the younger Evelin Gerbier.

There are other, and innumerable, neurotic modern women in decadent literature. Indeed their presence, with the passive male and a peculiar sensibility, goes far in defining decadent literature. Many of these women have already been studied in the chapter on the pervert. Verlaine's lesbians are among them, and even more numerous are the many androgynes: Mademoiselle de Maupin (Gautier), Tullia Fabriana (Villiers de l'Isle-Adam, *Isis*), the transvestites of Rollinat's *Les Névroses*, Péladan's *L'Androgyne*, Huysmans' Urania (*A Rebours*), and numberless sado-masochists from Lorrain, Gourmont, Lombard. They occur with startling frequency and cross the artificial boundaries of the so-called literary schools. Who, for instance, would think of the whimsical Alphonse Daudet as a portrayer of sado-masochists? Yet the heroine of *Sapho*, Fanny Legrand, is certainly a *femme fatale*. Sidonie Schèbe is an infamous bitch in *Froment jeune et Risler aîné*. Other sado-masochistic women lurk in seemingly unlikely places. Indeed they are so numerous and appear in such a jumble from 1850 or so to the close of the century that descriptive chronology becomes unimportant. The essential thing is the portrait of modern woman that emerges from decadent literature—a woman described by Baudelaire and Verlaine, with perfect justification, as a satanic vampire. For it is modern woman, the great temptress, the ageless vampire, appearing in many guises and protean forms, who has broken the natural bond of love, i.e., communion of man and woman in nature; and it is she who has usurped man's historic role only to let it slip from her grasp as a tortured, destructive, sado-masochistic neurotic. She begins as a *femme fatale* and ends as a pitiable wreck.

NINE

THE DECADENT IN CATACLYSM: PROBLEMS OF THE GÖTTERDÄMMERUNG

WE have now defined the decadent hero and placed him in one of the bleakest worldviews ever visualized. He is a metaphysical hero living *à rebours*, against the grain, a cerebral hero who is an aesthete, cosmopolitan, pervert, or all three at once. His roles are inextricably entwined. He is an ambiguous figure who personifies yet hates his society, one which he wishes to destroy yet cannot live without. This is the decadent agony. He is a megalopolitan primitive sentenced to life in the prison of the modern world. He abhors but feeds upon its artificiality. Surely there has never been a more enigmatic hero than the decadent.

He poses many problems.

The first problem is the matter of his very appearance in decadent literature. Is he an accurate social projection of the times? The decadent writers seem to feel that they are portraying nineteenth century France as it really is. But are they rather venting a personal *weltschmerz* atypical of the national ethos? This problem is cardinal. In a sense the literature of the decadence is bluntly plain. Decadence is an obsessive

theme, whether it appears as cosmic pessimism, pathological
degeneration, erotic titillation, or an actual eclipse of society
with all the overtones of a Wagnerian twilight of the gods.
This is true. But while they voice a common concern, decadent writers are, after all, only a tiny minority of their
society. Perhaps their portrait of the Western World, and
particularly of France, is biased, unjust, and unduly fatalistic.

How can one be sure?

A modern parallel is instructive. Consider the South of
contemporary American fiction and contrast it with the
South of diurnal reality. According to William Faulkner,
Truman Capote, Tennessee Williams, Erskine Caldwell, and
innumerable other Southern writers, the South is in a state of
suppurating decay. Gone with the wind, indeed, and forever, are Scarlett O'Hara and Rhett Butler wooing under
the omnipresent and often moss-bedecked magnolia, or delicate Southern belles fanning their cameo faces coquettishly
before the stark columns of great mansions while neighborhood swains wax poetic, syrup in their resonant voices, to
the sound of Negroes humming while they happily work in
the cotton fields. Now the romantic South has been replaced
by a vision of the decadent South.

The contemporary portrait is antithetical in every way.
The cotton fields have become red clay cracking under the
enervating and dehumanizing sun. The Delta country is
dotted with numberless plantations all in ruins. In one an
idiot daughter of an impoverished family, with an invalid
mother and besotted father to support, seduces an upstart
townsman under a chinaberry tree, that noble tree assumedly
supplying a protective veil to all illicit lovers throughout
the South. Children discover the facts of life while playing
with one another and fondling themselves in the cornshucks.
An impotent sadistic killer like Popeye, in Faulkner's *Sanc-
tuary,* ravishes a young bitch like Temple Drake with a
corncob while he neighs psychotically like a horse. Or a
sweet, somewhat hypersexual old lady like dear Miss Emily,
in the familiar story, kills her lover and daily fondles his
decaying body, year in and year out, in a desperate and path-

ological attempt to hold his fidelity. Or the familiar poor white trash squat in the charred remnant of a great house, spitting out watermelon seeds, swigging moonshine, and committing adultery in deserted rooms, if such their unsophisticated act may be called. Or a darky is jerked trembling from his tarpaper shack, while his tearful wife and innumerable pickaninnies look helplessly on, by blond and blue-eyed Anglo-Saxon sadists, their shotguns in hand, and led to the dismal swamp never to return again: the Negro, it seems, had the audacity to stare at a white woman, who is often a prostitute. And since in Southern literature the white woman usually has a repressed yen for the black man, she has falsely accused him in her twisted mental processes. Thus justice must be summarily executed. These familiar themes are liberally spiced with other perversions, like homosexuality and incest and sado-masochism. Miscegenation is a constant motif. Thus the South unenviably emerges as the most lurid land ever portrayed in any age or by any literature: it is one of unmitigated ignorance, poverty, bigotry, disease, perversion, vice.

The nation as a whole has responded with willing credulity to this portrait. Millions of Americans and tens of millions in other nations who know the South only through its literature (and it is a great literature) have lost all powers of discrimination. Everything is believed. The Mason-Dixon line is an invisible iron curtain that condemns one half of the nation to eternal doom, suffering from the curse of slavery, while the other prospers and looks upon it with indignant horror. The South is a country of ignorance and degradation. It is a modern citadel of gothic horrors, sexual and otherwise, usually perpetrated against the colored man by the white bigot.

To some extent—a very, very small extent—the situation is true.

Yet the picture is of course ludicrous, though Southern literature has given it wide currency. The South of reality is a region of bursting energy with humming mills, great dams, expanding industry, dynamic entrepreneurs. The difference between Atlanta and Milwaukee, from this point of view, is primarily one of regional accent and unimportant folkways. In both cities the Negro policeman is likely to stop the white traffic offender with a curt question: Where's the fire, mister? To be sure there are perverted and ruined aristocrats, scions of the decadent South, though the South has a monopoly on neither aristocracy nor homosexuality. This picture, while immortalized in great literature, is obviously distorted and incredibly one-sided. A bit of truth is magnified beyond recognition. Any observer who knows the South of fact and that of fiction is quite aware of this fundamental dichotomy between reality and literature.

We know that this image of the decadent South is almost totally inaccurate because we can verify the situation with our eyes. We may wonder, then, about a literature that portrays the Second Empire and Third Republic peopled by androgynes, perverts, sado-masochists, megalopolitans, and psychotics. If we could verify that situation too, we might discover that the literature of the epoch is completely divorced from its factual history.

In fact the Second Empire seems to be a period of general prosperity and optimism. Under Louis-Napoléon the magic name Bonaparte gives confidence to a mighty nation that is still respected and honored, and even looked upon with something like awe, throughout the earth. France is still the greatest landpower on earth. She is to lose this title not in the débâcle of 1870, as one might suppose in retrospect, but only in 1940 when the intrepid Heinz Guderian breaks loose with three panzer corps, delaying orders *not* to advance till the last moment, against the numerically superior forces of the allied armies, while Adolf Hitler actually trembles for fear of the French army. It is a little-known but factually proved chapter in military history. We mention the fact because military strength seems always to be equated with national grandeur.

France of the second half of the nineteenth century has great economic strength. Its agricultural production is at an all-time high, its ships sail the most distant waters, and its factories hum with the luxury products for which France has always been justly famous. Even the family life, understood within its own context, can hardly be called decadent when one reflects that the French *père de famille,* while deeply devoted to his wife and children, has throughout history seemed something of a philanderer to the puritanical Anglo-Saxon. A middle-aged "fling" can hardly be considered as a symptom of general decadence. The France of 1850 to the Great War is a nation of conservative bourgeoisie. Though prosperous businessmen may frequent the theater to leer, say, at Nana, they hardly spend their lives in brothels or opium dens. A few floozies from Offenbach do not overthrow the mighty French Empire, just as Rome did not collapse because a few senators gave an orgy or two. In fact France has so much *élan vital* that it is even imperialistic during the entire period. Bismarck has excellent reasons to fear the French. They are a threat to Prussia. France expands her African policy, invades Indo-China during the Second Empire, and is even ready to fight both Britain and Germany by the end of the century, if need be, to protect her farflung colonial interests. She almost declares war over territorial conflicts in North Africa. Thus France is not only willing to fight but perhaps actually spoiling for a fight to regain her prestige lost in 1870. France of this period is belligerent, not decadent.

Surely, too, only the crassest spirit would interpret the *élan vital* of a nation exclusively in materialistic terms. Nineteenth-century France, from a cultural standpoint, is even more vigorous than the Grand Siècle in artistic, intellectual, and scientific matters. With the exceptions of Periclean Athens and Elizabethan England there has perhaps never been a more brilliant period of human achievement. The literary production of the nineteenth century may not equal the perfection of the seventeenth, but it is more extensive, original, individualistic, and reflects a greater intellectual activity. Certainly the history of modern art, from Cézanne to the present day, is largely a French interval. Criticism has no more perspicacious critics, despite certain flaws, than

Sainte-Beuve, Taine, Faguet, Fromentin, Baudelaire. Bergson, Comte, and Boutroux are three luminaries in a galaxy of great philosophers. Pasteur, Berthelot, and the Curies are among the many great scientists of the age. Literary movements multiply geometrically because the intellectual agitation is so great and fruitful. The writers of the nineteenth century are so fine and so numerous that no other nation, at any period of its development, can equal France in sheer quantity and general achievement, and few if any periods of culture equal France in its ultimate quality. France is not moribund during this century of success. She glows with true greatness.

With the refutation of France as a decadent nation, then, a second and more fundamental question arises: Is the entire idea of decadence false, meaningless, even absurd?

The evidence seems overwhelming that an equation of political and economic stagnation with moral and social decay is not only nonsensical but idiotic. In his famous preface to *Aphrodite,* as we have seen, Pierre Louÿs points out the historical fact that every megalopolis has reached its apogee of cultural contribution when it supposedly reached its moral nadir. One might pray, then, for vice in order to have its concomitant greatness. Remy de Gourmont, who is an astute critic in the decadence, develops this very position. In "Stéphane Mallarmé et l'idée de décadence," from his perceptive *La Culture des idées,* he argues bluntly that Roman political history has proved how ridiculous the current idea of decadence is in reality. He maintains that Frenchmen have been duped by the specious philosophy of Montesquieu into believing that social decadence, if there is such a thing, results also in literary decadence. He suggests, with biting truth, that one might be nearer actuality in declaring that political decadence is the most favorable of all possible states for intellectual growth and cultural contribution.

It is certainly difficult for a historian to equate moral probity with grandeur and licentiousness with decay. The eighteenth century in France is the great erotic epoch, not the nineteenth. The first century after Christ in Rome shows Roman expansion at its height and intellectual development in full flower; yet this is the era of its greatest moral depravity or, at least, ethical looseness. The idea popularized by historical novelists that Nero was succeeded on the throne by Heliogabalus and that the two reigned as supreme tyrants of daily orgies, thus causing the immediate downfall of Rome, ignores the obvious fact that Rome is to fall only four hundred years after Nero fiddles before the burning city. Just who are these hedonistic decadents, anyway, who so wickedly incur the wrath of the gods upon themselves and Rome for their sensual excesses? Are they wicked imperial Romans like Vespasian? Are they dishonest administrators like Agricola, Tacitus, Pliny? Are they corrupt emperors like Marcus Aurelius and the "epicurean" Antonines? Are they wastrels like the Flavians? Are they weaklings like Probus, Claudius II, Aurelian, Diocletian? The questions are of course ironic. All these men are effective and even ideal administrators. They are good and sometimes great men. The Roman Senate, despite Hollywood, is a moral if not always wise deliberative body throughout its long history.

As a matter of fact one is tempted to argue, following Gourmont, that perhaps virtue brings decline. At least Rome is great when she is wicked. Chronology shows quite clearly that after Christianity is recognized as the state religion, after the gladiatorial contests are abolished, after moral regeneration and the suppression of prostitution, Rome totters most precariously. One should thereby conclude that sexual activity is a sign of *élan vital,* and be as nefarious and depraved as humanly possible. Indeed, the *élan vital* is a sexual energy, the libido, an overflowing of the exuberance of life, and nothing sinful or decadent in itself. There is much evidence for this position.

Gibbon might even be correct in pointing out that Christians, so-called paragons of morality, are largely responsible for the Roman decline and fall, hence the Roman decadence. He argues cogently in *The Decline and Fall of the Roman*

Empire, it must be admitted. The early Christians are often uneducated riffraff, slaves, prostitutes, pickpockets, neurotics, in fact the scum of the Roman Empire. They usually refuse to pay taxes, to serve in the armed forces, and of course they do not pay homage to the state gods, symbolizing their obeisance to the political state. They disrupt society. They are supremely irritating. And why? Because they worship another minor deity imported from the Middle-East, a section of the world overflowing with crackpots and religious cults. To see an unwashed Christian of antiquity, ignorant and insolent in his mystic faith, flout the laws of a supremely sophisticated society and reject with his arrogant and unjustified fanaticism the arguments of, say, the stoic philosophers would have been, frankly, a nauseating sight to any modern man transported to the original scene. The cross is to Roman justice what the electric chair is to modern American law; it symbolizes punishment for transgression. Jesus of Nazareth, then, is a common criminal. The Christian who dies for such an ignominious symbol and for such a man must have looked like a lunatic. Putting the Christian out of his misery is a kind of euthanasia for the mentally unfit.

Perhaps, if we pursue this line of reasoning, Christian morality is responsible for the decay of the Roman Empire, and by extension morality everywhere should be eschewed as being anti-natural. Nature, one might well argue, clearly means for man to fornicate and enjoy his senses. The supreme symbol of Christian morality might be that of the spineless Honorius trembling fearfully in Ravenna, surrounded by ignorant if not fraudulent priests and by petulant eunuchs, while the mighty Empire of Rome falls asunder. And when the German barbarians come to crash the gates of Rome, they do not bring morality. They bring the vigor of murder and rapine and total amorality if not immorality. They are above all men of nature, warriors of blood and the soil.

All these things are perhaps true each in its own way. Certainly they are valid to a point, like our portrait of the South.

Yet they are also false inasmuch as they are only part of the story. The facts that are undeniable from one standpoint, from one coherent scheme, are after all a single side of the coin. The opposite picture exists as inevitably as its shadow. Which is true? the modern logician might ask. He thereby shows his semantic predisposition to define and to resolve always by assuming opposites and by an *either . . . or* approach. Perhaps the logic of the future will be more inclusive. It will allow for *both . . . and* in an attempt to reconcile opposites, knowing that man is reason and nonreason, being and nonbeing, life and death, and that he is these things, and more, not in a definable but rather an inseparable way. Is there, indeed, such a state as nonbeing? What could possibly exemplify nonbeing that could not be better understood as being? The future logician, strange as this logic may now seem, will no longer be obsessed with opposites that have no correspondence with reality. He will recognize them for the artificial distinctions and inaccurate categories of the human understanding that they are. Yet his supreme refutation of the semantic approach, which at first seems illogical, is a testimony to his utter reliance upon semantics; just as the positivist is his most characteristic when, going beyond himself and the system he represents, he tears down the positivist position as the logical conclusion of his own system. Decadence is nothing if not an enigma.

Thus everything that has been used to prove that France is not decadent may be reversed, and vice versa. Of course France seems at its greatest, one might say, just at the point of ripeness: the rich red apple glows at its fullest, most beautiful, a moment before it begins to decay. Decadence coexists in grandeur, decay in national ripeness. A piece of meat is succulent one moment, gamy the next. Furthermore, growth and decline are relative factors that can never be understood out of context. France is great in the eighteenth century because it operates in a context where Germany is weak. But in the nineteenth century France may be stronger but seem weaker because in the changing context Germany has grown strong. Comparison and contrast alone make such terms as "weak" or "decadent" meaningful, and they are modes of understanding within a particular context. Thus French *élan vital* declines not of itself but in comparison with that of other powers. Germany is to grow at a greater rate than France, and England is to expand faster than either. Does that mean the slower nation is decadent? The failure of the *élan vital* to respond to a menace, one might conclude, is an infallible sign of decadence. It evidences that the energy of a nation is waning and not waxing.

One should not understress, moreover, the great importance of morality. Whereas it is perhaps true that the great nation blooms most luxuriantly at the precise moment of completest depravity, decadence is nonetheless a force in play. At that precise time destruction begins to operate as catabolism, the payment for metabolism as life, the final wages of sin. The sinner, or decadent, as he might be called, does not reap his whirlwind at once. He sows first and he reaps later. But he does reap. The harvest of death and damnation shall be gathered, and its taste shall be exceedingly bitter.

One might argue, too, that naturally only a small minority, the cultural élite so to speak, is cognizant of the profound movements of the times. If the writer has any justification at all for his function, it is that he is sensitive to his ethos, that he perceives truths of which the herdman with his more limited sensibility is supinely unaware. The decadent writers, then, are quite right. It is not a serious charge that they do not reflect current and general thinking: a pooling of ignorance has rarely produced knowledge. The masses have never been completely right. There is no reason to suppose that the masses of the pleasure-seeking Second Empire have as much perspicacity as their writers.

One might also say that the Roman administrators, able as they admittedly were, merely maintained a shaky empire on an uncertain footing. But the *élan vital* had run out, and the institutions which it incarnated lumbered on to an ultimate doom. In similar fashion, despite its great reputation, the French army at its greatest moment, the triumph of Moscow, begins to decline and will continue to decline until the terrible catastrophe of 1940. Perhaps even the interlude of 1914, a more devastating war for France by far than the second world war, is more an apparent than real time of greatness. The French generals so foolishly persist in attacking, in great wave after wave, that the Germans actually develop a system of defense predicated on the incredible waste and carnage of the French onslaughts. Their bravery is ineffectual, even suicidal, like that of the Confederates under Pickett advancing against the Union lines at Gettysburg. After such horrible bloodletting it is no wonder that France, by 1940, has lost the will to fight, that its destiny as a military power has seemingly come to an end.

All these things, like their opposites, are perhaps true.

Ultimate truth lies in reconciling the antipodal positions, not by fitting them together like pieces of a giant puzzle. Such piecemeal construction is manifestly impossible. One must rather recognize that claim and counter-claim both exist in a complex totality. The logic of such understanding is for the critic not to be too "logical" as he attempts to assess the various positions which all clamor for attention, which all have good claims to validity, and which all demand total acceptance. Indeed everything must be accounted for, but logical assessment by itself does not suffice. Analysis is valuable only in terms of synthesis. What will be the synthetic agent formulating the French decadent worldview, allowing for the reconciliation of the opposite positions? The answer to this question suggests a word that is no longer acceptable in polite critical society.

That word is intuition.

The French decadent writers are, from this point of view, supremely intuitive. They instinctively understand that a great social change is being effected in France and by extension throughout the Western world. France is especially important because, as the most culturally advanced nation since Greece, she responds hypersensitively to the stimuli that more lethargic nations at first ignore. The decadent authors sense the spirit of their times although they do not always comprehend it intellectually. Perhaps it is too much to expect full intellectual understanding. That kind of knowledge can come only later, much later, if at all.

A restatement of the decadent message is appropriate at this point of the argument. From Montesquieu to Spengler there flows a common cyclical idea of history. Civilization is not a state of unilinear progress or decadence. It is cyclical movement. History is composed of many cultures recurring in similar patterns, evolving along familiar biological lines of birth, growth, maturity, age, and death. Hence each culture is unique in space and time with an essentially different *élan vital* that activates it and that is almost mystically the soul of a nation. In this theory nations have souls, or natural instincts, no less than animals. Of course writers are rarely philosophers, and when they are, after a fashion, like Péladan they tend to be wretched artists. But they are usually attuned to the cultural ethos of the age; at least the better writers are, so that they realize not only where the nation is for the moment but also and more importantly where it is going in the future.

Decadent writers know, consequently, that the capitalist society before 1914 is destined to end in the cataclysm of the Great War. This is the kind of *Götterdämmerung* that they envision. Nobility will be replaced by surging mobs acting in the guise of democracy, and the triumph of money will ironically be complete. The masses do not seek to do away with money; they simply want it for themselves. Socialism will be the guiding spirit of the new age. It will oppose the group-soul of the new society to the atomistic soul of the great European heritage from the Renaissance through the Second Empire and up to the Great War. The individual will lose his unique station in life. He will be increasingly subordinated in new ways to the organism, the social structure, the state, the faceless society, in the revolt of the masses, whether that mass insurrection expresses itself as fascism, naziism, or communism. The constant factor is that the individual is dead, that the atomistic soul cannot exist in the group-conscious society. Lorrain and Bourges, among others, are explicit on this point in their many predictions. They are also correct. Other decadent writers, while voicing no prophecies that may later be verified, portray their society with amazing exactitude. The countryside is deserted for the megalopolis, Paris. The newspaper world of mass communication, advertisement, conditioned reflex, and group thinking congeals. The bourgeoisie completes its financial triumphs over the dying aristocracy. The world becomes ugly, vulgar, petty. It is significant that the hero of the decadent literature is invariably an individualistic protagonist who reacts against the spirit of his times. That is, indeed, why he is a hero. This is the decadent message. In retrospect, from the vantage-point of 1960, when the new social order has already assumed form, the decadent world-view seems to be a just depiction.

The role of the sensitive man, the hero, the artist, is difficult in such a society, as the decadent writers sense and say. He has no recourse other than to aesthetics. He must turn to art as his decadent metaphysics. He has no other reality. Art is his religion, his salvation, his *raison d'être*. From the fictional Des Esseintes to the actual Oscar Wilde art is his dogmatic creed. He lives for it. As a hero he no longer has the enthusiasm of the romantic protagonist. First given to despair, then victimized by a paralyzing abulia, he is a cerebral hero who does not have the volition to act. Time is a transient nightmare and his society will vanish in smoke. He knows this. But he is condemned to watch the destruction of his world and his own impending collapse. Thus he recollects the past for which he yearns, and he glimpses the future to which he can never belong. The decadent's values are those of the aristocratic past and the atomistic soul: individualism, art, the measured life, dignity, solitude. In reaction against the crumbling society, like Prince Noronsoff, he may often turn sour. His decay is inevitable under unbearable social pressures and tensions. Society is too much for him. His values cannot withstand the collective strength of the brave new world. He is too much the creature and victim of his own era and its value-structure to change, like the surging masses, into a member of the new organism, the totality of the socialist state of the future, with its values antithetical to those of the aristocratic past. A new civilization entails, as the decadents intimate, a transvaluation of all ethical, social, religious values. The white man's burden of 1890 becomes bestial imperialism in 1960. The actions of the colonist are the same, but the interpretations given them are diametrically opposed. A new value-scheme is in effect in the different civilization.

The decadent prefers to die because he cannot become a member of the new social order. And he does expire, sometimes with dignity. But more often he dies like a wretched coward, sniveling with fear, clutching desperately for crutches like sex, dope, and liquor, even for *l'art pour l'art*. His death is miserable and cheap as attested to by innumerable decadent heroes.

The decadent writers are right. Their society is dying. After the Great War Europe begins to assume the socialistic forms foreshadowed in the nineteenth century and hardened into a scheme of values in our own day. The nineteenth-century man, an individualist, who might return today, would confront a totally different society. He will speak French, indeed, but his values are not those of the modern Frenchman. As the decadent writers maintain, those values perished in the apocalypse of the Second Empire and vanished from history in 1914 except as they remain as empty forms and hollow catchwords mouthed by the semanticist and cultural historian.

The callous reader errs if he curtly dismisses the decadent writers, despite all their inconsistencies, errors, and artistic failures, as curious figures who anticipated a holocaust of world-destruction. This common misunderstanding of the decadent message is unwarranted. The decadent writers are far too subtle to make such a gross error. Montesquieu, Adams, Spengler, the host of minor historians of the cyclical theory, maintain no such worldview. The decadent writers merely reflect their sophisticated ideas, which are current and common domain, even when they do not directly know them, by portraying not the end of man and of civilization, as critics have naïvely assumed, but rather the terminus of a *kind* of man and of the *kind* of civilization which he incarnates. That man is the decadent, that civilization his own peculiar creation and province. It has now passed nameless and unnoticed into the dynamic present.

The reader has his choice of these theories. I have offered at least three, and I have suggested several others that have ramifications which no one could fully understand. This is no cause for concern. Let the reader serve as his own critic in following these devious paths of comprehension.

The reader may choose to regard decadent literature as the curious mouthings of a tiny, unimportant, and ineffectual literary clique, an interesting episode in literary history without relationship to the world of historical fact. There is evidence for such a view. Or he may believe, somewhat religiously, that the world will pay for its transgressions against nature with a holocaust of death, doom, damnation, and total destruction. There is evidence for such an opinion. Or he may feel, as I do, that the decadent writers are simply hypersensitive men who intuit a passing age, lament its decline and fall, and uneasily await the breaking of the new dawn. Their literature, then, is the portrait of the hero or ideal man in stress, the social projection of the nineteenth-century age of uneasiness, as he reacts to his often unconscious but sometimes fully realized knowledge that his role on the stage of history, glittering as it is for the moment, will soon come to an abrupt and most inglorious end. All that will remain of his world, perhaps, is an overstuffed chair, a gilded mirror, or a hauntingly beautiful and quite meaningless waltz from Offenbach that lingers subliminally and evokes a brief nostalgic pain before passing into final oblivion in the twentieth-century mind.

NOTES

CHAPTER ONE

1. Arthur Symons, *Dramatis Personae* (Indianapolis: Bobbs-Merrill, n. d), p. 96.
2. *Ibid.*, pp. 96-97.
3. Madeleine G. Rudler, *Parnassiens, symbolistes, et décadents* (Paris: Messein, 1938), p. 30.
4. *Ibid.*, p. 54.
5. G. L. van Roosbroeck, *Legend of the Decadents* (New York: Columbia U. P., 1927), p. 10.
6. Rudler, p. 26.
7. Gustave Kahn, *Symbolistes et décadents* (Paris: Vanier, 1902), pp. 33-34.
8. Rudler, p. 72.
9. James M. Smith, *Elements of Decadence and Their Convergence in the French Literature of the Late Nineteenth Century* (Chapel Hill: unpub. diss., 1948), p. 10.
10. Paul Bourget, *Essais de psychologie contemporaine* (Paris: Plon, 1899), I, p. 20.
11. Désiré Nisard, *Etudes sur les poëtes latins de la décadence* (Paris: Hachette, 1888), II, p. 387.
12. *Ibid.*, p. 388.
13. *Ibid.*
14. Théophile Gautier, "Charles Baudelaire," preface to *Les Fleurs du mal* (Paris: Calmann-Lévy, n. d.), p. xvi.
15. Kahn, p. 37.
16. *Ibid.*, p. 38.
17. Remy de Gourmont, "Stéphane Mallarmé et l'idée de décadence," in *La Culture des idées* (Paris: Mercure de France, 1916), p. 112.
18. A. E. Carter, *The Idea of Decadence in French Literature, 1830-1900* (Toronto: Toronto U. P., 1958), pp. 123-43.
19. See James M. Smith's "Concept of Decadence in Nineteenth-Century French Literature," *Studies in Philology* (L, October 1953), 646 f. Also cf. Smith, "Does Art Follow Life or Does Life Follow Art? A Controversy in Nineteenth-Century French Literature," *Studies in Philology* (LIII, October 1956), 635-38.
20. Carter, *ibid.*

21. Smith, *Elements of Decadence,* pp. 153-54.
22. Cf. Roosbroeck, pp. 14 f.
23. For a glimpse into this cultural ethos, see William Gaunt, "A Continental State of Mind," *The Aesthetic Adventure* (New York: Harcourt, Brace, 1945). It is an informative chapter in the intellectual history of the French decadence.
24. John B. Wolf, "The *Elan Vital* of France: A Problem in Historical Perspective," in Edward Mead Earle, ed., *Modern France* (Princeton: Princeton U. P., 1959), p. 21. Prof. Wolf is the most vocal and able proponent of this concept of modern France.
25. *Ibid.,* p. 23.
26. Wallace Fowlie, *Mallarmé* (Chicago U. P., 1953), p. 257.
27. Brooks Adams, *The Law of Civilization and Decay* (New York: Vintage, 1955), pp. 292-93.
28. Arthur de Gobineau, "L'Essai sur l'inégalité des races humaines," *Pages choisies* (Paris: Mercure de France, 1905), p. 66.
29. Carter, p. 137.
30. Pierre Martino, *Parnasse et symbolisme (1850-1900)* (Paris: Colin, 1947), p. 144.
31. D. G. Charleton, *Positivist Thought in France during the Second Empire* (Oxford: Oxford U. P., 1959), p. 163.
32. André Barre, *Le Symbolisme* (Paris: Jouve, 1911), p. 22.
33. *Ibid.,* p. 398.
34. *Ibid.,* p. 399.
35. Max Nordau, *Degeneration* (New York: Appleton, 1895), p. 31. A translation from the German *Entartung.*
36. Renato Poggioli, "Qualis Artifex Pereo! or Barbarism and Decadence," *Harvard Library Bulletin,* XIII, 1 (Winter 1959), 136-37.
37. Anatole Baju, *L'Ecole décadente* (Paris: Vanier, 1887), p. 9.
38. *Ibid.,* p. 10.

CHAPTER TWO

1. Oswald Spengler, *The Decline of the West* (New York: Knopf, 1959), II, pp. 98-99.
2. Octave Mirbeau, *Les Vingt et un jours d'un neurasthénique* (Paris: Charpentier, 1904), p. 89.
3. Lucien Victor-Meunier, "Le Rappel," 21 mars 1898, in Emile Zola, *Paris,* from *Oeuvres complètes,* ed. Maurice Le Blond (Paris: Bernouard, 1929), pp. 574-75.
4. Edmond and Jules de Goncourt, *Germinie Lacerteux* (Paris: Flammarion, 1921), p. 279.
5. *Ibid.,* p. 95.
6. Edmond and Jules de Goncourt, *Charles Demailly* (Paris: Flammarion, 1926), p. 152.
7. *Ibid.,* p. 262.
8. *Ibid.,* p. 80.
9. Paul Bourget, *Cosmopolis* (Paris: Lemerre, 1898), p. ii.
10. Catulle Mendès, *Zo'har* (Paris: Charpentier, 1922), p. 54.
11. Spengler, p. 102.
12. Remy de Gourmont, *Les Chevaux de Diomède* (Paris: La Connaissance, 1921), p. 104.
13. Goncourt, *Charles Demailly,* p. 138.
14. Jean Lorrain, *Monsieur de Phocas* (Paris: Ollendorff, 1901), p. 11.
15. Jean Lorrain, *Buveurs d'âmes* (Paris: Charpentier, 1893), from the *avertissement.*
16. Joséphin Péladan, *Le Vice suprême* (Paris: Editions du monde moderne, 1926), p. 86.
17. Elémir Bourges, *Le Crépuscule des dieux,* ed. André Lebois (Paris: Le Cercle du livre, 1954), p. ciii.
18. Goncourt, *Charles Demailly,* pp. 236-37.
19. Catulle Mendès, *Méphistophéla* (Paris: Fasquelle, 1903), p. 169.

20. Catulle Mendès, *La Première maîtresse* (Paris: Charpentier, 1922), p. 2.

21. Pierre Louÿs, *La Femme et le pantin* (Paris: Michel, 1948), p. 54.

22. *Ibid.*, p. 238.

23. Pierre Louÿs, *Aphrodite* (Paris: Fasquelle, n. d.), pp. 268-69.

24. Péladan, *Le Vice suprême*, p. 122.

25. Paul Verlaine, *Oeuvres poétiques complètes* (Paris: Gallimard, 1948), p. 544.

26. *Ibid.*, pp. 343-44.

27. Emile Zola, *La Fortune des Rougon* (Paris: Bernouard, 1927), p. 73.

28. Mendès, *La Première maîtresse*, pp. 112-13.

29. Péladan, *Le Vice suprême*, p. 185.

30. Joris-Karl Huysmans, *A Rebours* (Paris: Crès, 1928), p. 157.

31. *Ibid.*, p. 158.

32. Péladan, *Le Vice suprême*, p. 62-63.

33. Théophile Gautier, *Mademoiselle de Maupin* (Paris: Garnier, 1930), p. 342. This novel is a harbinger of the French decadence and its themes.

34. *Ibid.*, p. 419.

35. Jean Lorrain, *Princesses d'ivoire et d'ivresse* (Paris: Ollendorff, 1902), pp. 8-9.

36. Joséphin Péladan, *Curieuse!* (Paris: Laurent, 1886), p. 8.

37. Joséphin Péladan, *Finis latinorum* (Paris: Flammarion, 1899), p. 254.

38. A. E. Carter, *The Idea of Decadence in French Literature, (1830-1900)* (Toronto: Toronto U. P., 1958), p. 105.

39. Spengler, pp. 103-104.

40. James M. Smith, *Elements of Decadence and Their Convergence in French Literature of the Late Nineteenth Century* (Chapel Hill: unpub. diss., 1948), p. 59.

41. Anatole Baju, *L'Ecole décadente* (Paris: Vanier, 1887), p. 7.

42. *Ibid.*, p. 8.

43. Renato Poggioli, "Qualis Artifex Pereo! or Barbarism and Decadence," *Harvard Library Bulletin*, XIII, 1 (Winter 1959), 141-42.

44. *Ibid.*, p. 138.

CHAPTER THREE

1. Marcel Schwob, *Coeur double* (Paris: Bernouard, 1927), p. xx.

2. Maurice Barrès, *Un Homme libre* (Paris: Plon, 1922), p. 65.

3. Maurice Barrès, *Le Jardin de Bérénice* (Paris: Plon, 1921), p. 66.

4. Pierre Martino, *Parnasse et symbolisme (1850-1900)* (Paris: Colin, 1947), p. 145.

5. Pierre Martino, *Le Naturalisme français (1870-1895)* (Paris: Colin, 1945), p. 217.

6. René Dumesnil, *L'Epoque réaliste et naturaliste* (Paris: Tallandier, 1945), p. 27.

7. Paul Verlaine, *Oeuvres poétiques complètes* (Paris: Gallimard, 1948), p. 49.

8. Villiers de l'Isle-Adam, *L'Eve future* (Paris: Charpentier, 1891), p. 110.

9. Edmond and Jules de Goncourt, *Charles Demailly* (Paris: Flammarion, 1926), p. 139.

10. Remy de Gourmont, *Une Nuit au Luxembourg* (Paris: Mercure de France, 1923), p. 101.

11. *Ibid.*, pp. 96-97.

12. Remy de Gourmont, *Les Chevaux de Diomède* (Paris: La Connaissance, 1921), p. 160.

13. *Ibid.*, p. 162.

14. Remy de Gourmont, *Sixtine* (Paris: Mercure de France, n.d.), pp. 75-76.

15. *Ibid.*, p. 76.

16. E.g., Villiers de l'Isle-Adam, *Derniers contes* (Paris: Mercure de France, 1921), pp. 99-100.

17. Joséphin Péladan, *Le Vice suprême* (Paris: Editions du monde moderne, 1926), p. 75.

18. *Ibid.*, p. 169.
19. Elémir Bourges, *Le Crépuscule des dieux*, ed. André Lebois (Paris: Le Cercle du livre, 1954), p. 239.
20. Gustave Flaubert, *L'Education sentimentale* (Paris: Librairie de France, 1922), p. 19.
21. *Ibid.*, p. 513.

CHAPTER FOUR

1. Oswald Spengler, *Decline of the West* (New York: Knopf, 1957), II, pp. 102-103.
2. Gustave Flaubert, *L'Education sentimentale* (Paris: Librairie de France, 1922), p. 155.
3. Catulle Mendès, *Monstres parisiens* (Paris: Charpentier, 1902), p. 232.
4. *Ibid.*, p. 97.
5. Jean Lorrain, *Le Crime des riches* (Paris: Douville, 1905), unnumbered page in the frontispiece.
6. Joséphin Péladan, *Curieuse!* (Paris: Laurent, 1886), pp. 278-79.
7. Pierre Louÿs, *Aphrodite* (Paris: Fasquelle, n. d.), unnumbered page in the préface.
8. Paul Bourget, *Cosmopolis* (Paris: Lemerre, 1898), pp. ii-iii.
9. Octave Mirbeau, *Les Vingt et un jours d'un neurasthénique* (Paris: Charpentier, 1904), p. 434.
10. Edmond and Jules de Goncourt, *Charles Demailly* (Paris: Flammarion, 1926), p. 262.
11. *Ibid.*, p. 80.
12. Edmond and Jules de Goncourt, *Germinie Lacerteux* (Paris: Flammarion, 1921), p. 95.
13. Emile Zola, *La Curée* (Paris: Bernouard, 1927), p. 52.
14. Emile Zola, *Au Bonheur des dames* (Paris: Bernouard, 1928), p. 467. It is Zola's own note.
15. Emile Zola, *Le Ventre de Paris* (Paris: Bernouard, 1927), p. 335. Zola's note.

16. Emile Zola, *L'Argent* (Paris: Bernouard, 1928), p. 437. Zola's note.
17. Emile Zola, *Paris* (Paris: Bernouard, 1929), p. 558. Zola's note.
18. *Ibid.*, pp. 574-75. Victor-Meunier's criticism of Zola's *Paris*.
19. Emile Zola, *Nana* (Paris: Bernouard, 1928), p. 447. Zola's note.
20. Spengler, p. 96.
21. *Ibid.*, pp. 96, 103.

CHAPTER FIVE

1. Joris-Karl Huysmans, *A Rebours* (Paris: Crès, 1928), p. 337.
2. Joris-Karl Huysmans, *Là-Bas* (Paris: Crès, 1928), p. 246.
3. Charles Baudelaire, *Oeuvres complètes* (Paris: Gallimard, 1954), p. 377.
4. Arthur Rimbaud, *Oeuvres* (Paris: Mercure de France, 1924), p. 269.
5. Ernest Raynaud, *La Mêlée symboliste (1870-1900)* (Paris: La Renaissance du livre, 1918), p. 64.
6. Marcel Schwob, *Coeur double* (Paris: Bernouard, 1927), p. xv.
7. Remy de Gourmont, *Les Chevaux de Diomède* (Paris: La Connaissance, 1921), p. 67.
8. *Ibid.*, p. 85.
9. *Ibid.*, pp. 210-11.
10. *Ibid.*, pp. 200-201.
11. Remy de Gourmont, *Sixtine* (Paris: Mercure de France, n. d.), p. 13.
12. *Ibid.*, p. 136.
13. *Ibid.*, p. 18.
14. *Ibid.*, p. 264.
15. *Ibid.*, p. 66.
16. *Ibid.*, pp. 235-36.
17. *Ibid.*, pp. 75-76.
18. Paul Verlaine, *Oeuvres Poétiques complètes* (Paris: Gallimard, 1948), p. 206.
19. Stéphane Mallarmé, *Oeuvres complètes* (Paris: Gallimard, 1956), p. 38.
20. *Ibid.*,
21. *Ibid.*, pp. 67-68.

CHAPTER SIX

1. See my earlier study on the protagonist of the first half of the nineteenth century for which this work is the sequel, *The Hero in French Romantic Literature* (Athens: Univ. of Georgia Press, 1959), the chapter entitled "The Rebel and the Dandy," for a differentiation between the two.

2. John C. Prevost, *Le Dandysme en France (1817-1839)* (Genève: Droz, 1957), p. 163.

3. Arthur Symons, *Dramatis Personae* (Indianapolis: Bobbs-Merrill, n. d.), p. 116.

4. Théophile Gautier, "Charles Baudelaire," the preface to *Les Fleurs du mal* (Paris: Calmann-Lévy, n. d.), p. xviii.

5. Albert Cassagne, *La Théorie de l'art pour l'art en France* (Paris: Dorbon, 1959), pp. 464-65.

6. Ralph Adams Cram, *The Decadent: Being the Gospel of Inaction* (Boston: privately printed, 1893), p. 27.

7. G. L. van Roosbroeck, *The Legend of the Decadents* (New York: Columbia U. P., 1927), p. 3.

8. Joris-Karl Huysmans, *A Rebours* (Paris: Crès, 1928), p. 271.

9. Théophile Gautier, *Emaux et camées* (Genève: Droz, 1947), pp. 130, 131, 132.

10. Leconte de Lisle, *Poèmes barbares* (Paris: Lemerre, 1881), p. 356.

11. Leconte de Lisle, *Poèmes antiques* (Paris: Lemerre, 1881), pp. 134, 135, 136.

12. José-Maria de Heredia, *Les Trophées* (Paris: Lemerre, n. d.), p. 156.

13. Charles Baudelaire, *Les Fleurs du mal* (Paris: Corti, 1950), pp. 9-10.

14. Paul Verlaine, *Oeuvres poétiques complètes* (Paris: Gallimard, 1948), p. 206.

15. Wallace Fowlie, *Mallarmé* (Univ. Chicago Press, 1953), p. 264.

16. Arthur Rimbaud, *Oeuvres* (Paris: Mercure de France, 1924), pp. 34-35.

17. André Barre, *Le Symbolisme* (Paris: Jouve, 1911), p. 23.

18. Rimbaud, pp. 93-94.

19. Arthur Rimbaud, "Lettre du Voyant," *Oeuvres complètes* (Montréal: Valignette, n. d.), p. 205.

20. Stéphane Mallarmé, *Oeuvres complètes* (Paris: Gallimard, 1945), p. 50.

21. Guy Michaud, *Message poétique du symbolisme* (Paris: Nizet, 1947), p. 232.

22. Quoted in Ernest Raynaud, *La Mêlée symboliste (1870-1890)* (Paris: La Renaissance du livre, 1918), p. 64.

23. Remy de Gourmont, *Les Chevaux de Diomède* (Paris: La Connaissance, 1921), p. 118.

24. Baudelaire, pp. 40-41.

25. Remy de Gourmont, *Une Nuit au Luxembourg* (Paris: Mercure de France, 1923), p. 101.

26. Jean Lorrain, *Monsieur de Phocas* (Paris: Ollendorff, 1906), pp. 45-46.

27. Remy de Gourmont, *Sixtine* (Paris: Mercure de France, n. d.), pp. 75-76.

CHAPTER SEVEN

1. For the important difference between the romantic hero and the decadent hero in this regard, see my chapter entitled "Hypersensibility and the Pathological Hero," in *The Hero in French Romantic Literature* (Athens: Univ. of Georgia Press, 1959).

2. Charles Baudelaire, *Les Fleurs du mal* (Paris: Corti, 1950), p. 173.

3. *Ibid.*, p. 176.

4. Joséphin Péladan, *Finis latinorum* (Paris: Flammarion, 1899), p. 254.

5. Jean Lorrain, *Princesses d'ivoire et d'ivresse* (Paris: Ollendorff, 1902), p. 8.

6. Remy de Gourmont, *Lettres à l'amazone* (Paris: Mercure de France, 1917), p. 22.

7. Rachilde, *Monsieur Vénus* (Paris: Flammarion, 1926), p. 96.

8. Joris-Karl Huysmans, *A Rebours* (Paris: Crès, 1928), p. 158.

9. Emile Zola, *La Curée* (Paris: Bernouard, 1927), p. 187.

10. Catulle Mendès, *La Première maîtresse* (Paris: Charpentier, 1922), p. 290.

11. Rachilde, *La Sanglante ironie* (Paris: Mercure de France, 1902), p. v.

12. Jean Lorrain, *Buveurs d'âmes* (Paris: Charpentier, 1893), unnumbered page from the préface.

13. Jean Lorrain, *Monsieur de Phocas* (Paris: Ollendorff, 1901), p. 25.

14. Catulle Mendès, *Gog* (Paris: Charpentier, 1896), p. 2.

15. Elémir Bourges, *Le Crépuscule des dieux* (Paris: Le Cercle du livre, 1954), p. cvi.

CHAPTER EIGHT

1. Roger L. Williams, *Gaslight and Shadow* (New York: Macmillan, 1957), p. 111.

2. See Ferdinand Lundberg and Marynia F. Farnham, *Modern Woman: The Lost Sex* (New York: Harper, 1947), for a comprehensive survey of the psychological origins of the "modern woman." Much of the book is intensely Freudian, but there is a sound undercurrent of philosophical understanding.

3. Brooks Adams, *The Law of Civilization and Decay* (New York: Knopf, 1943), sections on the civilized woman, *passim*.

4. Joséphin Péladan, *Finis latinorum* (Paris: Flammarion, 1899), p. 217.

5. James M. Smith, *Elements of Decadence and Their Convergence in the French Literature of the Late Nineteenth Century* (Chapel Hill: unpub. diss., 1948), p. 207.

6. Catulle Mendès, *Méphistophéla* (Paris: Fasquelle, 1903), p. 168.

7. Gustave Flaubert, *Salammbô* (Paris: Librairie de France, 1922), p. 51.

8. Villiers de l'Isle-Adam, *Axël* (Paris: Mercure de France, 1923), p. 47.

9. Octave Mirbeau, *Le Jardin des supplices* (Paris: Charpentier, 1911), p. ii.

10. *Ibid.*, p. 158.

11. *Ibid.*, p. 294.

12. Joséphin Péladan, *Le Vice suprême* (Paris: Editions du monde moderne, 1926), p. 83.

13. *Ibid.*, p. 87.

14. *Ibid.*, p. 122.

15. *Ibid.*, p. 244.

16. Pierre Louÿs, *Aphrodite* (Paris: Fasquelle, n. d.), p. 212.

17. *Ibid.*, pp. 268-69.

18. Pierre Louÿs, *La Femme et le pantin* (Paris: Michel, 1948), p. 238.

19. Catulle Mendès, *Zo'har* (Paris: Charpentier, 1922), p. 27.

20. *Ibid.*, pp. 288-89.

21. E.g., Edmond and Jules de Goncourt, *Charles Demailly* (Paris: Flammarion, 1926), pp. 236-37, an exemplary section on the modern woman as seen by the contemporary novelist. There are numerous other passages throughout.

22. Marcel Schwob, *Le Livre de Monelle* (Paris: Bernouard, 1927), pp. 11-12.

23. Remy de Gourmont, *Les Chevaux de Diomède* (Paris: La Connaissance, 1921), p. 154.

24. Joris-Karl Huysmans, *Là-Bas* (Paris: Crès, 1928), p. 34.

25. *Ibid.*, p. 246.

26. Jean Lorrain, *Le Vice errant* (Paris: Ollendorff, 1902), pp. 362-63.
27. Emile Zola, *La Fortune des Rougon* (Paris: Bernouard, 1927), p. 1.
28. *Ibid.,* p. 73.
29. Edmond and Jules de Goncourt, *Germinie Lacerteux* (Paris: Flammarion, 1921), p. 225.
30. *Ibid.,* p. 233.
31. Rachilde, *La Sanglante ironie* (Paris: Mercure de France, 1902), p. v.
32. Rachilde, *L'Animale* (Paris: Empris, 1893), p. 176.
33. *Ibid.,* p. 298.
34. Joséphin Péladan, *Curieuse!* (Paris: Laurent, 1886), pp. 278-79.
35. Catulle Mendès, *La Première maîtresse* (Paris: Charpentier, 1922), pp. 255-56.

BIBLIOGRAPHY

The complete bibliography of the French decadent literature includes most if not all works from Baudelaire to the outbreak of World War I. This is the literature that is concerned with the idea of decadence, of decline and fall, whether interpreted as cosmic pessimism, pathological degeneration, or an eclipse of society.

The books in this select bibliography are those which most explicitly treat the themes which are implicit throughout the literature of the epoch. They comprise a core bibliography for anyone who wishes to study the French decadence. They are among the texts that I consulted in the preparation of this work.

Adams, Brooks. *The Law of Civilization and Decay*. New York: Knopf, 1943.

Arnold, Matthew. *Culture and Anarchy*. London: Smith, Elder, 1875.

Audiat, Pierre. *L'Aurélia de Gérard de Nerval*. Paris: Champion, 1926.

Babbitt, Irving. *The New Laokoön*. Boston: Houghton Mifflin, 1910.

————. *Rousseau and Romanticism*. Boston: Houghton Mifflin, 1935.

Baju, Anatole. *L'Ecole décadente*. Paris: Vanier, 1887.

Balfour, Arthur James. *Decadence*. Cambridge: Cambridge U. P., 1908.

Balzac, Honoré de. *Traité de la vie élégante*. Paris: Librairie nouvelle, 1853.

Barbey d'Aurevilly, Jules. *Les Diaboliques*. Paris: Dentu, 1874.

——————. *Du Dandysme et de G. Brummell*. Paris: Poulet-Malassis, 1861.

——————. *Un Prêtre marié*. Paris: Faure, 1865.

——————. *Une Vieille maîtresse*. Paris: Faure, 1866.

Barre, André. *Le Symbolisme*. Paris: Jouve, 1911.

Barrès, Maurice. *Un Homme libre*. Paris: Plon, 1922.

——————. *Le Jardin de Bérénice*. Paris: Plon, 1921.

——————. *Sous l'oeil des barbares*. Paris: Plon, 1922.

Baudelaire, Charles. *Oeuvres complètes*. Paris: Gallimard, 1954.

Bourges, Elémir. *Le Crépuscule des dieux*. Paris: Le Cercle du livre, 1954.

——————. *Sous la hache*. Paris: Colin, 1895.

Bertrand, Aloysius. *Gaspard de la nuit*. Angers: Pavie, 1842.

Bibesco, Alexandre. *La Question du vers français et la tentative des poètes décadents*. Paris: Fischbacher, 1896.

Borel, Pétrus. *Champavert: Contes immoraux*. Amsterdam: Imprimerie de la Société des bibliophiles Brabançons, 1870.

——————. *Madame Putiphar*. Paris: Ollivier, 1839.

Boulenger, Jacques. *Les Dandys*. Paris: Calmann-Lévy, 1932.

Bourget, Paul. *Cosmopolis*. Paris: Lemerre, 1898.

——————. *Physiologie de l'amour moderne*. Paris: Plon, n. d.

——————. *Portraits d'écrivains et notes d'esthétique*. Paris: Plon, 1883.

Burdett, Osbert. *The Beardsley Period*. London: John Lane, 1925.

Carter, A. E. *The Idea of Decadence in French Literature, 1830-1900*. Toronto: Toronto U. P., 1958.

Cassagne, Albert. *La Théorie de l'art pour l'art en France*. Paris: Dorbon, 1959.

Charlton, D. G. *Positivist Thought in France during the Second Empire*. Oxford: Oxford U. P., 1959.

Cohn, Robert Greer. *Mallarmé's Un coup de dés*. New Haven: Yale French Studies, 1949.

Cornell, Kenneth. *The Symbolist Movement*. New Haven: Yale U. P., 1951.

Cram, Ralph Adams. *The Decadent: Being the Gospel of Inaction*. Boston: Privately printed, 1893.

Creed, Elizabeth. *Le Dandysme de Jules Barbey d'Aurevilly.* Paris: Droz, 1938.

Doumic, René. *Etudes sur la littérature française.* lere série. Paris: Perrin, 1896.

————. ————. 6eme série. Paris: Perrin, 1909.

Dujardin, Edouard. *Les Lauriers sont coupés.* Paris: Messein, 1924.

Dumesnil, René. *L'Epoque réaliste et naturaliste.* Paris: Tallandier, 1945.

Earle, Edward Mead, ed. *Modern France: Problems of the Third and Fourth Republics.* Princeton: Princeton U. P., 1951.

Farrère, Claude. *Fumée d'opium.* Paris: Flammarion, 1924.

Flaubert, Gustave. *L'Education sentimentale.* Paris: Librairie de France, 1922.

————. *Salammbô.* Paris: Charpentier, 1893.

————. *La Tentation de Saint-Antoine.* Parris: Fasquelle, 1900.

————. *Trois contes.* Paris: Charpentier, 1877.

Fontainas, André. *Dans la lignée de Baudelaire.* Paris: Nouvelle Revue critique, 1930.

Fowlie, Wallace. *Mallarmé.* Chicago: Univ. of Chicago Press, 1953.

Gaunt, William. *The Aesthetic Adventure.* New York: Harcourt, Brace, 1945.

Gautier, Théophile. *Mademoiselle de Maupin.* Paris: Garnier, 1930.

————. *Emaux et camées.* Genève: Droz, 1947.

Ghil, René. *Oeuvres complètes.* Paris: Messein, 1938.

Gobineau, Arthur de. *Nouvelles Asiatiques.* Paris: Perrin, 1925.

————. *Pages choisies.* Paris: Mercure de France, 1905.

Goncourt, Edmond and Jules de. *Charles Demailly.* Paris: Flammarion, 1926.

————. *Germinie Lacerteux.* Paris: Flammarion, 1921.

————. *Soeur Philomène.* Paris: Lemerre, 1890.

Gourmont, Remy de. *Les Chevaux de Diomède.* Paris: La Connaissance, 1921.

————. *La Culture des idées.* Paris: Mercure de France, 1916.

————. *Lettres à l'amazone.* Paris: Mercure de France, 1917.

————. *Lettres d'un satyre.* Paris: Mercure de France, 1923.

————————. *Une Nuit au Luxembourg.* Paris: Mercure de France, 1923.

————————. *Le Pèlerin du silence.* Paris: Mercure de France, n. d.

————————. *Sixtine.* Paris: Mercure de France, n. d.

Heredia, José-Maria de. *Les Trophées.* Paris: Lemerre, n. d.

Huysmans, Joris-Karl. *Oeuvres complètes.* Paris: Crès, 1928.

Kahn, Gustave. *Symbolistes et décadents.* Paris: Vanier, 1902.

Laforgue, Jules. *Oeuvres complètes.* Paris: Mercure de France, 1946.

Laurent, Emile. *La Poésie décadente devant la science psychiatrique.* Paris: Maloine, 1897.

Leconte de Lisle. *Poèmes antiques.* Paris: Lemerre, 1881.

————————. *Poèmes barbares.* Paris: Lemerre, 1881.

————————. *Poèmes tragiques.* Paris: Lemerre, n. d.

Le Rouge, Gustave. *Verlainiens et décadents.* Paris: Seheur, 1928.

Lorrain, Jean. *Buveurs d'âmes.* Paris: Charpentier, 1893.

————————. *Le Crime des riches.* Paris: Douville, 1905.

————————. *La Forêt bleue.* Paris: Lemerre, 1883.

————————. *Monsieur de Phocas.* Paris: Ollendorff, 1901.

————————. *Pelléastres.* Paris: Méricant, n. d.

————————. *Princesses d'ivoire et d'ivresse.* Paris: Ollendorff, 1902.

————————. *Le Vice errant.* Paris: Ollendorff, 1902.

Louÿs, Pierre. *Aphrodite.* Paris: Fasquelle, n. d.

————————. *La Femme et le pantin.* Paris: Michel, 1948.

Lundberg, Ferdinand and Farnham, Marynia F. *Modern Woman: The Lost Sex.* New York: Harper, 1947.

Maeterlinck, Maurice. *Serres chaudes.* Paris: Pelletan, 1927.

Mallarmé, Stéphane. *Oeuvres complètes.* Paris: Gallimard, 1945.

Martino, Pierre. *Le Naturalisme français (1870-1895).* Paris: Colin, 1945.

————————. *Parnasse et symbolisme (1850-1900).* Paris: Colin, 1947.

Maurras, Charles. *Barbarie et poésie.* Paris: Nouvelle Librairie nationale, 1925.

Mendès, Catulle. *Arc-en-ciel et Sourcil-Rouge.* Paris: Charpentier, 1897.

————————. *Le Chercheur de Tares.* Paris: Charpentier, 1898.

————————. *La Femme-Enfant.* Paris: Charpentier, 1891.

————————. *Gog.* Paris: Charpentier, 1896.

————————. *L'Homme tout nu.* Paris: Victor-Havard, 1887.

——————. *Lesbia.* Paris: Charpentier, 1899.

——————. *Méphistophéla.* Paris: Fasquelle, 1903.

——————. *La Messe rose.* Paris: Charpentier, 1892.

——————. *Monstres parisiens.* Paris: Charpentier, 1902.

——————. *Le Mouvement poétique français de 1867 à 1900.* Paris: Fasquelle, 1903.

——————. *La Première maîtresse.* Paris: Charpentier, 1922.

——————. *Rue des Filles-Dieu, 56.* Paris: Charpentier, 1895.

——————. *Le Roi vierge.* Paris: Carpentier, 1900.

——————. *Les Romans d'innocence.* Paris: Charpentier, 1904.

——————. *Zo'har.* Paris: Charpentier, 1922.

Michaud, Guy. *Message poétique du symbolisme.* Paris: Nizet, 1947.

Mirbeau, Octave. *Le Jardin des supplices.* Paris: Chapentier, 1911.

——————. *Le Journal d'une femme de chambre.* Paris: Charpentier, 1908.

——————. *Les Vingt et un jours d'un neurasthénique.* Paris: Charpentier, 1904.

Moréas, Jean. *Le Pèlerin passionné.* Paris: Vanier, 1891.

Morice, Charles. *La Littérature de tout à l'heure.* Paris: Didier, 1889.

Mougenot, Joseph-Fabien. *Hugo et les décadents (1830-1890).* Paris: Le Chat noir, 1889.

Nisard, Désiré. *Etudes sur les poëtes latins de la décadence.* Paris: Hachette, 1888.

Nordau, Max. *Degeneration (Entartung).* New York: Appleton, 1895.

Péladan, Joséphin. *Curieuse!* Paris: Laurent, 1886.

——————. *Finis latinorum.* Paris: Flammarion, 1899.

——————. *Istar.* Paris: Edinger, 1888.

——————. *Le Vice suprême.* Paris: Editions du monde moderne, 1926.

Poggioli, Renato. "Qualis Artifex Pereo! or Barbarism and Decadence," *Harvard Library Bulletin,* XIII, 1 (Winter 1959), 135-59.

Powert, Jacques (i.e., Paul Adam). *Petit glossaire pour servir à l'intelligence des auteurs décadents et symbolistes.* Paris: Vanier, 1888.

Prevost, John C. *Le Dandysme en France (1817-1839).* Paris: Minard, 1957.

Rachilde. *L'Animale*. Paris: Empris, 1893.

————. *Les Hors nature*. Paris: Mercure de France, n.d.

————. *Monsieur Vénus*. Paris: Flammarion, 1926.

————. *La Sanglante ironie*. Paris: Mercure de France, 1902

————. *La Tour d'amour*. Paris: Mercure de France, n. d.

Raudot, M. *De la Décadence de la France*. Paris: Amyot, 1850.

Raynaud, Ernest. *La Mêlée symboliste* (1870-1890). Paris: La Renaissance du livre, 1918.

Rimbaud, Arthur. *Oeuvres complètes*. Paris: Gallimard, 1954.

Rollinat, Maurice. *Les Névroses*. Paris: Charpentier, 1896.

Rudler, Madeleine G. *Parnassiens, symbolistes, et décadents*. Paris: Messein, 1938.

Sabatier, Pierre. *L'Esthétique des Goncourt*. Paris: Hachette, 1920.

Saint-Beuve, Charles Augustin. *Volupté*. Paris: Presses françaises, 1927.

Schwob, Marcel. *Coeur double*. Paris: Bernouard, 1927.

————. *Le Livre de Monelle*. Paris: Bernouard, 1927.

Seylaz, Louis. *Edgar Poë et les premiers symbolistes français*. Lausanne: Imprimerie la Concorde, 1923.

Smith, James M. *Elements of Decadence and Their Convergence in the French Literature of the Late Nineteenth Century*. Chapel Hill: unpub. diss., 1948.

————. "Preconception of Reality, and Abulia, in Nineteenth Century French Literature," in *Romance Studies Presented to William Morton Day*. Chapel Hill: Univ. of North Carolina Press, 1950.

Spengler, Oswald. *The Decline of the West*. New York: Knopf, 1950.

Symons, Arthur. *Dramatis personae*. Indianapolis: Bobbs-Merrill, n.d.

Van Roosbroeck, G. L. *The Legend of the Decadents*. New York: Columbia U. P., 1927.

Verlaine, Paul. *Oeuvres poétiques complètes*. Paris: Gallimard, 1948.

Vicaire, Gabriel. *Les Déliquescences d'Adoré Floupette, poète décadent*. Byzance (i.e., Paris): Lion Vanné (i.e., Léon Vanier), 1885.

Villiers de l'Isle-Adam. *Contes cruels*. Paris: Mercure de France, 1928.

————. *Derniers contes*. Paris: Mercure de France, 1921.

————————. *L'Eve future*. Paris: Charpentier, 1891.

————————. *Isis*. Paris: Librairie internationale, n.d.

Vyverberg, Henry. *Historical Pessimism in the French Enlightenment*. Cambridge: Harvard U.P., 1958.

Weinstein, Leo. *The Metamorphoses of Don Juan*. Stanford: Stanford U. P., 1959.

Williams, Roger L. *Gaslight and Shadow*. New York: Macmillan, 1957.

Zola, Emile. *Oeuvres complètes*. Paris: Bernouard, 1926-31.

INDEX

192